DASH DIET
COOKBOOK 2024
FOR BEGINNERS

*1800 Days of Delightful Low-Sodium Recipes to Lower
Your Blood Pressure and Preserve Your Heart Health.*

60 Days Meal Plan + BONUS Included

Violet Harmond

Table of Content

Introduction

What is the DASH Diet?

DASH stands for Dietary Approaches to Stop Hypertension, and it was initially developed by the National Heart, Lung, and Blood Institute (NHLBI) in collaboration with several leading research institutions. The primary objective of the DASH diet is to lower blood pressure levels, but it has also been widely recognized for its ability to promote overall cardiovascular health, reduce the risk of chronic diseases, and contribute to sustainable weight management.

The Origins of the DASH Diet

The DASH diet was originally created as a result of extensive research conducted in the 1990s. A team of scientists sought to investigate the relationship between diet and hypertension, with the aim of finding an effective non-pharmacological approach to manage high blood pressure. Through rigorous studies, they discovered that certain dietary patterns had a profound impact on blood pressure levels, leading to the development of the DASH diet.

Key Principles of the DASH Diet

The DASH diet is based on a balanced and flexible approach to eating. It emphasizes consuming nutrient-dense foods while limiting the intake of certain nutrients known to negatively affect blood pressure, such as sodium and saturated fats. Here are the key principles of the DASH diet:

Emphasis on Fruits and Vegetables: The DASH diet encourages the consumption of a variety of fruits and vegetables, which are excellent sources of essential vitamins, minerals, and fiber. These foods form the foundation of a healthy eating plan and provide numerous health benefits.

Whole Grains: Whole grains, such as whole wheat, brown rice, and oats, are rich in fiber, which helps to maintain healthy blood pressure levels and reduce the risk of heart disease. The DASH diet promotes the inclusion of whole grains in meals and snacks.

Lean Protein Sources: The DASH diet recommends lean protein sources, such as poultry, fish, beans, and legumes, as they provide important nutrients without the added saturated fats often found in fatty meats.

Low-Fat Dairy Products: The DASH diet suggests incorporating low-fat or fat-free dairy products into the diet. These products are excellent sources of calcium, potassium, and vitamin D, which are essential for maintaining healthy blood pressure.

Limited Sodium Intake: Excessive sodium intake has been linked to increased blood pressure levels. The DASH diet encourages reducing sodium consumption by choosing fresh ingredients, using herbs and spices for flavor, and minimizing the consumption of processed foods high in sodium.

Health Benefits of the DASH Diet

Numerous studies have highlighted the remarkable health benefits associated with the DASH diet. By following this dietary pattern, individuals have experienced improvements in blood pressure levels, lowered cholesterol levels, reduced risk of heart disease and stroke, and enhanced overall well-being. Additionally, the DASH diet has shown positive effects on weight management and the prevention of type 2 diabetes. Your Journey Begins

As you embark on this journey to embrace the DASH diet, remember that it is more than just a short-term fix. It is a sustainable lifestyle approach to healthy eating, backed by scientific research. This cookbook will serve as your guide, offering delicious and nutritious recipes that align with the principles of the DASH diet.

Get ready to savor a wide variety of flavors, explore creative culinary options, and nourish your body with wholesome ingredients. By embracing the DASH diet, you are taking an important step towards improving your health and well-being. Let's dive into the world of delicious and heart-healthy recipes together!

Conversion Tables

VOLUME EQUIVALENTS (DRY)

US STANDARD	METRIC (APPROXIMATE)
1/8 Teaspoon	0.5 ml
1/4 Teaspoon	1 ml
1/2 Teaspoon	2 ml
3/4 Teaspoon	4 ml
1 Teaspoon	5 ml
1 Tablespoon	15 ml
1/4 Cup	59 ml
1/2 Cup	118 ml
3/4 Cup	177 ml
1 Cup	235 ml
2 Cups	475 ml
3 Cups	700 ml
4 Cups	1 l

WEIGHT EQUIVALENTS

US STANDARD	METRIC (APPROXIMATE)
1 Ounce	28 g
2 Ounces	57 g
5 Ounces	142 g
10 Ounces	284 g
15 Ounces	425 g
16 Ounces (1 Pound)	455g
1.5 Pounds	680 g
2 Pounds	907 g

VOLUME EQUIVALENTS (LIQUID)

US STANDARD	US STANDARD (OUNCES)	METRIC (APPROXIMATE)
2 Tablespoons	1 fl.oz.	30 ml
1/4 Cup	2 fl.oz.	60 ml
1/2 Cup	4 fl.oz.	120 ml
1 Cup	8 fl.oz.	240 ml
1 1/2 Cups	12 fl.oz.	355 ml
2 Cups or 1 Pint	16 fl.oz.	475 ml
4 Cups or 1 Quart	32 fl.oz.	1 l
1 Gallon	128 fl.oz.	4 l

TEMPERATURES EQUIVALENTS

FAHRENHEIT (F)	CELSIUS (C) (APPROXIMATE)
225 °F	107 °C
250 °F	120 °C
275 °F	135 °C
300 °F	150 °C
325 °F	160 °C
350 °F	180 °C
375 °F	190 °C
400 °F	205 °C
425 °F	220 °C
450 °F	235 °C
475 °F	245 °C
500 °F	260 °C

Breakfast

1. Spinach Veggie Omelet

Preparation time: 10 minutes
Servings: 1

Ingredients:

- 2 large eggs
- 1 cup fresh spinach leaves, chopped
- 1/4 cup bell peppers, diced
- 1/4 cup onions, diced
- 1/4 cup tomatoes, diced
- 1/4 teaspoon black pepper
- 1/4 teaspoon dried oregano
- Cooking spray

Instructions:

1. In a bowl, whisk the eggs until well beaten.
2. Heat a non-stick skillet over medium heat and coat it with cooking spray.
3. Add the diced bell peppers and onions to the skillet and sauté for 2-3 minutes until they start to soften.
4. Add the chopped spinach leaves and tomatoes to the skillet and sauté for another 2 minutes until the spinach wilts.
5. Pour the beaten eggs into the skillet, spreading them evenly over the vegetables.
6. Sprinkle black pepper and dried oregano on top of the omelet.
7. Cook the omelet for 3-4 minutes until the edges are set.
8. Carefully flip the omelet using a spatula and cook for an additional 2-3 minutes until cooked through.
9. Slide the omelet onto a plate, fold it in half, and serve hot.

Nutritional Information (per serving):
Cal: 190 | Fat: 10g | Chol: 370mg | Sod: 80mg | Carbs: 11g | Fiber: 3g | Sugars: 5g | Pro: 16g

2. Berry Overnight Oats

Preparation time: 10 minutes (plus overnight refrigeration)
Servings: 1

Ingredients:

- 1/2 cup rolled oats
- 1/2 cup unsweetened almond milk (or any milk of your choice)
- 1/4 cup plain Greek yogurt
- 1/4 cup mixed berries (such as blueberries, raspberries, and strawberries)
- 1 tablespoon chia seeds
- 1/2 tablespoon honey or maple syrup (optional, for added sweetness)
- 1/4 teaspoon vanilla extract

Instructions:

1. In a jar or container with a tight-fitting lid, combine the rolled oats, almond milk, Greek yogurt, chia seeds, honey or maple syrup (if using), and vanilla extract.
2. Stir well to ensure all the ingredients are well combined.
3. Add the mixed berries to the mixture and gently stir to distribute them evenly.
4. Cover the jar or container with the lid and refrigerate overnight or for at least 4-6 hours.
5. In the morning, give the oats a good stir and add additional toppings if desired, such as more berries or a sprinkle of nuts.
6. Enjoy the overnight oats chilled straight from the refrigerator.

Nutritional Information (per serving):
Cal: 290 | Fat: 8g | Chol: 2mg | Sod: 62mg | Carbs: 45g | Fiber: 9g | Sugars: 12g | Pro: 14g

3. Whole Wheat Pancake Delight

Preparation time: 15 minutes
Servings: 2-3

Ingredients:

- 1 cup whole wheat flour
- 1 tablespoon honey or maple syrup
- 1 teaspoon baking powder
- 1/4 teaspoon baking soda
- 1/4 teaspoon cinnamon
- 1 cup unsweetened almond milk (or any milk of your choice)
- 1 large egg
- 1 tablespoon unsalted butter, melted
- Cooking spray (for greasing the pan)
- Fresh berries or sliced fruits (for serving, optional)

Instructions:

1. In a mixing bowl, combine the whole wheat flour, honey or maple syrup, baking powder, baking soda, and cinnamon. Mix well.
2. In a separate bowl, whisk together the almond milk, egg, and melted butter until well combined.
3. Pour the wet ingredients into the dry ingredients and stir until just combined. Do not overmix; a few lumps are okay.
4. Heat a non-stick skillet or griddle over medium heat and coat it with cooking spray.
5. Pour about 1/4 cup of batter onto the skillet for each pancake. Cook until bubbles form on the surface, then flip and cook the other side until golden brown.

6. Repeat the process with the remaining batter, adding more cooking spray as needed.
7. Serve the whole wheat pancakes warm with fresh berries or sliced fruits, if desired.

Nutritional Information (per serving):
Cal: 320 | Fat: 9g | Chol: 85mg | Sod: 100mg | Carbs: 52g | Fiber: 6g | Sugars: 10g | Pro: 10g

4. Mushroom Scrambled Eggs

Preparation time: 10 minutes
Servings: 2

Ingredients:

- 4 large eggs
- 1 cup sliced mushrooms
- 1/4 cup diced onions
- 1/4 cup diced bell peppers
- 1 tablespoon olive oil
- 1/4 teaspoon black pepper
- 1/4 teaspoon dried thyme
- Cooking spray
- Fresh parsley, chopped (for garnish, optional)

Instructions:

1. Heat a non-stick skillet over medium heat and add the olive oil.
2. Add the diced onions and bell peppers to the skillet and sauté for 2-3 minutes until they start to soften.
3. Add the sliced mushrooms to the skillet and continue to cook for another 3-4 minutes until the mushrooms release their moisture and start to brown.
4. Meanwhile, in a bowl, whisk the eggs until well beaten. Season with black pepper and dried thyme.
5. Push the sautéed mushrooms, onions, and bell peppers to one side of the skillet and coat the other side with cooking spray.
6. Pour the beaten eggs onto the greased side of the skillet and let them cook for a few seconds until they start to set.
7. Using a spatula, scramble the eggs while incorporating the sautéed mushrooms, onions, and bell peppers.
8. Continue to cook and scramble until the eggs are cooked to your desired consistency.
9. Remove from heat and garnish with fresh parsley, if desired.
10. Serve the mushroom scrambled eggs hot.

Nutritional Information (per serving):
Cal: 180 | Fat: 13g | Chol: 370mg | Sod: 75mg | Carbs: 4g | Fiber: 1g | Sugars: 2g | Pro: 12g

5. Yogurt Berry Parfait

Preparation time: 10 minutes
Servings: 2

Ingredients:

- 1 cup non-fat Greek yogurt
- 1 cup mixed berries (such as strawberries, blueberries, and raspberries)
- 2 tablespoons chopped nuts (such as almonds or walnuts)
- 2 tablespoons honey or maple syrup
- 1/4 teaspoon vanilla extract
- Fresh mint leaves (for garnish, optional)

Instructions:

1. In a small bowl, mix the non-fat Greek yogurt, honey or maple syrup, and vanilla extract until well combined.
2. In two serving glasses or bowls, layer the yogurt mixture, mixed berries, and chopped nuts.
3. Repeat the layers until all the ingredients are used, finishing with a layer of berries and nuts on top.
4. Garnish with fresh mint leaves, if desired.
5. Serve the yogurt berry parfait immediately or refrigerate for later consumption.

Nutritional Information (per serving):
Cal: 180 | Fat: 4g | Chol: 5mg | Sod: 35mg | Carbs: 28g | Fiber: 4g | Sugars: 21g | Pro: 13g

6. Avocado Toast with Tomatoes

Preparation time: 10 minutes
Servings: 2

Ingredients:

- 2 slices whole wheat bread
- 1 ripe avocado
- 1 small tomato, sliced
- 1 tablespoon lemon juice
- 1/4 teaspoon black pepper
- 1/4 teaspoon red pepper flakes (optional, for added heat)
- Fresh cilantro or basil leaves (for garnish, optional)

Instructions:

1. Toast the slices of whole wheat bread until golden brown.
2. While the bread is toasting, cut the avocado in half, remove the pit, and scoop out the flesh into a bowl.
3. Mash the avocado with a fork until it reaches a

creamy consistency.

4. Add the lemon juice, black pepper, and red pepper flakes (if using) to the mashed avocado. Mix well to combine.
5. Once the bread is toasted, spread the mashed avocado evenly on each slice.
6. Top the avocado toast with sliced tomatoes.
7. Garnish with fresh cilantro or basil leaves, if desired.
8. Serve the avocado toast with tomatoes immediately.

Nutritional Information (per serving):
Cal: 170 | Fat: 10g | Chol: 0mg | Sod: 140mg | Carbs: 18g | Fiber: 6g | Sugars: 2g | Pro: 4g

7. Veggie Breakfast Burrito

Preparation time: 20 minutes
Servings: 2

Ingredients:

- 4 eggs
- 1/4 cup diced onions
- 1/4 cup diced bell peppers
- 1/4 cup diced tomatoes
- 1/4 cup sliced mushrooms
- 1/4 tsp. ground cumin
- 1/4 tsp. paprika
- 1/4 tsp. pepper
- 2 whole wheat tortillas
- 1/4 cup shredded low-fat cheddar cheese
- Cooking spray
- Fresh cilantro (for garnish, optional)

Instructions:

1. In a bowl, whisk the eggs until well beaten. Set aside.
2. Heat a non-stick skillet over medium heat and coat it with cooking spray.
3. Add the diced onions, bell peppers, tomatoes, and mushrooms to the skillet. Sauté for 3-4 minutes until the vegetables start to soften.
4. Sprinkle the ground cumin, paprika, and pepper over the sautéed vegetables. Stir well to coat the vegetables with the spices.
5. Pour the beaten eggs into the skillet with the vegetables. Cook, stirring occasionally, until the eggs are scrambled and fully cooked.
6. Warm the whole wheat tortillas in a separate skillet or microwave.
7. Divide the scrambled eggs and vegetable mixture evenly between the tortillas.
8. Sprinkle the shredded low-fat cheddar cheese over the filling.
9. Roll up the tortillas, tucking in the sides as you go, to form the breakfast burritos.

10. Optional: Heat the burritos in a skillet for a few minutes to melt the cheese and crisp up the tortilla.
11. Garnish with fresh cilantro, if desired.
12. Serve the veggie breakfast burritos warm.

Nutritional Information (per serving):
Cal: 280 | Fat: 11g | Chol: 350mg | Sod: 220mg | Carbs: 26g | Fiber: 5g | Sugars: 4g | Pro: 19g

8. Quinoa Apple Bowl

Preparation time: 20 minutes
Servings: 2

Ingredients:

- 1 cup cooked quinoa
- 1 medium apple, diced
- 2 tablespoons chopped walnuts
- 2 tablespoons dried cranberries
- 1 tbsp. honey or maple syrup
- 1/4 tsp. cinnamon
- 1/4 tsp. vanilla extract
- Fresh mint leaves (for garnish, optional)

Instructions:

1. In a bowl, combine the cooked quinoa, diced apple, chopped walnuts, and dried cranberries.
2. In a separate small bowl, whisk together the honey or maple syrup, cinnamon, and vanilla extract.
3. Pour the sweetener mixture over the quinoa and apple mixture. Toss well to coat all the ingredients.
4. Divide the quinoa apple mixture into serving bowls.
5. Garnish with fresh mint leaves, if desired.
6. Serve the quinoa apple bowls at room temperature or chilled.

Nutritional Information (per serving):
Cal: 300 | Fat: 9g | Chol: 0mg | Sod: 10mg | Carbs: 53g | Fiber: 7g | Sugars: 20g | Pro: 7g

9. Smoked Salmon Bagel Delight

Preparation time: 10 minutes
Servings: 2

Ingredients:

- 2 whole grain bagels
- 4 ounces smoked salmon
- 2 tablespoons low-fat cream cheese
- 1/4 cup sliced red onions
- 1/4 cup sliced cucumbers
- 2 tablespoons capers

- Fresh dill (for garnish, optional)
- Lemon wedges (for serving)

Instructions:

1. Slice the whole grain bagels in half horizontally.
2. Toast the bagel halves until lightly crispy.
3. Spread 1 tbsp. of low-fat cream cheese on each bagel half.
4. Layer the smoked salmon evenly on each bagel half.
5. Top with sliced red onions, sliced cucumbers, and capers.
6. Garnish with fresh dill, if desired.
7. Serve the smoked salmon bagel delight with lemon wedges on the side.

Nutritional Information (per serving):
Cal: 320 | Fat: 10g | Chol: 20mg | Sod: 460mg | Carbs: 43g | Fiber: 5g | Sugars: 4g | Pro: 20g

10. Blueberry Spinach Smoothie

Preparation time: 5 minutes
Servings: 2

Ingredients:

- 1 cup frozen blueberries
- 1 cup fresh spinach leaves
- 1 ripe banana
- 1/2 cup plain low-fat Greek yogurt
- 1/2 cup unsweetened almond milk (or any other non-dairy milk)
- 1 tbsp. honey or maple syrup (optional, for added sweetness)
- Ice cubes (optional, for extra chill)

Instructions:

1. In a blender, combine the frozen blueberries, fresh spinach leaves, ripe banana, low-fat Greek yogurt, and unsweetened almond milk.
2. If desired, add the honey or maple syrup for extra sweetness.
3. Blend on high speed until smooth and creamy.
4. If desired, add a few ice cubes and blend again until well incorporated.
5. Pour the blueberry spinach smoothie into glasses.
6. Serve the smoothie immediately.

Nutritional Information (per serving):
Cal: 120 | Fat: 1g | Chol: 0mg | Sod: 60mg | Carbs: 25g | Fiber: 4g | Sugars: 14g | Pro: 6g

11. Zucchini Frittata Delight

Preparation time: 20 minutes
Servings: 4

Ingredients:

- 6 eggs
- 1 medium zucchini, thinly sliced
- 1/2 cup diced red bell pepper
- 1/4 cup diced onion
- 1/4 cup grated Parmesan cheese
- 2 tablespoons chopped fresh basil
- 1/2 tsp. dried oregano
- 1/4 tsp. pepper
- Cooking spray

Instructions:

1. Preheat the oven to 350°F (175°C).
2. In a bowl, whisk the eggs until well beaten. Set aside.
3. Heat a non-stick skillet over medium heat and coat it with cooking spray.
4. Add the sliced zucchini, diced red bell pepper, and diced onion to the skillet. Sauté for 5-6 minutes until the vegetables are tender.
5. In a separate bowl, combine the grated Parmesan cheese, chopped fresh basil, dried oregano, and pepper.
6. Add the sautéed vegetables to the egg mixture. Stir well to combine.
7. Spray a baking dish with cooking spray and pour the egg and vegetable mixture into the dish.
8. Bake in the preheated oven for 15-20 minutes until the frittata is set and slightly golden on top.
9. Remove from the oven and let it cool for a few minutes.
10. Slice the frittata into wedges and serve.

Nutritional Information (per serving):
Cal: 130 | Fat: 8g | Chol: 235mg | Sod: 90mg | Carbs: 4g | Fiber: 1g | Sugars: 2g | Pro: 11g

12. Almond Butter Toast Delight

Preparation time: 5 minutes
Servings: 2

Ingredients:

- 2 slices whole grain bread
- 4 tablespoons almond butter
- 1 medium banana, sliced
- 2 teaspoons honey (optional, for added sweetness)
- 1 tbsp. chopped almonds (optional, for garnish)

Instructions:

1. Toast the slices of whole grain bread until lightly crispy.
2. Spread 2 tablespoons of almond butter on each slice of toasted bread.
3. Arrange the sliced banana on top of the almond butter.
4. Drizzle with honey, if desired, for added sweetness.
5. Sprinkle chopped almonds on top for extra crunch and garnish.
6. Serve the almond butter toast delight immediately.

Nutritional Information (per serving):
Cal: 280 | Fat: 15g | Chol: 0mg | Sod: 140mg | Carbs: 33g | Fiber: 6g | Sugars: 11g | Pro: 8g

13. Turkey Mushroom Egg Scramble

Preparation time: 15 minutes
Servings: 2

Ingredients:

- 4 eggs
- 4 ounces lean ground turkey
- 1 cup sliced mushrooms
- 1/4 cup diced onions
- 1/4 cup diced bell peppers (any color)
- 1/2 tsp. dried thyme
- 1/4 tsp. pepper
- Cooking spray
- Fresh parsley (for garnish, optional)

Instructions:

1. Heat a non-stick skillet over medium heat and coat it with cooking spray.
2. Add the lean ground turkey to the skillet and cook until browned, breaking it into smaller pieces.
3. Add the sliced mushrooms, diced onions, and diced bell peppers to the skillet. Sauté for 5-6 minutes until the vegetables are tender.
4. In a bowl, whisk the eggs until well beaten.
5. Pour the beaten eggs into the skillet with the cooked turkey and vegetables.
6. Sprinkle dried thyme and pepper over the mixture. Stir gently to combine.
7. Continue cooking and stirring until the eggs are fully cooked and scrambled.
8. Remove from heat and garnish with fresh parsley, if desired.
9. Serve the turkey mushroom egg scramble immediately.

Nutritional Information (per serving):
Cal: 240 | Fat: 14g | Chol: 410mg | Sod: 120mg | Carbs: 5g | Fiber: 1g | Sugars: 2g | Pro: 23g

14. Berry Kale Yogurt Smoothie

Preparation time: 5 minutes
Servings: 2

Ingredients:

- 1 cup frozen mixed berries (such as strawberries, blueberries, raspberries)
- 1 cup chopped kale leaves
- 1 ripe banana
- 1/2 cup plain low-fat Greek yogurt
- 1/2 cup unsweetened almond milk (or any other non-dairy milk)
- 1 tbsp. honey or maple syrup (optional, for added sweetness)
- Ice cubes (optional, for extra chill)

Instructions:

1. In a blender, combine the frozen mixed berries, chopped kale leaves, ripe banana, low-fat Greek yogurt, and unsweetened almond milk.
2. If desired, add the honey or maple syrup for extra sweetness.
3. Blend on high speed until smooth and creamy.
4. If desired, add a few ice cubes and blend again until well incorporated.
5. Pour the Berry Kale Yogurt Smoothie into glasses.
6. Serve the smoothie immediately.

Nutritional Information (per serving):
Cal: 120 | Fat: 1.5g | Chol: 0mg | Sod: 70mg | Carbs: 25g | Fiber: 4g | Sugars: 14g | Pro: 6g

15. Cottage Cheese Peach Delight

Preparation time: 5 minutes
Servings: 2

Ingredients:

- 1 cup low-fat cottage cheese
- 2 ripe peaches, sliced
- 2 tablespoons chopped walnuts (optional, for garnish)
- 1 tbsp. honey or maple syrup (optional, for added sweetness)
- Fresh mint leaves (for garnish, optional)

Instructions:

1. In a bowl, scoop 1/2 cup of low-fat cottage cheese for each serving.
2. Top each portion of cottage cheese with sliced

peaches.
3. Drizzle honey or maple syrup over the peaches for added sweetness, if desired.
4. Sprinkle chopped walnuts on top for extra crunch and garnish.
5. Garnish with fresh mint leaves, if desired, for a pop of color and freshness.
6. Serve the Cottage Cheese Peach Delight immediately.

Nutritional Information (per serving):
Cal: 170 | Fat: 4g | Chol: 10mg | Sod: 170mg | Carbs: 24g | Fiber: 3g | Sugars: 20g | Pro: 12g

16. Mango Coconut Quinoa Bowl

Preparation time: 20 minutes
Servings: 2

Ingredients:

- 1 cup cooked quinoa
- 1 ripe mango, diced
- 1/4 cup unsweetened shredded coconut
- 2 tablespoons chopped almonds (optional, for garnish)
- 1 tbsp. honey or maple syrup (optional, for added sweetness)
- Fresh mint leaves (for garnish, optional)

Instructions:

1. In a bowl, combine the cooked quinoa, diced mango, and unsweetened shredded coconut.
2. Stir gently until well mixed.
3. If desired, drizzle honey or maple syrup over the mixture for added sweetness.
4. Sprinkle chopped almonds on top for extra crunch and garnish.
5. Garnish with fresh mint leaves, if desired, for a pop of color and freshness.
6. Serve the Mango Coconut Quinoa Bowl immediately.

Nutritional Information (per serving):
Cal: 280 | Fat: 7g | Chol: 0mg | Sod: 10mg | Carbs: 52g | Fiber: 6g | Sugars: 23g | Pro: 6g

17. Fruit Topped Waffle Delight

Preparation time: 15 minutes
Servings: 2

Ingredients:

- 2 whole grain waffles
- 1 cup mixed fresh berries (such as strawberries, blueberries, raspberries)
- 1/4 cup low-fat Greek yogurt

- 1 tbsp. chopped nuts (such as almonds or walnuts)
- 1 tbsp. honey or maple syrup (optional, for added sweetness)
- Fresh mint leaves (for garnish, optional)

Instructions:

1. Toast the whole grain waffles according to the package instructions.
2. Place each waffle on a plate.
3. Top each waffle with the mixed fresh berries.
4. Spoon the low-fat Greek yogurt over the berries.
5. Sprinkle the chopped nuts on top for added crunch and flavor.
6. Drizzle honey or maple syrup over the waffles if desired, for added sweetness.
7. Garnish with fresh mint leaves, if desired, for a pop of color and freshness.
8. Serve the Fruit-Topped Waffle Delight immediately.

Nutritional Information (per serving):
Cal: 250 | Fat: 8g | Chol: 5mg | Sod: 160mg | Carbs: 41g | Fiber: 6g | Sugars: 15g | Pro: 8g

18. Spinach Mushroom Wrap

Preparation time: 15 minutes
Servings: 2

Ingredients:

- 4 large whole wheat tortillas
- 1 cup fresh spinach leaves
- 1 cup sliced mushrooms
- 1/2 cup diced tomatoes
- 4 eggs
- Salt and pepper to taste
- Cooking spray or olive oil for cooking

Instructions:

1. Heat a non-stick skillet over medium heat and lightly coat it with cooking spray or olive oil.
2. Add the sliced mushrooms to the skillet and sauté for 2-3 minutes until they start to soften.
3. Add the fresh spinach leaves to the skillet and cook until wilted, about 1-2 minutes.
4. In a separate bowl, beat the eggs and season with salt and pepper.
5. Push the mushrooms and spinach to one side of the skillet and pour the beaten eggs into the other side.
6. Cook the eggs, gently stirring occasionally, until they are scrambled and fully cooked.
7. Warm the whole wheat tortillas in a separate skillet or microwave.
8. Divide the scrambled eggs, mushroom-spinach mixture, and diced tomatoes evenly among the

tortillas.

9. Fold the sides of the tortillas inward and roll them up tightly to create the breakfast wraps.
10. Serve the Spinach Mushroom Breakfast Wraps immediately.

Nutritional Information (per serving):
Cal: 290 | Fat: 10g | Chol: 370mg | Sod: 300mg | Carbs: 35g | Fiber: 8g | Sugars: 5g | Pro: 18g

19. Kiwi Chia Pudding Delight

Preparation time: 5 minutes (plus chilling time)
Servings: 2

Ingredients:

- 2 ripe kiwis, peeled and diced
- 1 cup unsweetened almond milk (or any non-dairy milk)
- 1/4 cup chia seeds
- 1 tbsp. honey or maple syrup (optional, for added sweetness)
- Fresh mint leaves (for garnish, optional)

Instructions:

1. In a bowl or container, mash the diced kiwis with a fork until they become slightly mashed but still chunky.
2. Add the almond milk and chia seeds to the mashed kiwis. Stir well to combine.
3. Let the mixture sit for 5 minutes, then give it another stir to prevent clumping of the chia seeds.
4. Cover the bowl or container and refrigerate for at least 2 hours or overnight, allowing the chia seeds to absorb the liquid and create a pudding-like consistency.
5. Before serving, give the mixture a final stir. If desired, you can add honey or maple syrup for added sweetness.
6. Divide the Kiwi Chia Pudding into serving bowls or glasses.
7. Garnish with fresh mint leaves, if desired, for a pop of color and freshness.
8. Serve the Kiwi Chia Pudding Delight chilled.

Nutritional Information (per serving):
Cal: 160 | Fat: 7g | Chol: 0mg | Sod: 10mg | Carbs: 22g | Fiber: 10g | Sugars: 8g | Pro: 5g

20. Almond Cereal with Berries

Preparation time: 5 minutes
Servings: 1

Ingredients:

- 1 cup unsweetened almond milk (or any non-dairy milk)
- 1/2 cup whole grain cereal (such as rolled oats or bran flakes)
- 1/4 cup fresh mixed berries (such as blueberries, raspberries, or strawberries)
- 1 tbsp. sliced almonds
- 1 tsp. honey or maple syrup (optional, for added sweetness)

Instructions:

1. In a bowl, pour the unsweetened almond milk over the whole grain cereal.
2. Let the cereal soak in the milk for a few minutes to soften.
3. Top the cereal with fresh mixed berries and sliced almonds.
4. Drizzle with honey or maple syrup, if desired, for added sweetness.
5. Serve the Almond Cereal with Berries immediately.

Nutritional Information (per serving):
Cal: 230 | Fat: 8g | Chol: 0mg | Sod: 70mg | Carbs: 35g | Fiber: 8g | Sugars: 7g | Pro: 6g

21. Sweet Potato Hash Browns

Preparation time: 20 minutes
Servings: 2

Ingredients:

- 2 medium sweet potatoes
- 1 small onion, diced
- 1 tbsp. olive oil
- 1/2 tsp. paprika
- 1/2 tsp. garlic powder
- 1/4 tsp. salt
- 1/4 tsp. pepper
- Fresh parsley, chopped (for garnish, optional)

Instructions:

1. Peel the sweet potatoes and grate them using a box grater or food processor.
2. Place the grated sweet potatoes in a clean kitchen towel and squeeze out any excess moisture.
3. In a large skillet, heat the olive oil over medium heat.
4. Add the diced onion to the skillet and sauté until it becomes translucent and slightly golden.
5. Add the grated sweet potatoes to the skillet and spread them out evenly.
6. Sprinkle the paprika, garlic powder, salt, and pepper over the sweet potatoes.
7. Cook for about 10-12 minutes, stirring

occasionally, until the sweet potatoes are cooked through and crispy.

8. Remove from heat and garnish with fresh parsley, if desired.
9. Serve the Sweet Potato Hash Browns hot.

Nutritional Information (per serving):
Cal: 180 | Fat: 5g | Chol: 0mg | Sod: 140mg | Carbs: 32g | Fiber: 5g | Sugars: 9g | Pro: 3g

22. Turkey Bacon Sandwich

Preparation time: 10 minutes
Servings: 1

Ingredients:

- 1 whole wheat English muffin
- 2 slices turkey bacon
- 1 large egg
- 1/4 cup baby spinach leaves
- 1 slice low-fat cheese
- Salt and pepper, to taste

Instructions:

1. Preheat a non-stick skillet over medium heat.
2. Place the turkey bacon slices in the skillet and cook until crispy. Remove from the skillet and set aside.
3. In the same skillet, crack the egg and cook to your desired doneness, seasoning with salt and pepper.
4. While the egg is cooking, split the English muffin and lightly toast it.
5. Place the baby spinach leaves on one side of the English muffin.
6. Top with the cooked turkey bacon slices.
7. Slide the cooked egg onto the other side of the English muffin.
8. Place the slice of low-fat cheese on top of the egg.
9. Close the sandwich with the other half of the English muffin.
10. Serve the Turkey Bacon Breakfast Sandwich immediately.

Nutritional Information (per serving):
Cal: 320 | Fat: 11g | Chol: 220mg | Sod: 400mg | Carbs: 31g | Fiber: 5g | Sugars: 2g | Pro: 25g

23. Cottage Cheese Fruit Salad

Preparation time: 10 minutes
Servings: 2

Ingredients:

- 1 cup low-fat cottage cheese

- 1 cup mixed fresh fruits (such as berries, sliced peaches, and grapes)
- 1 tbsp. honey (optional)
- 1 tbsp. chopped nuts (such as almonds or walnuts)
- Fresh mint leaves for garnish (optional)

Instructions:

1. In a mixing bowl, combine the low-fat cottage cheese and mixed fresh fruits.
2. Drizzle the honey over the fruit and cottage cheese mixture, if desired, and gently toss to coat.
3. Sprinkle the chopped nuts over the salad and gently stir.
4. Divide the Cottage Cheese Fruit Salad into serving bowls or plates.
5. Garnish with fresh mint leaves, if desired.
6. Serve immediately.

Nutritional Information (per serving):
Cal: 170 | Fat: 4g | Chol: 5mg | Sod: 200mg | Carbs: 22g | Fiber: 3g | Sugars: 17g | Pro: 13g

24. Veggie Breakfast Quesadilla

Preparation time: 15 minutes
Servings: 2

Ingredients:

- 4 small whole wheat tortillas
- 4 eggs
- 1/2 cup diced bell peppers (any color)
- 1/2 cup diced tomatoes
- 1/2 cup chopped spinach
- 1/4 cup diced red onion
- 1/4 cup shredded reduced-fat cheddar cheese
- Cooking spray
- Salt and pepper to taste

Instructions:

1. In a mixing bowl, beat the eggs and season with salt and pepper.
2. Heat a non-stick skillet over medium heat and lightly coat it with cooking spray.
3. Add the diced bell peppers, tomatoes, spinach, and red onion to the skillet. Sauté for 2-3 minutes until the vegetables are slightly softened.
4. Push the vegetables to one side of the skillet and pour the beaten eggs into the other side. Cook the eggs, stirring occasionally, until scrambled and cooked through.
5. Place two tortillas on a clean surface. Divide the scrambled eggs and sautéed vegetables evenly between the tortillas.
6. Sprinkle shredded cheddar cheese over the eggs and vegetables. Top with the remaining

two tortillas.

7. Heat a large non-stick skillet over medium heat and lightly coat it with cooking spray.
8. Carefully transfer one assembled quesadilla to the skillet and cook for 2-3 minutes on each side until the tortilla is crispy and the cheese is melted. Repeat with the second quesadilla.
9. Remove the quesadillas from the skillet and let them cool for a minute. Cut each quesadilla into wedges.
10. Serve hot and enjoy!

Nutritional Information (per serving):
Cal: 295 | Fat: 12g | Chol: 377mg | Sod: 250mg | Carbs: 28g | Fiber: 6g | Sugars: 4g | Pro: 19g

25. Banana Almond Butter Smoothie

Preparation time: 5 minutes
Servings: 1

Ingredients:

- 1 ripe banana
- 1 tbsp. almond butter (unsalted)
- 1 cup unsweetened almond milk
- 1/2 tsp. honey (optional)
- 1/2 tsp. vanilla extract
- 1/2 cup ice cubes

Instructions:

1. Peel the ripe banana and break it into chunks.
2. In a blender, combine the banana chunks, almond butter, unsweetened almond milk, honey (if using), vanilla extract, and ice cubes.
3. Blend on high speed until all the ingredients are well combined and the smoothie is creamy and smooth.
4. If the smoothie is too thick, you can add a little more almond milk and blend again.
5. Pour the smoothie into a glass and serve immediately.

Nutritional Information (per serving):
Cal: 250 | Fat: 12g | Chol: 0mg | Sod: 90mg | Carbs: 33g | Fiber: 5g | Sugars: 16g | Pro: 5g

Side Dishes and Appetizers

1. Lemon Garlic Roasted Asparagus

Preparation time: 15 minutes
Servings: 4

Ingredients:

- 1 bunch asparagus, ends trimmed
- 2 tablespoons olive oil
- 2 cloves garlic, minced
- Zest of 1 lemon
- Juice of 1/2 lemon
- Salt and pepper to taste

Instructions:

1. Preheat the oven to 425°F (220°C).
2. Place the trimmed asparagus on a baking sheet.
3. In a small bowl, whisk together the olive oil, minced garlic, lemon zest, lemon juice, salt, and pepper.
4. Drizzle the lemon garlic mixture over the asparagus, tossing to coat evenly.
5. Arrange the asparagus in a single layer on the baking sheet.
6. Roast in the preheated oven for 10-12 minutes, or until the asparagus is tender and slightly crispy.
7. Remove from the oven and serve immediately.

Nutritional Information (per serving):
Cal: 70 | Fat: 5g | Chol: 0mg | Sod: 10mg | Carbs: 5g | Fiber: 2g | Sugars: 2g | Pro: 2g

2. Caprese Salad Skewers

Preparation time: 15 minutes
Servings: 4

Ingredients:

- 1 pint cherry tomatoes
- 8 small mozzarella balls (about 1 inch in diameter)
- 16 fresh basil leaves
- 2 tablespoons balsamic glaze
- Freshly ground pepper, to taste

Instructions:

1. Rinse the cherry tomatoes and pat them dry.
2. Skewer one cherry tomato, followed by a mozzarella ball, and then a basil leaf. Repeat the sequence until all the ingredients are used.
3. Arrange the skewers on a serving platter.
4. Drizzle the balsamic glaze over the skewers.
5. Sprinkle freshly ground pepper over the skewers for added flavor.
6. Serve immediately.

Nutritional Information (per serving):
Cal: 125 | Fat: 9g | Chol: 25mg | Sod: 75mg | Carbs: 4g | Fiber: 1g | Sugars: 3g | Pro: 7g

3. Baked Zucchini Fries

Preparation time: 30 minutes
Servings: 4

Ingredients:

- 2 medium zucchini
- 1/4 cup whole wheat flour
- 1/2 tsp. garlic powder
- 1/2 tsp. paprika
- 1/4 tsp. salt
- 1/4 tsp. pepper
- 2 eggs, beaten
- Cooking spray

Instructions:

1. Preheat the oven to 425°F (220°C). Line a baking sheet with parchment paper and lightly coat it with cooking spray.
2. Wash the zucchini and cut them into long, thin strips resembling fries.
3. In a shallow bowl, combine the whole wheat flour, garlic powder, paprika, salt, and pepper.
4. Dip each zucchini strip into the beaten eggs, allowing the excess to drip off, then coat it in the flour mixture. Shake off any excess flour.
5. Place the coated zucchini strips on the prepared baking sheet, leaving space between each fry.
6. Lightly spray the fries with cooking spray to help them crisp up in the oven.
7. Bake for 15-20 minutes, or until the zucchini fries are golden brown and crispy.
8. Remove from the oven and let them cool for a few minutes before serving.

Nutritional Information (per serving):
Cal: 82 | Fat: 3g | Chol: 93mg | Sod: 185mg | Carbs: 10g | Fiber: 2g | Sugars: 2g | Pro: 5g

4. Greek Cucumber Salad

Preparation time: 15 minutes
Servings: 4

Ingredients:

- 2 English cucumbers, sliced
- 1 cup cherry tomatoes, halved
- 1/2 cup red onion, thinly sliced
- 1/4 cup Kalamata olives, pitted and halved
- 1/4 cup crumbled feta cheese
- 2 tablespoons extra-virgin olive oil

- 1 tbsp. lemon juice
- 1 tbsp. red wine vinegar
- 1 tsp. dried oregano
- Salt and pepper, to taste
- Fresh parsley, for garnish (optional)

Instructions:

1. In a large bowl, combine the sliced cucumbers, cherry tomatoes, red onion, Kalamata olives, and crumbled feta cheese.
2. In a separate small bowl, whisk together the olive oil, lemon juice, red wine vinegar, dried oregano, salt, and pepper to make the dressing.
3. Pour the dressing over the cucumber mixture and toss gently to coat all the ingredients evenly.
4. Taste and adjust the seasoning if needed.
5. Let the salad marinate in the refrigerator for at least 15 minutes to allow the flavors to meld together.
6. Before serving, garnish with fresh parsley if desired.

Nutritional Information (per serving):
Cal: 110 | Fat: 8g | Chol: 6mg | Sod: 200mg | Carbs: 8g | Fiber: 2g | Sugars: 4g | Pro: 3g

5. Spicy Edamame Stir Fry

Preparation time: 15 minutes
Servings: 4

Ingredients:

- 2 cups frozen edamame, shelled
- 1 red bell pepper, thinly sliced
- 1 small carrot, thinly sliced
- 1 cup snap peas
- 1 tbsp. low-sodium soy sauce
- 1 tbsp. rice vinegar
- 1 tsp. sesame oil
- 1/2 tsp. crushed red pepper flakes
- 2 cloves garlic, minced
- 1 tbsp. vegetable oil
- Sesame seeds, for garnish (optional)
- Green onions, sliced, for garnish (optional)

Instructions:

1. In a pot of boiling water, cook the edamame according to package instructions. Drain and set aside.
2. In a small bowl, whisk together the soy sauce, rice vinegar, sesame oil, crushed red pepper flakes, and minced garlic to make the sauce.
3. Heat the vegetable oil in a large skillet or wok over medium-high heat.
4. Add the red bell pepper, carrot, and snap peas to the skillet and stir-fry for 3-4 minutes until the

vegetables are crisp-tender.
5. Add the cooked edamame and the sauce to the skillet, tossing everything together to coat the vegetables and edamame evenly.
6. Continue to stir-fry for another 2-3 minutes until the sauce is heated through.
7. Remove from heat and garnish with sesame seeds and sliced green onions if desired.

Nutritional Information (per serving):
Cal: 160 | Fat: 7g | Chol: 0mg | Sod: 130mg | Carbs: 16g | Fiber: 6g | Sugars: 5g | Pro: 9g

6. Stuffed Mushroom Caps

Preparation time: 20 minutes
Servings: 4

Ingredients:

- 16 large mushroom caps
- 1 tbsp. olive oil
- 1 small onion, finely chopped
- 2 cloves garlic, minced
- 1/2 cup whole wheat breadcrumbs
- 1/4 cup grated Parmesan cheese
- 2 tablespoons chopped fresh parsley
- 1/2 tsp. dried oregano
- 1/4 tsp. salt
- 1/4 tsp. pepper

Instructions:

1. Preheat the oven to 375°F (190°C).
2. Remove the stems from the mushroom caps and finely chop them.
3. Heat the olive oil in a skillet over medium heat. Add the chopped mushroom stems, onion, and garlic, and sauté until softened, about 5 minutes.
4. In a mixing bowl, combine the sautéed mushroom mixture with the breadcrumbs, Parmesan cheese, parsley, oregano, salt, and pepper. Stir well to combine.
5. Spoon the filling mixture into the mushroom caps, filling each one generously.
6. Place the stuffed mushroom caps on a baking sheet and bake in the preheated oven for 15 minutes or until the mushrooms are tender and the filling is golden brown.
7. Remove from the oven and let cool for a few minutes before serving.

Nutritional Information (per serving):
Cal: 120 | Fat: 5g | Chol: 2mg | Sod: 180mg | Carbs: 14g | Fiber: 3g | Sugars: 4g | Pro: 6g

7. Fresh Tomato Bruschetta

Preparation time: 15 minutes
Servings: 4

Ingredients:

*   4 ripe tomatoes, diced
*   2 cloves garlic, minced
*   1/4 cup fresh basil leaves, chopped
*   2 tablespoons extra-virgin olive oil
*   1 tbsp. balsamic vinegar
*   1/4 tsp. salt
*   1/4 tsp. pepper
*   8 slices whole wheat baguette

Instructions:

1. In a mixing bowl, combine the diced tomatoes, minced garlic, chopped basil leaves, olive oil, balsamic vinegar, salt, and pepper. Toss well to combine.
2. Let the tomato mixture sit for about 10 minutes to allow the flavors to meld together.
3. Meanwhile, lightly toast the slices of whole wheat baguette.
4. Spoon the tomato mixture onto the toasted baguette slices, dividing it evenly.
5. Serve the bruschetta immediately and enjoy!

Nutritional Information (per serving):
Cal: 140 | Fat: 7g | Chol: 0mg | Sod: 240mg | Carbs: 18g | Fiber: 3g | Sugars: 4g | Pro: 3g

8. Avocado Cucumber Salsa

Preparation time: 10 minutes
Servings: 4

Ingredients:

*   1 large avocado, diced
*   1 medium cucumber, diced
*   1/4 cup red onion, finely chopped
*   1 jalapeno pepper, seeded and finely chopped
*   2 tablespoons fresh cilantro, chopped
*   1 tbsp. lime juice
*   1/2 tsp. cumin
*   1/4 tsp. salt
*   1/4 tsp. pepper

Instructions:

1. In a mixing bowl, combine the diced avocado, cucumber, red onion, jalapeno pepper, cilantro, lime juice, cumin, salt, and pepper.
2. Gently toss the ingredients together until well combined.
3. Taste and adjust the seasonings if needed.

4. Serve the avocado cucumber salsa immediately as a dip or topping for grilled meats, tacos, or salads.

Nutritional Information (per serving):
Cal: 80 | Fat: 6g | Chol: 0mg | Sod: 150mg | Carbs: 7g | -Fiber: 4g | Sugars: 2g | Pro: 1g

9. Steamed Broccoli with Lemon

Preparation time: 15 minutes
Servings: 4

Ingredients:

*   1 head of broccoli, cut into florets
*   1 tbsp. lemon juice
*   1 tbsp. extra-virgin olive oil
*   1/4 tsp. salt
*   1/4 tsp. pepper
*   Lemon wedges for garnish (optional)

Instructions:

1. Fill a pot with 1-2 inches of water and place a steamer basket inside. Bring the water to a boil over medium heat.
2. Add the broccoli florets to the steamer basket and cover the pot with a lid. Steam the broccoli for about 5-7 minutes or until it becomes tender but still vibrant green.
3. Remove the steamed broccoli from the pot and transfer it to a serving dish.
4. In a small bowl, whisk together the lemon juice, olive oil, salt, and pepper.
5. Drizzle the lemon dressing over the steamed broccoli and toss gently to coat.
6. Garnish with lemon wedges if desired.
7. Serve the steamed broccoli with lemon as a side dish or enjoy it on its own.

Nutritional Information (per serving):
Cal: 50 | Fat: 3.5g | Chol: 0mg | Sod: 160mg | Carbs: 5g | Fiber: 2g | Sugars: 1g | Pro: 2g

10. Baked Sweet Potato Wedges

Preparation time: 30 minutes
Servings: 4

Ingredients:

*   2 large sweet potatoes
*   1 tbsp. olive oil
*   1/2 tsp. paprika
*   1/4 tsp. garlic powder
*   1/4 tsp. onion powder
*   1/4 tsp. salt (optional)

- 1/4 tsp. pepper

Instructions:

1. Preheat your oven to 425°F (220°C).
2. Wash and scrub the sweet potatoes, then cut them into wedges.
3. In a large bowl, combine the olive oil, paprika, garlic powder, onion powder, salt (if using), and pepper. Mix well.
4. Add the sweet potato wedges to the bowl and toss them until they are evenly coated with the oil and spice mixture.
5. Arrange the sweet potato wedges in a single layer on a baking sheet lined with parchment paper or a silicone baking mat.
6. Bake the sweet potato wedges in the preheated oven for about 25-30 minutes, or until they are golden brown and crispy on the outside, flipping them halfway through.
7. Once baked, remove the sweet potato wedges from the oven and let them cool slightly before serving.

Nutritional Information (per serving):
Cal: 120 | Fat: 3g | Chol: 0mg | Sod: 160mg | Carbs: 22g | Fiber: 4g | Sugars: 5g | Pro: 2g

11. Spinach and Feta Peppers

Preparation time: 45 minutes
Servings: 4

Ingredients:

- 4 large bell peppers (any color)
- 1 tbsp. olive oil
- 1 small onion, finely chopped
- 2 cloves garlic, minced
- 4 cups fresh spinach, chopped
- 1/2 cup crumbled feta cheese
- 1/4 cup grated Parmesan cheese
- 1/4 cup breadcrumbs
- 1/2 tsp. dried oregano
- 1/4 tsp. pepper
- Optional toppings: chopped fresh parsley, red pepper flakes

Instructions:

1. Preheat your oven to 375°F (190°C).
2. Slice off the tops of the bell peppers and remove the seeds and membranes from the inside. Set aside.
3. In a large skillet, heat the olive oil over medium heat. Add the chopped onion and minced garlic, and sauté until the onion is translucent.
4. Add the chopped spinach to the skillet and cook until wilted, stirring occasionally.

5. Remove the skillet from heat and stir in the crumbled feta cheese, grated Parmesan cheese, breadcrumbs, dried oregano, and pepper. Mix well until the filling is evenly combined.
6. Stuff each bell pepper with the spinach and feta filling, packing it tightly.
7. Place the stuffed peppers in a baking dish and cover with foil.
8. Bake in the preheated oven for 25 minutes. Then, remove the foil and bake for an additional 10 minutes, or until the peppers are tender and the tops are golden brown.
9. Remove from the oven and let the stuffed peppers cool for a few minutes before serving.

Nutritional Information (per serving):
Cal: 180 | Fat: 9g | Chol: 20mg | Sod: 210mg | Carbs: 18g | Fiber: 5g | Sugars: 8g | Pro: 10g

12. Cilantro Lime Quinoa Salad

Preparation time: 20 minutes
Servings: 4

Ingredients:

- 1 cup quinoa
- 2 cups water
- 1 cup cherry tomatoes, halved
- 1/2 cup diced cucumber
- 1/4 cup chopped red onion
- 1/4 cup chopped fresh cilantro
- 2 tablespoons fresh lime juice
- 1 tbsp. extra-virgin olive oil
- 1/2 tsp. ground cumin
- Salt and pepper to taste

Instructions:

1. Rinse the quinoa thoroughly under cold water.
2. In a medium saucepan, bring the water to a boil. Add the quinoa and reduce the heat to low. Cover and simmer for 15 minutes, or until the water is absorbed and the quinoa is tender. Remove from heat and let it cool.
3. In a large bowl, combine the cooked quinoa, cherry tomatoes, cucumber, red onion, and chopped cilantro.
4. In a small bowl, whisk together the lime juice, olive oil, ground cumin, salt, and pepper.
5. Pour the dressing over the quinoa mixture and toss to combine, ensuring all ingredients are well coated.
6. Serve the Cilantro Lime Quinoa Salad chilled or at room temperature.

Nutritional Information (per serving):
Cal: 225 | Fat: 6g | Chol: 0mg | Sod: 25mg | Carbs: 37g | Fiber: 5g | Sugars: 3g | Pro: 6g

13. Roasted Brussels Sprouts

Preparation time: 25 minutes
Servings: 4

Ingredients:

- 1 pound Brussels sprouts
- 2 tablespoons olive oil
- 1/2 tsp. garlic powder
- 1/2 tsp. onion powder
- 1/2 tsp. paprika
- Salt and pepper to taste

Instructions:

1. Preheat the oven to 425°F (220°C).
2. Trim the ends of the Brussels sprouts and remove any discolored outer leaves. Cut larger Brussels sprouts in half.
3. In a large bowl, toss the Brussels sprouts with olive oil, garlic powder, onion powder, paprika, salt, and pepper until evenly coated.
4. Spread the Brussels sprouts in a single layer on a baking sheet.
5. Roast in the preheated oven for 20-25 minutes, or until the Brussels sprouts are tender and golden brown, tossing them halfway through cooking for even browning.
6. Remove from the oven and let them cool slightly before serving.

Nutritional Information (per serving):
Cal: 108 | Fat: 7g | Chol: 0mg | Sod: 22mg | Carbs: 10g | Fiber: 4g | Sugars: 2g | Pro: 4g

14. Greek Yogurt Vegetable Dip

Preparation time: 10 minutes
Servings: 4

Ingredients:

- 1 cup plain Greek yogurt
- 1/2 cup diced cucumber
- 1/4 cup diced red bell pepper
- 1/4 cup diced red onion
- 1 clove garlic, minced
- 2 tablespoons chopped fresh dill
- 1 tbsp. lemon juice
- Salt and pepper to taste

Instructions:

1. In a bowl, combine the Greek yogurt, cucumber, red bell pepper, red onion, minced garlic, chopped fresh dill, lemon juice, salt, and pepper.
2. Stir well to combine all the ingredients.
3. Taste and adjust the seasoning if needed.

4. Cover the bowl and refrigerate for at least 30 minutes to allow the flavors to blend.
5. Serve the dip chilled with a variety of fresh vegetables for dipping.

Nutritional Information (per serving):
Cal: 61 | Fat: 1g | Chol: 2mg | Sod: 24mg | Carbs: 7g | Fiber: 1g | Sugars: 4g | Pro: 7g

15. Grilled Eggplant Slices

Preparation time: 15 minutes
Servings: 4

Ingredients:

- 1 large eggplant
- 2 tablespoons olive oil
- 1 tsp. dried oregano
- 1/2 tsp. garlic powder
- Salt and pepper to taste
- Fresh lemon juice (optional)

Instructions:

1. Preheat the grill to medium-high heat.
2. Slice the eggplant into 1/2-inch thick rounds.
3. In a small bowl, combine the olive oil, dried oregano, garlic powder, salt, and pepper.
4. Brush both sides of the eggplant slices with the oil mixture.
5. Place the eggplant slices on the preheated grill and cook for about 4-5 minutes on each side, or until tender and grill marks appear.
6. Remove the grilled eggplant slices from the grill and transfer them to a serving platter.
7. Optional: Drizzle the slices with fresh lemon juice for added flavor.
8. Serve the grilled eggplant slices as a side dish or use them in sandwiches, salads, or as a topping for pizzas.

Nutritional Information (per serving):
Cal: 90 | Fat: 7g | Chol: 0mg | Sod: 4mg | Carbs: 7g | Fiber: 4g | Sugars: 3g | Pro: 1g

16. Black Bean Hummus

Preparation time: 10 minutes
Servings: 6

Ingredients:

- 1 can (15 ounces) black beans, drained and rinsed
- 2 tablespoons tahini
- 2 tablespoons lemon juice
- 1 clove garlic, minced

- 1/2 tsp. ground cumin
- 1/2 tsp. paprika
- 1/4 tsp. salt (optional)
- 2 tablespoons olive oil
- Fresh parsley or cilantro, for garnish (optional)

Instructions:

1. In a food processor or blender, combine the black beans, tahini, lemon juice, garlic, cumin, paprika, and salt (if using).
2. Process the ingredients until smooth and well combined, scraping down the sides as needed.
3. While the food processor is running, slowly drizzle in the olive oil until the mixture reaches a creamy consistency.
4. Taste and adjust the seasonings if needed, adding more lemon juice, garlic, or salt to taste.
5. Transfer the black bean hummus to a serving bowl and garnish with fresh parsley or cilantro if desired.
6. Serve the black bean hummus with fresh vegetables, whole grain crackers, or as a spread in sandwiches or wraps.

Nutritional Information (per serving):
Cal: 105 | Fat: 6g | Chol: 0mg | Sod: 81mg | Carbs: 10g | Fiber: 4g | Sugars: 0g | Pro: 4g

17. Stuffed Cherry Tomatoes

Preparation time: 15 minutes
Servings: 6

Ingredients:

- 24 cherry tomatoes
- 4 ounces low-fat cream cheese
- 2 tablespoons chopped fresh herbs (such as basil, parsley, or chives)
- 1 tbsp. lemon juice
- 1/4 tsp. garlic powder
- Salt and pepper to taste
- Optional toppings: sliced olives, chopped cucumber, or crumbled feta cheese

Instructions:

1. Slice off the top of each cherry tomato and use a small spoon or melon baller to scoop out the seeds and pulp, creating small tomato cups. Set aside.
2. In a mixing bowl, combine the cream cheese, chopped fresh herbs, lemon juice, garlic powder, salt, and pepper. Stir until well mixed.
3. Using a small spoon or piping bag, fill each tomato cup with the cream cheese mixture.
4. Optional: Top the stuffed tomatoes with sliced olives, chopped cucumber, or crumbled feta

cheese for added flavor and texture.
5. Arrange the stuffed cherry tomatoes on a serving platter and refrigerate until ready to serve.

Nutritional Information (per serving):
Cal: 58 | Fat: 3g | Chol: 10mg | Sod: 45mg | Carbs: 6g | Fiber: 1g | Sugars: 3g | Pro: 2g

18. Baked Parmesan Zucchini

Preparation time: 20 minutes
Servings: 4

Ingredients:

- 2 medium zucchini
- 2 tablespoons olive oil
- 1/4 cup grated Parmesan cheese
- 1/4 tsp. garlic powder
- 1/4 tsp. dried oregano
- Salt and pepper to taste

Instructions:

1. Preheat the oven to 425°F (220°C) and line a baking sheet with parchment paper.
2. Wash the zucchini and slice them into 1/4-inch thick rounds.
3. In a mixing bowl, combine the olive oil, grated Parmesan cheese, garlic powder, dried oregano, salt, and pepper. Stir until well mixed.
4. Dip each zucchini round into the Parmesan mixture, coating both sides. Place them in a single layer on the prepared baking sheet.
5. Bake in the preheated oven for 15-18 minutes or until the zucchini rounds are tender and the Parmesan cheese is golden brown.
6. Remove from the oven and let them cool slightly before serving.

Nutritional Information (per serving):
Cal: 105 | Fat: 9g | Chol: 4mg | Sod: 111mg | Carbs: 3g | Fiber: 1g | Sugars: 2g | Pro: 3g

19. Cucumber Greek Yogurt Dip

Preparation time: 10 minutes
Servings: 4

Ingredients:

- 1 large cucumber
- 1 cup plain Greek yogurt
- 1 clove garlic, minced
- 1 tbsp. fresh lemon juice
- 1 tbsp. chopped fresh dill
- Salt and pepper to taste

Instructions:

1. Peel the cucumber, then grate or finely chop it. Place the grated cucumber in a clean kitchen towel and squeeze out any excess moisture.
2. In a mixing bowl, combine the Greek yogurt, minced garlic, lemon juice, chopped dill, salt, and pepper. Stir well to combine.
3. Add the grated cucumber to the yogurt mixture and mix until well combined.
4. Taste and adjust the seasoning if needed.
5. Transfer the dip to a serving bowl and garnish with additional chopped dill, if desired.
6. Serve with fresh vegetables or whole-grain pita bread.

Nutritional Information (per serving):
Cal: 54 | Fat: 0g | Chol: 2mg | Sod: 27mg | Carbs: 6g | - Fiber: 1g | Sugars: 4g | Pro: 8g

20. Roasted Cauliflower Bites

Preparation time: 10 minutes
Cooking time: 25 minutes
Servings: 4

Ingredients:

- 1 medium head cauliflower
- 2 tablespoons olive oil
- 1 tsp. garlic powder
- 1 tsp. paprika
- 1/2 tsp. salt
- 1/4 tsp. pepper
- Optional toppings: fresh parsley, grated Parmesan cheese

Instructions:

1. Preheat your oven to 425°F (220°C) and line a baking sheet with parchment paper.
2. Cut the cauliflower into bite-sized florets and place them in a large bowl.
3. In a small bowl, mix together the olive oil, garlic powder, paprika, salt, and pepper.
4. Drizzle the olive oil mixture over the cauliflower florets and toss to coat them evenly.
5. Spread the cauliflower florets in a single layer on the prepared baking sheet.
6. Roast in the preheated oven for about 25 minutes, or until the cauliflower is golden brown and tender, stirring halfway through.
7. Remove from the oven and let the roasted cauliflower cool slightly.
8. Optional: Sprinkle with fresh parsley and grated Parmesan cheese before serving.
9. Serve the roasted cauliflower bites as a side dish or a healthy snack.

Nutritional Information (per serving):
Cal: 98 | Fat: 7g | Chol: 0mg | Sod: 300mg | Carbs: 8g | - Fiber: 3g | Sugars: 3g | Pro: 3g

21. Mediterranean Stuffed Olives

Preparation time: 15 minutes
Servings: 4

Ingredients:

- 1 cup pitted green olives
- 1/4 cup crumbled feta cheese
- 1 tbsp. chopped fresh parsley
- 1 tbsp. chopped sun-dried tomatoes (packed in oil)
- 1 tsp. lemon zest
- 1 tsp. extra virgin olive oil
- Freshly ground pepper to taste

Instructions:

1. In a small bowl, combine the feta cheese, chopped parsley, chopped sun-dried tomatoes, lemon zest, and extra virgin olive oil.
2. Mix the ingredients until well combined.
3. Take each pitted green olive and stuff it with a small amount of the feta cheese mixture.
4. Repeat the process until all the olives are stuffed.
5. Arrange the stuffed olives on a serving plate.
6. Sprinkle freshly ground pepper over the stuffed olives.
7. Serve the Mediterranean Stuffed Olives as an appetizer or a snack.

Nutritional Information (per serving):
Cal: 65 | Fat: 6g | Chol: 8mg | Sod: 264mg | Carbs: 2g | - Fiber: 1g | Sugars: 0g | Pro: 2g

22. Steamed Green Beans Almonds

Preparation time: 15 minutes
Servings: 4

Ingredients:

- 1 pound fresh green beans, ends trimmed
- 2 tablespoons slivered almonds
- 1 tbsp. extra virgin olive oil
- 1 garlic clove, minced
- 1/2 tsp. lemon zest
- Salt and pepper to taste

Instructions:

1. Fill a large pot with water and bring it to a boil.
2. Add the green beans to the boiling water and cook for 3-5 minutes, until the beans are ten

der-crisp.

3. Drain the green beans and immediately transfer them to a bowl of ice water to stop the cooking process and preserve their bright green color. Let them cool for a few minutes, then drain again.
4. In a skillet, toast the slivered almonds over medium heat until they turn golden brown and fragrant. Stir frequently to prevent burning.
5. In a small bowl, whisk together the extra virgin olive oil, minced garlic, lemon zest, salt, and pepper.
6. In a serving dish, toss the steamed green beans with the prepared dressing.
7. Sprinkle the toasted almonds over the green beans.
8. Serve the Steamed Green Beans with Almonds as a side dish or a light meal.

Nutritional Information (per serving):
Cal: 93 | Fat: 6g | Chol: 0mg | Sod: 8mg | Carbs: 9g | Fiber: 4g | Sugars: 3g | Pro: 3g

23. Quinoa Stuffed Bell Peppers

Preparation time: 20 minutes
Cooking time: 35 minutes
Servings: 4

Ingredients:

- 4 bell peppers (any color), tops removed and seeds removed
- 1 cup cooked quinoa
- 1 cup black beans, rinsed and drained
- 1/2 cup corn kernels (fresh or frozen)
- 1/2 cup diced tomatoes
- 1/4 cup diced red onion
- 2 cloves garlic, minced
- 1 tsp. cumin
- 1/2 tsp. paprika
- 1/2 tsp. dried oregano
- Salt and pepper to taste
- Optional toppings: fresh cilantro, avocado slices, lime wedges

Instructions:

1. Preheat the oven to 375°F (190°C).
2. In a large mixing bowl, combine the cooked quinoa, black beans, corn kernels, diced tomatoes, red onion, minced garlic, cumin, paprika, dried oregano, salt, and pepper. Mix well.
3. Stuff each bell pepper with the quinoa mixture, pressing it down gently to fill the pepper completely.
4. Place the stuffed bell peppers in a baking dish and cover with foil.
5. Bake in the preheated oven for 30-35 minutes, or until the bell peppers are tender.

6. Remove the foil and bake for an additional 5 minutes to lightly brown the tops.
7. Remove from the oven and let the stuffed bell peppers cool for a few minutes.
8. Serve the Quinoa Stuffed Bell Peppers with optional toppings such as fresh cilantro, avocado slices, and lime wedges.

Nutritional Information (per serving):
Cal: 259 | Fat: 2.5g | Chol: 0mg | Sod: 73mg | Carbs: 52g | Fiber: 13g | Sugars: 8g | Pro: 12g

24. Zesty Kale Chips

Preparation time: 10 minutes
Cooking time: 20 minutes
Servings: 4

Ingredients:

- 1 bunch of kale
- 1 tbsp. olive oil
- 1 tbsp. lemon juice
- 1 tsp. chili powder
- 1/2 tsp. garlic powder
- Salt to taste

Instructions:

1. Preheat the oven to 300°F (150°C).
2. Wash the kale thoroughly and pat it dry with a clean kitchen towel or paper towel.
3. Remove the tough stems from the kale leaves and tear the leaves into bite-sized pieces.
4. In a large mixing bowl, combine the olive oil, lemon juice, chili powder, garlic powder, and salt. Mix well.
5. Add the kale leaves to the bowl and toss them in the seasoning mixture until well coated.
6. Arrange the kale leaves in a single layer on a baking sheet lined with parchment paper.
7. Place the baking sheet in the preheated oven and bake for about 15-20 minutes, or until the kale chips are crispy and slightly browned. Keep an eye on them to prevent burning.
8. Remove from the oven and let the kale chips cool for a few minutes before serving.

Nutritional Information (per serving):
Cal: 60 | Fat: 4g | Chol: 0mg | Sod: 80mg | Carbs: 5g | Fiber: 1.5g | Sugars: 1g | Pro: 2g

25. Guacamole Stuffed Cucumber Bites

Preparation time: 15 minutes
Servings: 4

Ingredients:

- 2 large cucumbers
- 1 ripe avocado
- 1 small tomato, diced
- 1/4 cup red onion, finely chopped
- 1 tbsp. fresh lime juice
- 1 tbsp. chopped fresh cilantro
- Salt and pepper to taste

Instructions:

1. Wash the cucumbers and cut them into 1-inch thick slices.
2. Use a small spoon or melon baller to hollow out the center of each cucumber slice, creating a small well for the guacamole.
3. In a bowl, mash the avocado with a fork until creamy.
4. Add the diced tomato, red onion, lime juice, and chopped cilantro to the mashed avocado. Mix well.
5. Season the guacamole with salt and pepper to taste.
6. Spoon the guacamole mixture into the hollowed-out cucumber slices, filling them generously.
7. Arrange the stuffed cucumber bites on a serving platter and garnish with additional cilantro, if desired.
8. Serve immediately and enjoy!

Nutritional Information (per serving):
Cal: 90 | Fat: 7g | Chol: 0mg | Sod: 10mg | Carbs: 7g | -
Fiber: 4g | Sugars: 2g | Pro: 2g

Soups

1. Tomato Basil Soup

Preparation time: 30 minutes
Servings: 4

Ingredients:

- 1 tbsp. olive oil
- 1 onion, chopped
- 2 cloves garlic, minced
- 4 cups low-sodium vegetable broth
- 2 cans (14.5 ounces each) diced tomatoes
- 1/4 cup tomato paste
- 1/2 cup fresh basil leaves, chopped
- 1/2 tsp. dried oregano
- Salt and pepper to taste
- Optional toppings: fresh basil leaves, grated Parmesan cheese

Instructions:

1. Heat the olive oil in a large pot over medium heat.
2. Add the chopped onion and minced garlic to the pot. Sauté until the onion becomes translucent and fragrant, about 5 minutes.
3. Pour in the low-sodium vegetable broth, diced tomatoes (with their juices), and tomato paste. Stir to combine.
4. Add the chopped basil leaves and dried oregano to the pot. Season with salt and pepper to taste.
5. Bring the soup to a boil, then reduce the heat to low. Simmer uncovered for 15-20 minutes, allowing the flavors to meld together.
6. Once the soup has simmered, remove it from the heat and let it cool slightly.
7. Use an immersion blender or transfer the soup to a blender in batches to puree until smooth. Be careful when blending hot liquids.
8. Return the pureed soup to the pot and heat it gently if necessary.
9. Ladle the tomato basil soup into bowls and garnish with fresh basil leaves and grated Parmesan cheese, if desired.
10. Serve hot and enjoy!

Nutritional Information (per serving):
Cal: 110 | Fat: 4g | Chol: 0mg | Sod: 170mg | Carbs: 17g | Fiber: 4g | Sugars: 9g | Pro: 4g

2. Lentil Vegetable Stew

Preparation time: 45 minutes
Servings: 6

Ingredients:

- 1 tbsp. olive oil
- 1 onion, chopped
- 2 cloves garlic, minced
- 2 carrots, diced
- 2 celery stalks, diced
- 1 red bell pepper, diced
- 1 zucchini, diced
- 1 cup dried lentils, rinsed and drained
- 4 cups low-sodium vegetable broth
- 1 can (14.5 ounces) diced tomatoes
- 1 tsp. dried thyme
- 1 tsp. paprika
- Salt and pepper to taste
- Fresh parsley, chopped (for garnish)

Instructions:

1. Heat the olive oil in a large pot over medium heat.
2. Add the chopped onion and minced garlic to the pot. Sauté until the onion becomes translucent and fragrant, about 5 minutes.
3. Add the diced carrots, celery, red bell pepper, and zucchini to the pot. Stir and cook for another 5 minutes until the vegetables begin to soften.
4. Add the rinsed lentils, low-sodium vegetable broth, diced tomatoes (with their juices), dried thyme, and paprika to the pot. Season with salt and pepper to taste.
5. Bring the stew to a boil, then reduce the heat to low. Cover the pot and simmer for 30 minutes or until the lentils and vegetables are tender.
6. Once the stew is cooked, taste and adjust the seasoning if needed.
7. Ladle the lentil vegetable stew into bowls, garnish with fresh parsley, and serve hot.

Nutritional Information (per serving):
Cal: 220 | Fat: 3g | Chol: 0mg | Sod: 150mg | Carbs: 39g | Fiber: 14g | Sugars: 7g | Pro: 13g

3. Chicken Noodle Soup

Preparation time: 45 minutes
Servings: 6

Ingredients:

- 1 tbsp. olive oil
- 1 onion, chopped
- 2 carrots, sliced
- 2 celery stalks, sliced
- 2 cloves garlic, minced
- 6 cups low-sodium chicken broth
- 2 cups cooked chicken breast, shredded
- 2 cups egg noodles
- 1 tsp. dried thyme
- Salt and pepper to taste
- Fresh parsley, chopped (for garnish)

Instructions:

1. Heat the olive oil in a large pot over medium heat.
2. Add the chopped onion, sliced carrots, sliced celery, and minced garlic to the pot. Sauté for about 5 minutes until the vegetables begin to soften.
3. Pour in the low-sodium chicken broth and bring it to a boil.
4. Add the shredded chicken, egg noodles, dried thyme, salt, and pepper to the pot. Stir well to combine.
5. Reduce the heat to low and simmer for about 15 minutes or until the noodles are cooked and the vegetables are tender.
6. Taste the soup and adjust the seasoning if needed.
7. Ladle the chicken noodle soup into bowls, garnish with fresh parsley, and serve hot.

Nutritional Information (per serving):
Cal: 240 | Fat: 6g | Chol: 45mg | Sod: 120mg | Carbs: 24g | Fiber: 3g | Sugars: 3g | Pro: 20g

4. Minestrone Soup Delight

Preparation time: 40 minutes
Servings: 6

Ingredients:

- 1 tbsp. olive oil
- 1 onion, chopped
- 2 cloves garlic, minced
- 2 carrots, diced
- 2 celery stalks, diced
- 1 zucchini, diced
- 1 cup green beans, cut into 1-inch pieces
- 1 can (14 oz) diced tomatoes (low sodium, if available)
- 4 cups low-sodium vegetable broth
- 1 cup cooked kidney beans
- 1 cup cooked chickpeas
- 1 cup whole wheat pasta, such as penne or macaroni
- 1 tsp. dried basil
- 1 tsp. dried oregano
- Salt and pepper to taste
- Fresh parsley, chopped (for garnish)

Instructions:

1. Heat the olive oil in a large pot over medium heat.
2. Add the chopped onion and minced garlic to the pot. Sauté for about 5 minutes until the onion becomes translucent.
3. Add the diced carrots, diced celery, diced zucchini, and cut green beans to the pot. Cook for another 5 minutes, stirring occasionally.
4. Pour in the diced tomatoes (including the juice) and low-sodium vegetable broth. Stir well.
5. Add the cooked kidney beans, cooked chickpeas, and whole wheat pasta to the pot. Stir in the dried basil and dried oregano.
6. Bring the soup to a boil, then reduce the heat to low. Cover the pot and simmer for about 20 minutes or until the vegetables are tender and the pasta is cooked.
7. Season the soup with salt and pepper to taste.
8. Ladle the Minestrone Soup Delight into bowls, garnish with fresh parsley, and serve hot.

Nutritional Information (per serving):
Cal: 250 | Fat: 4g | Chol: 0mg | Sod: 150mg | Carbs: 46g | Fiber: 10g | Sugars: 6g | Pro: 11g

5. Butternut Squash Bisque

Preparation time: 45 minutes
Servings: 4

Ingredients:

- 1 medium butternut squash, peeled, seeded, and cubed
- 1 tbsp. olive oil
- 1 onion, chopped
- 2 cloves garlic, minced
- 2 carrots, chopped
- 2 celery stalks, chopped
- 4 cups low-sodium vegetable broth
- 1 tsp. dried thyme
- 1/2 tsp. ground nutmeg
- Salt and pepper to taste
- Fresh parsley, chopped (for garnish)

Instructions:

1. Heat the olive oil in a large pot over medium heat.
2. Add the chopped onion, minced garlic, chopped carrots, and chopped celery to the pot. Sauté for about 5 minutes until the vegetables start to soften.
3. Add the cubed butternut squash to the pot and cook for another 5 minutes, stirring occasionally.
4. Pour in the low-sodium vegetable broth and bring the mixture to a boil.
5. Reduce the heat to low and simmer for about 25-30 minutes until the butternut squash is tender.
6. Use an immersion blender or transfer the soup to a blender to puree until smooth and creamy.
7. Stir in the dried thyme and ground nutmeg. Season with salt and pepper to taste.
8. Ladle the Butternut Squash Bisque into bowls, garnish with fresh parsley, and serve hot.

6. Gazpacho with Fresh Veggies

Preparation time: 15 minutes
Servings: 4

Ingredients:

- 4 large tomatoes, diced
- 1 cucumber, peeled and diced
- 1 red bell pepper, diced
- 1 green bell pepper, diced
- 1 small red onion, finely chopped
- 2 cloves garlic, minced
- 2 tablespoons extra-virgin olive oil
- 2 tablespoons red wine vinegar
- 1 tbsp. lemon juice
- 1 tsp. dried basil
- 1/2 tsp. dried oregano
- Salt and pepper to taste
- Fresh basil leaves (for garnish)

Instructions:

1. In a large bowl, combine the diced tomatoes, cucumber, red bell pepper, green bell pepper, red onion, and minced garlic.
2. In a separate small bowl, whisk together the olive oil, red wine vinegar, lemon juice, dried basil, dried oregano, salt, and pepper.
3. Pour the dressing over the vegetable mixture and toss gently to combine.
4. Transfer half of the mixture to a blender and blend until smooth. Pour the blended mixture back into the bowl with the remaining vegetables and stir to combine.
5. Refrigerate the gazpacho for at least 1 hour to allow the flavors to meld.
6. Before serving, taste and adjust the seasoning if needed.
7. Ladle the chilled Gazpacho into bowls, garnish with fresh basil leaves, and serve.

Nutritional Information (per serving):
Cal: 100 | Fat: 6g | Chol: 0mg | Sod: 70mg | Carbs:
12g | Fiber: 3g | Sugars: 7g | Pro: 2g

7. Spinach Tortellini Soup

Preparation time: 30 minutes
Servings: 4

Ingredients:

- 1 tbsp. olive oil
- 1 small onion, diced
- 2 cloves garlic, minced
- 4 cups low-sodium vegetable broth
- 1 can (14.5 ounces) diced tomatoes, undrained
- 1 tsp. dried basil
- 1/2 tsp. dried oregano
- 1/4 tsp. crushed red pepper flakes (optional)
- Salt and pepper to taste
- 9 ounces refrigerated cheese tortellini
- 4 cups fresh spinach leaves
- Grated Parmesan cheese (for garnish)

Instructions:

1. In a large pot, heat the olive oil over medium heat. Add the diced onion and minced garlic, and sauté until the onion becomes translucent.
2. Pour in the vegetable broth and diced tomatoes (with their juice). Stir in the dried basil, dried oregano, crushed red pepper flakes (if using), salt, and pepper.
3. Bring the mixture to a boil, then reduce the heat and let it simmer for about 10 minutes to allow the flavors to meld.
4. Add the refrigerated cheese tortellini to the pot and cook according to the package instructions.
5. Once the tortellini is cooked, add the fresh spinach leaves to the pot and stir until they wilt.
6. Taste the soup and adjust the seasoning if needed.
7. Ladle the Spinach Tortellini Soup into bowls, garnish with grated Parmesan cheese, and serve.

Nutritional Information (per serving):
Cal: 320 | Fat: 13g | Chol: 20mg | Sod: 300mg | Carbs:
39g | Fiber: 5g | Sugars: 6g | Pro: 14g

8. Chunky Vegetable Chowder

Preparation time: 40 minutes
Servings: 6

Ingredients:

- 1 tbsp. olive oil
- 1 medium onion, diced
- 2 cloves garlic, minced
- 2 medium carrots, diced
- 2 celery stalks, diced
- 1 medium potato, peeled and diced
- 1 cup corn kernels (fresh or frozen)
- 1 cup diced zucchini
- 4 cups low-sodium vegetable broth
- 1 cup low-fat milk or unsweetened almond milk
- 1/2 tsp. dried thyme
- 1/2 tsp. dried rosemary
- Salt and pepper to taste
- Fresh parsley (for garnish)

Instructions:

1. In a large pot, heat the olive oil over medium heat. Add the diced onion and minced garlic, and sauté until the onion becomes translucent.
2. Add the diced carrots, celery, potato, corn kernels, and diced zucchini to the pot. Stir and cook for about 5 minutes until the vegetables start to soften.
3. Pour in the low-sodium vegetable broth and bring the mixture to a boil. Reduce the heat and let it simmer for about 15-20 minutes until the vegetables are tender.
4. Using an immersion blender or a countertop blender, blend a portion of the soup to create a creamy base while still leaving some chunky vegetables for texture.
5. Return the blended soup to the pot. Stir in the low-fat milk or unsweetened almond milk, dried thyme, dried rosemary, salt, and pepper. Simmer for an additional 5 minutes to allow the flavors to meld.
6. Taste the chowder and adjust the seasoning if needed.
7. Ladle the Chunky Vegetable Chowder into bowls, garnish with fresh parsley, and serve.

Nutritional Information (per serving):
Cal: 180 | Fat: 4g | Chol: 0mg | Sod: 120mg | Carbs: 32g | Fiber: 6g | Sugars: 7g | Pro: 7g

9. Mushroom Barley Soup

Preparation time: 50 minutes
Servings: 6

Ingredients:

- 1 tbsp. olive oil
- 1 medium onion, diced
- 2 cloves garlic, minced
- 8 ounces mushrooms, sliced
- 2 medium carrots, diced
- 2 celery stalks, diced
- 1/2 cup pearl barley
- 4 cups low-sodium vegetable broth
- 2 cups water
- 1 tsp. dried thyme
- 1 tsp. dried rosemary
- Salt and pepper to taste
- Fresh parsley (for garnish)

Instructions:

1. In a large pot, heat the olive oil over medium heat. Add the diced onion and minced garlic, and sauté until the onion becomes translucent.
2. Add the sliced mushrooms to the pot and cook for about 5 minutes until they start to brown.
3. Add the diced carrots, celery, and pearl barley to the pot. Stir and cook for an additional 2 minutes.
4. Pour in the low-sodium vegetable broth and water. Add the dried thyme, dried rosemary, salt, and pepper. Bring the mixture to a boil.
5. Reduce the heat and let the soup simmer for about 40 minutes until the barley is tender, stirring occasionally.
6. Taste the soup and adjust the seasoning if needed.
7. Ladle the Mushroom Barley Soup into bowls, garnish with fresh parsley, and serve.

Nutritional Information (per serving):
Cal: 160 | Fat: 4g | Chol: 0mg | Sod: 120mg | Carbs: 28g | Fiber: 6g | Sugars: 4g | Pro: 5g

10. Spicy Black Bean Soup

Preparation time: 40 minutes
Servings: 6

Ingredients:

- 1 tbsp. olive oil
- 1 medium onion, diced
- 2 cloves garlic, minced
- 2 teaspoons ground cumin
- 1 tsp. chili powder
- 1/2 tsp. smoked paprika
- 1/4 tsp. cayenne pepper (adjust to taste)
- 2 cans (15 ounces each) low-sodium black beans, drained and rinsed
- 1 can (14.5 ounces) diced tomatoes, undrained
- 3 cups low-sodium vegetable broth
- 1 cup frozen corn kernels
- Juice of 1 lime
- Salt and pepper to taste
- Fresh cilantro (for garnish)
- Plain Greek yogurt (optional, for serving)

Instructions:

1. In a large pot, heat the olive oil over medium heat. Add the diced onion and minced garlic, and sauté until the onion becomes translucent.
2. Add the ground cumin, chili powder, smoked paprika, and cayenne pepper to the pot. Stir and cook for about 1 minute to toast the spices.
3. Add the black beans, diced tomatoes (including the liquid), vegetable broth, and frozen corn kernels to the pot. Stir well to combine.
4. Bring the mixture to a boil, then reduce the heat and let it simmer for about 30 minutes to allow the flavors to meld together, stirring occasionally.
5. Using an immersion blender or a regular blender, carefully puree about half of the soup until smooth. This step is optional, but it helps to thicken the soup.

6. Stir in the lime juice and season with salt and pepper to taste.
7. Ladle the Spicy Black Bean Soup into bowls, garnish with fresh cilantro, and serve. You can also top each bowl with a dollop of plain Greek yogurt if desired.

Nutritional Information (per serving):
Cal: 190 | Fat: 3g | Chol: 0mg | Sod: 230mg | Carbs: 34g | Fiber: 10g | Sugars: 5g | Pro: 10g

11. Creamy Cauliflower Soup

Preparation time: 40 minutes
Servings: 4

Ingredients:

- 1 medium head cauliflower, cut into florets
- 1 tbsp. olive oil
- 1 medium onion, diced
- 2 cloves garlic, minced
- 4 cups low-sodium vegetable broth
- 1 cup unsweetened almond milk (or any other unsweetened plant-based milk)
- 1/2 tsp. dried thyme
- Salt and pepper to taste
- Chopped fresh parsley (for garnish)

Instructions:

1. In a large pot, bring water to a boil and blanch the cauliflower florets for about 5 minutes or until tender. Drain and set aside.
2. In the same pot, heat the olive oil over medium heat. Add the diced onion and minced garlic, and sauté until the onion becomes translucent.
3. Add the blanched cauliflower florets to the pot and stir to combine.
4. Pour in the vegetable broth and bring the mixture to a boil. Reduce the heat to low and let it simmer for about 15 minutes to allow the flavors to meld together.
5. Using an immersion blender or a regular blender, carefully puree the soup until smooth and creamy.
6. Return the soup to the pot and stir in the almond milk and dried thyme. Heat the soup over low heat until warmed through.
7. Season with salt and pepper to taste.
8. Ladle the Creamy Cauliflower Soup into bowls, garnish with chopped fresh parsley, and serve.

Nutritional Information (per serving):
Cal: 110 | Fat: 5g | Chol: 0mg | Sod: 150mg | Carbs: 15g | Fiber: 5g | Sugars: 6g | Pro: 4g

12. Chicken and Rice Soup

Preparation time: 45 minutes
Servings: 4

Ingredients:

- 1 tbsp. olive oil
- 1 medium onion, diced
- 2 cloves garlic, minced
- 2 medium carrots, peeled and sliced
- 2 celery stalks, sliced
- 4 cups low-sodium chicken broth
- 1 cup water
- 1 cup cooked chicken breast, shredded
- 1/2 cup long-grain brown rice
- 1 tsp. dried thyme
- Salt and pepper to taste
- Chopped fresh parsley (for garnish)

Instructions:

1. In a large pot, heat the olive oil over medium heat. Add the diced onion, minced garlic, sliced carrots, and sliced celery. Sauté for about 5 minutes or until the vegetables start to soften.
2. Pour in the chicken broth and water. Bring the mixture to a boil.
3. Add the shredded chicken, brown rice, dried thyme, salt, and pepper to the pot. Stir to combine.
4. Reduce the heat to low, cover the pot, and let the soup simmer for about 30 minutes or until the rice is cooked and the flavors have melded together.
5. Taste and adjust the seasoning with salt and pepper, if needed.
6. Ladle the Chicken and Rice Soup into bowls, garnish with chopped fresh parsley, and serve.

Nutritional Information (per serving):
Cal: 250 | Fat: 6g | Chol: 40mg | Sod: 150mg | Carbs: 27g | Fiber: 4g | Sugars: 4g | Pro: 21g

13. Carrot Ginger Soup

Preparation time: 40 minutes
Servings: 4

Ingredients:

- 1 tbsp. olive oil
- 1 medium onion, chopped
- 2 cloves garlic, minced
- 1 tbsp. fresh ginger, grated
- 1 pound carrots, peeled and chopped
- 4 cups low-sodium vegetable broth
- 1 cup water
- 1/2 cup unsweetened almond milk

- Salt and pepper to taste
- Fresh cilantro (for garnish)

Instructions:

1. In a large pot, heat the olive oil over medium heat. Add the chopped onion and minced garlic. Sauté for about 5 minutes or until the onion is translucent.
2. Add the grated ginger and chopped carrots to the pot. Stir to combine.
3. Pour in the vegetable broth and water. Bring the mixture to a boil.
4. Reduce the heat to low, cover the pot, and let the soup simmer for about 25 minutes or until the carrots are tender.
5. Use an immersion blender or transfer the soup to a blender in batches, and blend until smooth.
6. Return the soup to the pot and stir in the almond milk. Heat the soup over low heat until warmed through.
7. Season with salt and pepper to taste.
8. Ladle the Carrot Ginger Soup into bowls, garnish with fresh cilantro, and serve.

Nutritional Information (per serving):
Cal: 140 | Fat: 5g | Chol: 0mg | Sod: 160mg | Carbs: 22g | Fiber: 5g | Sugars: 9g | Pro: 3g

14. Italian Wedding Soup

Preparation time: 40 minutes
Servings: 6

Ingredients:

- 1 tbsp. olive oil
- 1 small onion, finely chopped
- 2 cloves garlic, minced
- 2 medium carrots, diced
- 2 celery stalks, diced
- 4 cups low-sodium chicken broth
- 4 cups water
- 1 cup whole wheat orzo pasta
- 1 pound lean ground turkey
- 1/4 cup whole wheat breadcrumbs
- 1/4 cup grated Parmesan cheese
- 1/4 cup fresh parsley, chopped
- 1 tsp. dried oregano
- 1/2 tsp. salt
- 1/4 tsp. pepper
- 4 cups fresh baby spinach

Instructions:

1. In a large pot, heat the olive oil over medium heat. Add the chopped onion, minced garlic, diced carrots, and diced celery. Sauté for about 5 minutes or until the vegetables are tender.
2. Pour in the chicken broth and water. Bring the

mixture to a boil.
3. Add the orzo pasta to the pot and cook according to package instructions until al dente.
4. In a separate bowl, combine the ground turkey, breadcrumbs, Parmesan cheese, chopped parsley, dried oregano, salt, and pepper. Mix well.
5. Roll the turkey mixture into small meatballs, about 1 inch in diameter.
6. Drop the meatballs into the boiling soup. Cook for about 10 minutes or until the meatballs are cooked through.
7. Stir in the fresh baby spinach and cook for an additional 2 minutes or until wilted.
8. Serve the Italian Wedding Soup hot.

Nutritional Information (per serving):
Cal: 230 | Fat: 8g | Chol: 50mg | Sod: 300mg | Carbs: 22g | Fiber: 3g | Sugars: 4g | Pro: 17g

15. Turkey Chili Concoction

Preparation time: 40 minutes
Servings: 6

Ingredients:

- 1 tbsp. olive oil
- 1 small onion, diced
- 2 cloves garlic, minced
- 1 pound lean ground turkey
- 1 can (15 ounces) low-sodium kidney beans, drained and rinsed
- 1 can (15 ounces) low-sodium black beans, drained and rinsed
- 1 can (15 ounces) low-sodium diced tomatoes
- 1 can (4 ounces) diced green chilies
- 1 cup low-sodium chicken broth
- 1 tbsp. chili powder
- 1 tsp. cumin
- 1/2 tsp. paprika
- 1/2 tsp. oregano
- 1/4 tsp. salt
- 1/4 tsp. pepper
- Optional toppings: chopped fresh cilantro, low-fat Greek yogurt, shredded low-fat cheese

Instructions:

1. Heat the olive oil in a large pot or Dutch oven over medium heat.
2. Add the diced onion and minced garlic to the pot. Sauté for about 5 minutes until the onion is translucent.
3. Add the ground turkey to the pot and cook until browned, breaking it up into crumbles with a spoon.
4. Drain any excess fat from the pot.
5. Add the kidney beans, black beans, diced tomatoes (with their juice), diced green chilies, chicken broth, chili powder, cumin, paprika,

oregano, salt, and pepper to the pot. Stir well to combine.

6. Bring the mixture to a boil, then reduce the heat and simmer uncovered for about 25 minutes, stirring occasionally.
7. Taste the chili and adjust the seasonings if needed.
8. Serve the turkey chili hot in bowls, and if desired, top with chopped fresh cilantro, a dollop of low-fat Greek yogurt, or a sprinkle of shredded low-fat cheese.

Nutritional Information (per serving):
Cal: 250 | Fat: 7g | Chol: 35mg | Sod: 320mg | Carbs: 27g | Fiber: 9g | Sugars: 3g | Pro: 21g

16. Broccoli Cheddar Soup

Preparation time: 30 minutes
Servings: 4

Ingredients:

- 1 tbsp. olive oil
- 1 small onion, diced
- 2 cloves garlic, minced
- 4 cups fresh broccoli florets
- 2 cups low-sodium vegetable broth
- 1 cup low-fat milk
- 1/2 tsp. dried thyme
- 1/4 tsp. pepper
- 1 cup shredded reduced-fat cheddar cheese
- Optional toppings: additional shredded cheddar cheese, chopped green onions

Instructions:

1. Heat the olive oil in a large pot or Dutch oven over medium heat.
2. Add the diced onion and minced garlic to the pot. Sauté for about 5 minutes until the onion is translucent.
3. Add the broccoli florets to the pot and cook for another 5 minutes, stirring occasionally.
4. Pour in the vegetable broth, low-fat milk, dried thyme, and pepper. Stir well to combine.
5. Bring the mixture to a boil, then reduce the heat and simmer for about 15 minutes until the broccoli is tender.
6. Use an immersion blender or transfer the soup to a blender or food processor to blend until smooth. Be careful when blending hot liquids.
7. Return the soup to the pot if needed, and stir in the shredded cheddar cheese until melted and well combined.
8. Taste the soup and adjust the seasonings if needed.
9. Serve the broccoli cheddar soup hot in bowls, and if desired, top with additional shredded

cheddar cheese and chopped green onions.

Nutritional Information (per serving):
Cal: 200 | Fat: 9g | Chol: 20mg | Sod: 200mg | Carbs: 19g | Fiber: 4g | Sugars: 8g | Pro: 12g

17. Corn and Potato Chowder

Preparation time: 40 minutes
Servings: 4

Ingredients:

- 1 tbsp. olive oil
- 1 small onion, diced
- 2 cloves garlic, minced
- 2 cups diced potatoes
- 2 cups low-sodium vegetable broth
- 2 cups frozen corn kernels
- 1 cup low-fat milk
- 1/2 tsp. dried thyme
- 1/4 tsp. pepper
- Optional toppings: chopped green onions, chopped fresh parsley

Instructions:

1. Heat the olive oil in a large pot or Dutch oven over medium heat.
2. Add the diced onion and minced garlic to the pot. Sauté for about 5 minutes until the onion is translucent.
3. Add the diced potatoes to the pot and cook for another 5 minutes, stirring occasionally.
4. Pour in the vegetable broth and bring the mixture to a boil. Reduce the heat to medium-low and simmer for about 10 minutes until the potatoes are tender.
5. Add the frozen corn kernels, low-fat milk, dried thyme, and pepper to the pot. Stir well to combine.
6. Continue cooking the chowder for another 10 minutes, stirring occasionally, until the corn is heated through.
7. Use a potato masher or immersion blender to partially blend the chowder, leaving some chunks of potatoes and corn for texture.
8. Taste the chowder and adjust the seasonings if needed.
9. Serve the corn and potato chowder hot in bowls, and if desired, top with chopped green onions and chopped fresh parsley.

Nutritional Information (per serving):
Cal: 200 | Fat: 5g | Chol: 2mg | Sod: 150mg | Carbs: 36g | Fiber: 4g | Sugars: 7g | Pro: 6g

18. Thai Coconut Curry Soup

Preparation time: 30 minutes
Servings: 4

Ingredients:

- 1 tbsp. olive oil
- 1 small onion, diced
- 2 cloves garlic, minced
- 1 tbsp. grated fresh ginger
- 2 tablespoons Thai red curry paste (check for low-sodium options)
- 2 cups low-sodium vegetable broth
- 1 can (14 ounces) light coconut milk
- 2 cups mixed vegetables (such as bell peppers, carrots, broccoli, and snow peas), thinly sliced
- 1 cup diced tofu or cooked chicken breast (optional)
- 2 tablespoons low-sodium soy sauce or tamari
- 1 tbsp. lime juice
- Fresh cilantro leaves, for garnish
- Optional toppings: sliced green onions, chopped fresh cilantro, lime wedges

Instructions:

1. Heat the olive oil in a large pot or Dutch oven over medium heat.
2. Add the diced onion, minced garlic, and grated ginger to the pot. Sauté for about 5 minutes until the onion is translucent.
3. Stir in the Thai red curry paste and cook for another minute until fragrant.
4. Pour in the vegetable broth and coconut milk. Stir well to combine.
5. Add the mixed vegetables and tofu or cooked chicken (if using) to the pot. Simmer for about 10 minutes until the vegetables are tender.
6. Stir in the low-sodium soy sauce or tamari and lime juice. Taste the soup and adjust the seasonings if needed.
7. Serve the Thai coconut curry soup hot in bowls. Garnish with fresh cilantro leaves and optional toppings such as sliced green onions, chopped fresh cilantro, and lime wedges.

Nutritional Information (per serving):
Cal: 180 | Fat: 11g | Chol: 0mg | Sod: 300mg | Carbs: 17g | Fiber: 4g | Sugars: 4g | Pro: 5g

19. Spinach and White Bean Soup

Preparation time: 40 minutes
Servings: 4

Ingredients:

- 1 tbsp. olive oil
- 1 small onion, diced
- 2 cloves garlic, minced
- 2 carrots, diced
- 2 celery stalks, diced
- 4 cups low-sodium vegetable broth
- 1 can (14 ounces) diced tomatoes (no salt added)
- 2 cans (15 ounces each) white beans (such as cannellini or Great Northern beans), drained and rinsed
- 4 cups fresh spinach leaves
- 1 tsp. dried thyme
- 1/2 tsp. dried rosemary
- Salt and pepper to taste

Instructions:

1. Heat the olive oil in a large pot or Dutch oven over medium heat.
2. Add the diced onion, minced garlic, diced carrots, and diced celery to the pot. Sauté for about 5 minutes until the vegetables are slightly tender.
3. Pour in the vegetable broth and diced tomatoes (including the liquid from the can). Stir well to combine.
4. Add the drained and rinsed white beans, dried thyme, and dried rosemary to the pot. Stir to combine.
5. Bring the soup to a boil, then reduce the heat to low and simmer for about 20 minutes to allow the flavors to meld together.
6. Stir in the fresh spinach leaves and cook for an additional 5 minutes until the spinach wilts.
7. Season the soup with salt and pepper to taste.
8. Serve the spinach and white bean soup hot in bowls.

Nutritional Information (per serving):
Cal: 220 | Fat: 3.5g | Chol: 0mg | Sod: 200mg | Carbs: 38g | Fiber: 10g | Sugars: 6g | Pro: 11g

20. Red Lentil Curry Soup

Preparation time: 40 minutes
Servings: 4

Ingredients:

- 1 tbsp. olive oil
- 1 small onion, diced
- 2 cloves garlic, minced
- 2 carrots, diced
- 2 celery stalks, diced
- 1 tbsp. curry powder
- 1 tsp. ground cumin
- 1/2 tsp. ground turmeric
- 1 cup red lentils
- 4 cups low-sodium vegetable broth
- 1 can (14 ounces) diced tomatoes (no salt added)

- 1 can (14 ounces) coconut milk (lite version)
- Salt and pepper to taste
- Fresh cilantro, chopped (for garnish)

Instructions:

1. Heat the olive oil in a large pot or Dutch oven over medium heat.
2. Add the diced onion, minced garlic, diced carrots, and diced celery to the pot. Sauté for about 5 minutes until the vegetables are slightly tender.
3. Add the curry powder, ground cumin, and ground turmeric to the pot. Stir well to coat the vegetables with the spices and cook for an additional 1-2 minutes.
4. Rinse the red lentils under cold water and add them to the pot.
5. Pour in the vegetable broth and diced tomatoes (including the liquid from the can). Stir well to combine.
6. Bring the soup to a boil, then reduce the heat to low and simmer for about 25 minutes until the lentils are cooked and tender.
7. Stir in the coconut milk and cook for an additional 5 minutes to heat through.
8. Season the soup with salt and pepper to taste.
9. Serve the red lentil curry soup hot in bowls, garnished with fresh chopped cilantro.

Nutritional Information (per serving):
Cal: 310 | Fat: 12g | Chol: 0mg | Sod: 240mg | Carbs: 40g | Fiber: 12g | Sugars: 7g | Pro: 12g

21. Beef and Barley Stew

Preparation time: 2 hours
Servings: 6

Ingredients:

- 1 pound lean beef stew meat, cut into small cubes
- 1 tbsp. olive oil
- 1 onion, diced
- 2 carrots, diced
- 2 celery stalks, diced
- 3 cloves garlic, minced
- 1 can (14 ounces) diced tomatoes (no salt added)
- 4 cups low-sodium beef broth
- 1 cup water
- 1/2 cup pearl barley
- 1 tsp. dried thyme
- 1 bay leaf
- Salt and pepper to taste
- Fresh parsley, chopped (for garnish)

Instructions:

1. Heat the olive oil in a large pot or Dutch oven

over medium heat.
3. Add the beef cubes to the pot and brown them on all sides. Remove the beef from the pot and set aside.
4. In the same pot, add the diced onion, diced carrots, diced celery, and minced garlic. Sauté for about 5 minutes until the vegetables are slightly tender.
5. Return the browned beef cubes to the pot.
6. Add the diced tomatoes (including the liquid from the can), beef broth, water, pearl barley, dried thyme, and bay leaf to the pot. Stir well to combine.
7. Bring the stew to a boil, then reduce the heat to low and cover the pot. Simmer for about 1.5 to 2 hours until the beef is tender and the barley is cooked.
8. Remove the bay leaf from the pot and season the stew with salt and pepper to taste.
9. Serve the beef and barley stew hot in bowls, garnished with fresh chopped parsley.

Nutritional Information (per serving):
Cal: 250 | Fat: 8g | Chol: 40mg | Sod: 200mg | Carbs: 22g | Fiber: 4g | Sugars: 5g | Pro: 22g

22. Creamy Asparagus Soup

Preparation time: 30 minutes
Servings: 4

Ingredients:

- 1 pound asparagus, woody ends trimmed
- 1 tbsp. olive oil
- 1 small onion, chopped
- 2 cloves garlic, minced
- 3 cups low-sodium vegetable broth
- 1 cup low-fat milk
- 1 tbsp. lemon juice
- Salt and pepper to taste
- Fresh herbs (such as chives or parsley) for garnish

Instructions:

1. In a large pot, bring water to a boil. Add the asparagus and cook for about 3-4 minutes until tender. Drain and set aside.
2. In the same pot, heat the olive oil over medium heat. Add the chopped onion and minced garlic. Sauté for about 5 minutes until the onion is translucent and fragrant.
3. Cut the cooked asparagus into small pieces, reserving a few tips for garnish if desired. Add the asparagus to the pot and stir well to combine with the onion and garlic.
4. Pour in the low-sodium vegetable broth and bring the mixture to a boil. Reduce the heat and simmer for about 10 minutes to allow the flavors to meld.

5. Using an immersion blender or a regular blender, puree the soup until smooth and creamy.
6. Return the soup to the pot and stir in the low-fat milk. Heat gently over low heat, stirring occasionally, until heated through.
7. Stir in the lemon juice and season the soup with salt and pepper to taste.
8. Serve the creamy asparagus soup hot in bowls, garnished with reserved asparagus tips and fresh herbs.

Nutritional Information (per serving):
Cal: 110 | Fat: 4g | Chol: 1mg | Sod: 120mg | Carbs: 15g | Fiber: 4g | Sugars: 7g | Pro: 5g

23. Moroccan Chickpea Soup

Preparation time: 40 minutes
Servings: 4

Ingredients:

- 1 tbsp. olive oil
- 1 onion, chopped
- 2 cloves garlic, minced
- 1 tsp. ground cumin
- 1 tsp. ground coriander
- 1/2 tsp. ground turmeric
- 1/2 tsp. ground cinnamon
- 1/4 tsp. cayenne pepper (optional, for added spice)
- 2 carrots, diced
- 2 celery stalks, diced
- 1 red bell pepper, diced
- 1 can (14 ounces) diced tomatoes, undrained
- 4 cups low-sodium vegetable broth
- 1 can (14 ounces) chickpeas, drained and rinsed
- 1 cup chopped kale or spinach
- Salt and pepper to taste
- Fresh cilantro or parsley for garnish

Instructions:

1. In a large pot, heat the olive oil over medium heat. Add the chopped onion and minced garlic. Sauté for about 5 minutes until the onion is translucent and fragrant.
2. Add the ground cumin, ground coriander, ground turmeric, ground cinnamon, and cayenne pepper (if using) to the pot. Stir well to coat the onions and garlic with the spices. Cook for an additional 1-2 minutes to toast the spices.
3. Add the diced carrots, diced celery, and diced red bell pepper to the pot. Stir and cook for about 5 minutes until the vegetables start to soften.
4. Pour in the diced tomatoes with their juice and the low-sodium vegetable broth. Bring the mixture to a boil, then reduce the heat and simmer for about 15 minutes to allow the flavors to meld.

5. Add the drained and rinsed chickpeas to the pot. Simmer for another 10 minutes to heat the chickpeas through.
6. Stir in the chopped kale or spinach and cook for an additional 5 minutes until the greens are wilted.
7. Season the soup with salt and pepper to taste.
8. Serve the Moroccan Chickpea Soup hot in bowls, garnished with fresh cilantro or parsley.

Nutritional Information (per serving):
Cal: 230 | Fat: 5g | Chol: 0mg | Sod: 220mg | Carbs: 38g | Fiber: 11g | Sugars: 10g | Pro: 11g

24. Sweet Potato and Kale Soup

Preparation time: 40 minutes
Servings: 4

Ingredients:

- 1 tbsp. olive oil
- 1 onion, chopped
- 2 cloves garlic, minced
- 2 medium sweet potatoes, peeled and diced
- 4 cups low-sodium vegetable broth
- 2 cups chopped kale
- 1 tsp. ground cumin
- 1/2 tsp. ground cinnamon
- 1/4 tsp. ground nutmeg
- Salt and pepper to taste
- Optional toppings: Greek yogurt, chopped fresh parsley

Instructions:

1. Heat the olive oil in a large pot over medium heat. Add the chopped onion and minced garlic. Sauté for about 5 minutes until the onion is translucent and fragrant.
2. Add the diced sweet potatoes to the pot and stir well to coat them in the oil. Cook for an additional 5 minutes to lightly brown the sweet potatoes.
3. Pour in the low-sodium vegetable broth and bring the mixture to a boil. Reduce the heat and simmer for about 15-20 minutes until the sweet potatoes are tender.
4. Using a blender or immersion blender, carefully blend the soup until smooth and creamy. If using a blender, blend the soup in batches and return it to the pot.
5. Stir in the chopped kale, ground cumin, ground cinnamon, and ground nutmeg. Simmer for an additional 5 minutes until the kale is wilted and the flavors are well combined.
6. Season the soup with salt and pepper to taste.
7. Ladle the Sweet Potato and Kale Soup into bowls. Optionally, top each serving with a dollop of Greek yogurt and a sprinkle of chopped fresh

parsley.

Nutritional Information (per serving):
Cal: 180 | Fat: 4g | Chol: 0mg | Sod: 160mg | Carbs:
34g | Fiber: 6g | Sugars: 7g | Pro: 5g

25. Navy Bean and Ham Soup

Preparation time: 8 hours 20 minutes
Servings: 6

Ingredients:

- 1 pound dried navy beans
- 1 ham hock or leftover ham bone
- 4 cups low-sodium chicken or vegetable broth
- 4 cups water
- 1 onion, chopped
- 2 carrots, diced
- 2 celery stalks, diced
- 3 cloves garlic, minced
- 1 bay leaf
- 1 tsp. dried thyme
- Salt and pepper to taste

Instructions:

1. Rinse the navy beans and remove any debris. Place them in a large bowl and cover with water. Soak overnight or for at least 8 hours. Drain and rinse the soaked beans.
2. In a large pot or Dutch oven, combine the soaked navy beans, ham hock or ham bone, low-sodium chicken or vegetable broth, water, chopped onion, diced carrots, diced celery, minced garlic, bay leaf, and dried thyme.
3. Bring the mixture to a boil over medium heat. Reduce the heat to low, cover the pot, and simmer for 1-2 hours, or until the beans are tender and cooked through. Stir occasionally.
4. Once the beans are cooked, remove the ham hock or ham bone from the pot. Remove any meat from the bone, chop it into small pieces, and return the meat to the pot. Discard the bone.
5. Use a potato masher or the back of a spoon to mash some of the beans against the side of the pot to thicken the soup. Alternatively, you can use an immersion blender to blend a portion of the soup for a smoother consistency.
6. Season the Navy Bean and Ham Soup with salt and pepper to taste.
7. Simmer the soup for an additional 10-15 minutes to allow the flavors to meld together.
8. Ladle the soup into bowls and garnish with chopped fresh parsley, if desired.

Nutritional Information (per serving):
Cal: 180 | Fat: 11g | Chol: 0mg | Sod: 300mg | Carbs:
17g | Fiber: 4g | Sugars: 4g | Pro: 5g

Poultry

1. Lemon Herb Roast Chicken

Preparation time: 10 minutes
Cooking time: 1 hour 30 minutes
Servings: 4

Ingredients:

- 1 whole chicken (about 4 pounds)
- 2 tablespoons olive oil
- 2 lemons, juiced and zested
- 2 cloves garlic, minced
- 1 tbsp. chopped fresh rosemary
- 1 tbsp. chopped fresh thyme
- Salt and pepper to taste
- Optional garnish: Fresh herbs (rosemary, thyme) and lemon slices

Instructions:

1. Preheat your oven to 375°F (190°C).
2. Rinse the whole chicken inside and out with cold water. Pat it dry with paper towels.
3. In a small bowl, combine the olive oil, lemon juice, lemon zest, minced garlic, chopped fresh rosemary, and chopped fresh thyme. Mix well.
4. Rub the mixture all over the chicken, including under the skin and inside the cavity. Season the chicken with salt and pepper to taste.
5. Place the chicken on a roasting pan or a baking dish with a wire rack.
6. Roast the chicken in the preheated oven for about 1 hour and 30 minutes, or until the internal temperature reaches 165°F (75°C) when measured with a meat thermometer inserted into the thickest part of the thigh without touching the bone.
7. Remove the chicken from the oven and let it rest for 10-15 minutes before carving.
8. Carve the chicken into serving pieces and transfer to a serving platter. Garnish with fresh herbs and lemon slices, if desired.

Nutritional Information (per serving):
Cal: 345 | Fat: 21g | Chol: 130mg | Sod: 100mg | Carbs: 3g | Fiber: 1g | Sugars: 1g | Pro: 36g

2. Grilled Lemon Pepper Chicken

Preparation time: 10 minutes
Marinating time: 1 hour
Grilling time: 12-15 minutes
Servings: 4

Ingredients:

- 4 boneless, skinless chicken breasts
- 2 lemons, juiced and zested
- 2 tablespoons olive oil
- 2 cloves garlic, minced
- 1 tbsp. freshly ground pepper
- Salt to taste
- Optional garnish: Lemon slices and fresh parsley

Instructions:

1. In a small bowl, combine the lemon juice, lemon zest, olive oil, minced garlic, freshly ground pepper, and a pinch of salt. Mix well.
2. Place the chicken breasts in a shallow dish and pour the marinade over them. Make sure the chicken is coated evenly. Cover the dish and refrigerate for at least 1 hour to allow the flavors to develop.
3. Preheat your grill to medium-high heat.
4. Remove the chicken breasts from the marinade, allowing any excess marinade to drip off.
5. Grill the chicken breasts for 6-8 minutes per side, or until they reach an internal temperature of 165°F (75°C) when measured with a meat thermometer.
6. Remove the chicken from the grill and let it rest for a few minutes.
7. Slice the chicken breasts and transfer them to a serving platter. Garnish with lemon slices and fresh parsley, if desired.

Nutritional Information (per serving):
Cal: 210 | Fat: 8g | Chol: 85mg | Sod: 90mg | Carbs: 5g | Fiber: 1g | Sugars: 1g | Pro: 30g

3. Baked Pesto Turkey Breast

Preparation time: 10 minutes
Cooking time: 1 hour 15 minutes
Servings: 4

Ingredients:

- 1.5 pounds boneless turkey breast
- 1/4 cup basil pesto (homemade or store-bought)
- 1 tbsp. olive oil
- 2 cloves garlic, minced
- 1 tsp. dried oregano
- Salt and pepper to taste

Instructions:

1. Preheat your oven to 350°F (175°C).
2. Place the turkey breast in a baking dish and season it with salt, pepper, and dried oregano.
3. In a small bowl, combine the basil pesto, olive oil, and minced garlic. Mix well.
4. Spread the pesto mixture evenly over the turkey breast, covering it entirely.
5. Cover the baking dish with foil and bake for approximately 1 hour, or until the turkey reaches an internal temperature of 165°F (75°C) when measured with a meat thermometer.

6. Remove the foil during the last 15 minutes of cooking to allow the top to brown slightly.
7. Once cooked, remove the turkey breast from the oven and let it rest for a few minutes before slicing.
8. Slice the turkey breast and serve it with your favorite side dishes or salads.

Nutritional Information (per serving):
Cal: 240 | Fat: 8g | Chol: 80mg | Sod: 150mg | Carbs: 2g | Fiber: 0g | Sugars: 0g | Pro: 37g

4. Garlic Parmesan Chicken Tenders

Preparation time: 15 minutes
Cooking time: 15 minutes
Servings: 4

Ingredients:

• 1 pound chicken tenders
• 1/2 cup whole wheat breadcrumbs
• 1/4 cup grated Parmesan cheese
• 1 tsp. garlic powder
• 1/2 tsp. dried oregano
• 1/2 tsp. paprika
• Salt and pepper to taste
• 1 large egg, beaten

Instructions:

1. Preheat your oven to 400°F (200°C). Line a baking sheet with parchment paper or lightly grease it.
2. In a shallow bowl, combine the breadcrumbs, grated Parmesan cheese, garlic powder, dried oregano, paprika, salt, and pepper. Mix well.
3. Dip each chicken tender into the beaten egg, allowing any excess to drip off, and then coat it in the breadcrumb mixture. Press the breadcrumbs onto the chicken to ensure they adhere well.
4. Place the coated chicken tenders on the prepared baking sheet, leaving a little space between each piece.
5. Bake for approximately 15 minutes or until the chicken is cooked through and the coating is golden and crispy.
6. Remove from the oven and let the chicken tenders cool slightly before serving.

Nutritional Information (per serving):
Cal: 230 | Fat: 6g | Chol: 130mg | Sod: 190mg | Carbs: 10g | Fiber: 1g | Sugars: 1g | Pro: 32g

5. Teriyaki Chicken Skewers

Preparation time: 10 minutes
Marinating time: 30 minutes
Cooking time: 10 minutes

Servings: 4

Ingredients:

• 1 pound boneless, skinless chicken breasts, cut into bite-sized pieces
• 1/4 cup low-sodium soy sauce
• 2 tablespoons honey
• 2 tablespoons rice vinegar
• 1 tbsp. minced garlic
• 1 tbsp. minced ginger
• 1 tbsp. sesame oil
• 1 tbsp. cornstarch
• 2 tablespoons water
• Optional garnish: sesame seeds and sliced green onions

Instructions:

1. In a bowl, whisk together the low-sodium soy sauce, honey, rice vinegar, minced garlic, minced ginger, and sesame oil to make the teriyaki marinade.
2. Place the chicken pieces in a shallow dish or zip-top bag and pour the teriyaki marinade over them. Make sure the chicken is evenly coated. Cover the dish or seal the bag and refrigerate for at least 30 minutes to marinate.
3. If using wooden skewers, soak them in water for 15 minutes to prevent them from burning during cooking.
4. Preheat your grill or grill pan over medium-high heat.
5. Thread the marinated chicken pieces onto the skewers.
6. In a small bowl, mix the cornstarch and water to create a slurry. This will be used to thicken the teriyaki sauce.
7. Place the chicken skewers on the preheated grill and cook for about 5 minutes on each side, or until the chicken is cooked through and slightly charred.
8. While the chicken is grilling, transfer the remaining marinade to a small saucepan and bring it to a boil. Reduce the heat and simmer for a few minutes until the sauce thickens. Stir in the cornstarch slurry and continue cooking for an additional minute.
9. Remove the cooked chicken skewers from the grill and brush them with the thickened teriyaki sauce.
10. Garnish with sesame seeds and sliced green onions, if desired, and serve hot.

Nutritional Information (per serving):
Cal: 240 | Fat: 5g | Chol: 73mg | Sod: 330mg | Carbs: 17g | Fiber: 0g | Sugars: 14g | Pro: 30g

6. Herb Crusted Turkey Cutlets

Preparation time: 15 minutes
Cooking time: 10 minutes
Servings: 4

Ingredients:

*   4 turkey cutlets (about 4-6 ounces each)
*   1/4 cup whole wheat breadcrumbs
*   1/4 cup grated Parmesan cheese
*   1 tbsp. chopped fresh parsley
*   1 tsp. dried oregano
*   1 tsp. dried thyme
*   1/2 tsp. garlic powder
*   1/2 tsp. paprika
*   1/4 tsp. pepper
*   2 tablespoons olive oil

Instructions:

1. Preheat your oven to 400°F (200°C).
2. In a shallow bowl, combine the breadcrumbs, grated Parmesan cheese, chopped parsley, dried oregano, dried thyme, garlic powder, paprika, and pepper. Mix well to create the herb crust mixture.
3. Pat the turkey cutlets dry with paper towels.
4. Dip each turkey cutlet into the herb crust mixture, pressing the mixture onto both sides to coat evenly.
5. In a large skillet, heat the olive oil over medium heat.
6. Add the coated turkey cutlets to the skillet and cook for 3-4 minutes on each side, or until they are golden brown and cooked through.
7. Transfer the browned turkey cutlets to a baking sheet and place them in the preheated oven for an additional 5 minutes to ensure they are fully cooked.
8. Remove the turkey cutlets from the oven and let them rest for a few minutes before serving.
9. Serve the herb-crusted turkey cutlets with your choice of sides, such as steamed vegetables or a salad.

Nutritional Information (per serving):
Cal: 240 | Fat: 10g | Chol: 85mg | Sod: 170mg | Carbs: 6g | Fiber: 1g | Sugars: 1g | Pro: 31g

7. Lemon Rosemary Chicken Thighs

Preparation time: 10 minutes
Marinating time: 30 minutes (optional)
Cooking time: 10 minutes
Servings: 4

Ingredients:

*   4 boneless, skinless chicken thighs
*   2 tablespoons fresh lemon juice
*   1 tbsp. olive oil
*   1 tbsp. chopped fresh rosemary
*   2 cloves garlic, minced
*   1/2 tsp. lemon zest
*   1/4 tsp. pepper
*   1/4 tsp. salt (optional, or to taste)

Instructions:

1. In a bowl, whisk together the lemon juice, olive oil, chopped rosemary, minced garlic, lemon zest, pepper, and salt (if using).
2. Place the chicken thighs in a shallow dish or a zip-top bag. Pour the marinade over the chicken and toss to coat evenly. Cover the dish or seal the bag and let the chicken marinate in the refrigerator for at least 30 minutes, or up to 4 hours for more flavor (optional).
3. Preheat your grill or grill pan over medium heat.
4. Remove the chicken thighs from the marinade, allowing any excess marinade to drip off.
5. Place the chicken thighs on the preheated grill or grill pan and cook for about 6-8 minutes per side, or until the chicken is cooked through and reaches an internal temperature of 165°F (74°C).
6. Remove the chicken from the grill and let it rest for a few minutes before serving.
7. Serve the lemon rosemary chicken thighs with your choice of sides, such as steamed vegetables or a salad.

Nutritional Information (per serving):
Cal: 210 | Fat: 10g | Chol: 95mg | Sod: 95mg | Carbs: 2g | Fiber: 0g | Sugars: 0g | Pro: 28g

8. Greek Yogurt Chicken Salad

Preparation time: 15 minutes
Servings: 4

Ingredients:

*   2 cups cooked chicken breast, diced
*   1/2 cup plain Greek yogurt
*   1/4 cup diced cucumber
*   1/4 cup diced red onion
*   1/4 cup diced celery
*   1/4 cup diced red bell pepper
*   2 tablespoons chopped fresh dill
*   2 tablespoons lemon juice
*   1 tbsp. extra-virgin olive oil
*   1/2 tsp. garlic powder
*   1/4 tsp. pepper
*   Salt to taste (optional)

Instructions:

1. In a large bowl, combine the diced chicken, Greek yogurt, cucumber, red onion, celery, red bell pepper, fresh dill, lemon juice, olive oil, garlic powder, pepper, and salt (if desired).
2. Stir the ingredients together until well combined, ensuring the chicken is coated with the yogurt mixture.
3. Taste and adjust the seasoning with salt and pepper, if needed.
4. Refrigerate the chicken salad for at least 30 minutes to allow the flavors to meld together.
5. Serve the Greek Yogurt Chicken Salad on its own, in a lettuce wrap, or with whole-grain bread or crackers.

Nutritional Information (per serving):
Cal: 180 | Fat: 7g | Chol: 70mg | Sod: 80mg | Carbs: 5g | Fiber: 1g | Sugars: 2g | Pro: 24g

9. Honey Mustard Glazed Turkey

Preparation time: 15 minutes
Cooking time: 1 hour 30 minutes
Servings: 8

Ingredients:

- 1 whole turkey (12-14 pounds)
- 1/4 cup Dijon mustard
- 1/4 cup honey
- 2 tablespoons olive oil
- 2 teaspoons dried thyme
- 2 teaspoons dried rosemary
- 1 tsp. garlic powder
- 1 tsp. onion powder
- 1/2 tsp. pepper
- Salt to taste (optional)

Instructions:

1. Preheat your oven to 325°F (165°C).
2. In a small bowl, whisk together the Dijon mustard, honey, olive oil, dried thyme, dried rosemary, garlic powder, onion powder, pepper, and salt (if desired).
3. Place the turkey on a rack in a roasting pan. Pat the turkey dry with paper towels.
4. Brush the honey mustard glaze all over the turkey, making sure to coat the entire surface.
5. Insert a meat thermometer into the thickest part of the turkey thigh, avoiding the bone.
6. Roast the turkey in the preheated oven, basting with the pan juices every 30 minutes, until the internal temperature reaches 165°F (74°C) and the turkey is golden brown and cooked through. This usually takes about 1 hour and 30 minutes, but cooking times may vary depending on the size of the turkey.

7. Once cooked, remove the turkey from the oven and let it rest for 15-20 minutes before carving.
8. Carve the turkey and serve with your favorite side dishes.

Nutritional Information (per serving):
Cal: 400 | Fat: 14g | Chol: 210mg | Sod: 140mg | Carbs: 10g | Fiber: 0g | Sugars: 10g | Pro: 56g

10. Buffalo Chicken Lettuce Wraps

Preparation time: 20 minutes
Cooking time: 15 minutes
Servings: 4

Ingredients:

- 1 pound boneless, skinless chicken breasts, cooked and shredded
- 1/2 cup hot sauce (such as Frank's RedHot)
- 2 tablespoons unsalted butter, melted
- 1 tbsp. apple cider vinegar
- 1/2 tsp. garlic powder
- 1/2 tsp. onion powder
- 1/4 tsp. pepper
- 8 large lettuce leaves (such as iceberg or butter lettuce)
- 1/2 cup diced tomatoes
- 1/2 cup diced celery
- 1/4 cup crumbled blue cheese (optional)
- Ranch or blue cheese dressing for serving (optional)

Instructions:

1. In a bowl, combine the hot sauce, melted butter, apple cider vinegar, garlic powder, onion powder, and pepper. Stir well to combine.
2. Add the shredded chicken to the buffalo sauce mixture and toss until the chicken is well coated.
3. Heat a non-stick skillet over medium heat. Add the buffalo chicken mixture and cook for 5-7 minutes, stirring occasionally, until heated through.
4. Arrange the lettuce leaves on a serving platter.
5. Spoon the buffalo chicken mixture onto each lettuce leaf.
6. Top with diced tomatoes, diced celery, and crumbled blue cheese (if using).
7. Serve the lettuce wraps with ranch or blue cheese dressing on the side, if desired.

Nutritional Information (per serving):
Cal: 220 | Fat: 9g | Chol: 95mg | Sod: 280mg | Carbs: 5g | Fiber: 2g | Sugars: 2g | Pro: 28g

11. Balsamic Glazed Chicken

Preparation time: 20 minutes
Cooking time: 15 minutes
Servings: 4

Ingredients:

- 8 chicken drumsticks
- 1/4 cup balsamic vinegar
- 2 tablespoons honey
- 1 tbsp. low-sodium soy sauce
- 1 tbsp. olive oil
- 2 cloves garlic, minced
- 1 tsp. dried rosemary
- 1/2 tsp. dried thyme
- 1/2 tsp. pepper
- Fresh parsley, chopped (for garnish, optional)

Instructions:

1. In a bowl, whisk together the balsamic vinegar, honey, soy sauce, olive oil, minced garlic, dried rosemary, dried thyme, and pepper.
2. Place the chicken drumsticks in a resealable plastic bag or a shallow dish. Pour the balsamic marinade over the drumsticks, ensuring they are well coated. Seal the bag or cover the dish and refrigerate for at least 30 minutes (or up to 4 hours) to marinate.
3. Preheat the oven to 400°F (200°C).
4. Line a baking sheet with foil and lightly grease with cooking spray.
5. Remove the chicken drumsticks from the marinade, allowing any excess marinade to drip off. Place the drumsticks on the prepared baking sheet, leaving space between them.
6. Bake the drumsticks in the preheated oven for 35-40 minutes or until cooked through, turning them halfway through and basting with the remaining marinade.
7. Once cooked, remove the drumsticks from the oven and let them rest for a few minutes.
8. Garnish with fresh parsley (optional) and serve hot.

Nutritional Information (per serving):
Cal: 275 | Fat: 11g | Chol: 140mg | Sod: 150mg | Carbs: 10g | Fiber: 0g | Sugars: 9g | Pro: 29g

12. Tomato Basil Turkey Meatballs

Preparation time: 15 minutes
Cooking time: 25 minutes
Servings: 4

Ingredients:

- 1 pound lean ground turkey
- 1/4 cup whole wheat breadcrumbs
- 1/4 cup grated Parmesan cheese
- 1/4 cup chopped fresh basil leaves
- 1/4 cup chopped sun-dried tomatoes (packed in oil, drained)
- 2 cloves garlic, minced
- 1/2 tsp. dried oregano
- 1/2 tsp. pepper
- 1/4 tsp. salt (optional)
- 1 large egg, beaten
- 1 can (14 ounces) low-sodium crushed tomatoes
- Fresh basil leaves, for garnish (optional)

Instructions:

1. Preheat the oven to 400°F (200°C). Line a baking sheet with foil and lightly grease with cooking spray.
2. In a large bowl, combine the ground turkey, breadcrumbs, grated Parmesan cheese, chopped fresh basil, chopped sun-dried tomatoes, minced garlic, dried oregano, pepper, salt (if desired), and beaten egg. Mix until well combined.
3. Shape the mixture into meatballs, about 1 inch in diameter, and place them on the prepared baking sheet.
4. Bake the meatballs in the preheated oven for 20-25 minutes or until cooked through and golden brown.
5. While the meatballs are baking, heat the crushed tomatoes in a saucepan over medium heat until warmed through.
6. Once the meatballs are cooked, transfer them to the saucepan with the crushed tomatoes. Gently stir to coat the meatballs with the sauce.
7. Serve the tomato basil turkey meatballs with additional sauce and garnish with fresh basil leaves, if desired.

Nutritional Information (per serving):
Cal: 255 | Fat: 11g | Chol: 124mg | Sod: 374mg | Carbs: 12g | Fiber: 3g | Sugars: 5g | Pro: 28g

13. Lemon Dill Chicken Kabobs

Preparation time: 15 minutes
Marinating time: 30 minutes
Cooking time: 10 minutes
Servings: 4

Ingredients:

- 1 pound boneless, skinless chicken breasts, cut into 1-inch cubes
- 2 tablespoons fresh lemon juice
- 2 tablespoons olive oil
- 1 tbsp. chopped fresh dill
- 2 cloves garlic, minced
- 1/2 tsp. lemon zest

- 1/4 tsp. pepper
- 1/4 tsp. salt (optional)
- 1 medium red bell pepper, cut into 1-inch pieces
- 1 medium red onion, cut into 1-inch pieces
- 8 cherry tomatoes

Instructions:

1. In a large bowl, combine the lemon juice, olive oil, chopped dill, minced garlic, lemon zest, pepper, and salt (if desired). Mix well to make the marinade.
2. Add the chicken cubes to the marinade and toss until they are evenly coated. Cover the bowl and refrigerate for 30 minutes to allow the flavors to develop.
3. Preheat the grill to medium-high heat.
4. Thread the marinated chicken cubes onto skewers, alternating with the red bell pepper, red onion, and cherry tomatoes.
5. Place the skewers on the preheated grill and cook for about 10 minutes, turning occasionally, until the chicken is cooked through and the vegetables are tender.
6. Remove the skewers from the grill and let them rest for a few minutes.
7. Serve the lemon dill chicken kabobs hot with a side of mixed greens or whole grain rice, if desired.

Nutritional Information (per serving):
Cal: 210 | Fat: 9g | Chol: 73mg | Sod: 96mg | Carbs: 7g | Fiber: 2g | Sugars: 3g | Pro: 25g

14. Mediterranean Turkey Burgers

Preparation time: 15 minutes
Cooking time: 12 minutes
Servings: 4

Ingredients:

- 1 pound lean ground turkey
- 1/4 cup chopped sun-dried tomatoes (packed in oil), drained
- 1/4 cup chopped Kalamata olives
- 2 tablespoons chopped fresh parsley
- 1 tsp. dried oregano
- 1/2 tsp. ground cumin
- 1/4 tsp. pepper
- 1/4 tsp. salt (optional)
- 4 whole wheat burger buns
- Lettuce leaves, tomato slices, and red onion slices for garnish

Instructions:

1. Preheat a grill or grill pan to medium-high heat.
2. In a large bowl, combine the ground turkey,

sun-dried tomatoes, Kalamata olives, chopped parsley, dried oregano, ground cumin, pepper, and salt (if desired). Mix well to combine all the ingredients.
3. Divide the turkey mixture into 4 equal portions. Shape each portion into a patty, about 1/2-inch thick.
4. Place the turkey patties on the preheated grill or grill pan. Cook for about 6 minutes per side, or until the internal temperature reaches 165°F (75°C) and the burgers are cooked through.
5. Remove the turkey burgers from the grill and let them rest for a few minutes.
6. Assemble the burgers by placing each turkey patty on a whole wheat bun. Top with lettuce leaves, tomato slices, and red onion slices.
7. Serve the Mediterranean turkey burgers with a side of mixed greens or a Greek salad, if desired.

Nutritional Information (per serving):
Cal: 282 | Fat: 10g | Chol: 81mg | Sod: 369mg | Carbs: 26g | Fiber: 5g | Sugars: 4g | Pro: 25g

15. Chicken Stuffed Sweet Potatoes

Preparation time: 10 minutes
Cooking time: 1 hour
Servings: 4

Ingredients:

- 4 medium sweet potatoes
- 1 tbsp. olive oil
- 1 small onion, diced
- 2 cloves garlic, minced
- 1 red bell pepper, diced
- 1 pound boneless, skinless chicken breasts, cooked and shredded
- 1 tsp. ground cumin
- 1/2 tsp. paprika
- 1/2 tsp. dried oregano
- 1/4 tsp. salt
- 1/4 tsp. pepper
- 1 cup baby spinach leaves
- Optional toppings: Greek yogurt, chopped green onions, chopped fresh cilantro

Instructions:

1. Preheat the oven to 400°F (200°C).
2. Wash the sweet potatoes and pierce them a few times with a fork. Place them on a baking sheet lined with parchment paper or foil.
3. Bake the sweet potatoes in the preheated oven for about 45-60 minutes, or until they are tender and easily pierced with a fork.
4. While the sweet potatoes are baking, heat the olive oil in a large skillet over medium heat. Add the diced onion, minced garlic, and diced red bell pepper. Sauté until the vegetables are softe

ned, about 5 minutes.

5. Add the cooked and shredded chicken, ground cumin, paprika, dried oregano, salt, and pepper to the skillet. Stir well to combine and cook for an additional 2-3 minutes.
6. Stir in the baby spinach leaves and cook until wilted, about 1-2 minutes.
7. Once the sweet potatoes are cooked, remove them from the oven and let them cool slightly. Cut a lengthwise slit on the top of each sweet potato and gently squeeze to open.
8. Divide the chicken and vegetable mixture evenly among the sweet potatoes, spooning it into the slit on top.
9. Top the stuffed sweet potatoes with optional toppings such as Greek yogurt, chopped green onions, or chopped fresh cilantro.
10. Serve the chicken stuffed sweet potatoes as a main dish. You can also serve them with a side salad or steamed vegetables.

Nutritional Information (per serving):
Cal: 342 | Fat: 6g | Chol: 63mg | Sod: 238mg | Carbs: 44g | Fiber: 7g | Sugars: 12g | Pro: 29g

16. Pesto Grilled Chicken Breast

Preparation time: 10 minutes
Marinating time: 30 minutes
Cooking time: 12 minutes
Servings: 4

Ingredients:

- 4 boneless, skinless chicken breasts
- 1/4 cup store-bought or homemade pesto sauce
- 1 tbsp. olive oil
- 1 tbsp. lemon juice
- 1/2 tsp. garlic powder
- 1/2 tsp. dried oregano
- 1/4 tsp. salt
- 1/4 tsp. pepper

Instructions:

1. In a small bowl, combine the pesto sauce, olive oil, lemon juice, garlic powder, dried oregano, salt, and pepper. Stir well to combine.
2. Place the chicken breasts in a shallow dish or a resealable plastic bag. Pour the pesto mixture over the chicken, making sure each breast is coated evenly. Marinate in the refrigerator for at least 30 minutes, or up to 4 hours for maximum flavor.
3. Preheat the grill to medium-high heat.
4. Remove the chicken breasts from the marinade, allowing any excess marinade to drip off.
5. Place the chicken breasts on the grill and cook for about 6 minutes per side, or until the internal temperature reaches 165°F (74°C). Cooking time

may vary depending on the thickness of the chicken breasts.

6. Once cooked, remove the chicken breasts from the grill and let them rest for a few minutes before serving.
7. Serve the pesto grilled chicken breasts with your favorite side dishes such as steamed vegetables, salad, or whole grains.

Nutritional Information (per serving):
Cal: 246 | Fat: 11g | Chol: 88mg | Sod: 280mg | Carbs: 2g | Fiber: 0g | Sugars: 0g | Pro: 34g

17. Orange Glazed Chicken Thighs

Preparation time: 10 minutes
Cooking time: 25 minutes
Servings: 4

Ingredients:

- 4 bone-in, skin-on chicken thighs
- 2 tablespoons orange marmalade
- 1 tbsp. low-sodium soy sauce
- 1 tbsp. olive oil
- 1 tsp. grated orange zest
- 1 clove garlic, minced
- 1/2 tsp. dried thyme
- 1/4 tsp. salt
- 1/4 tsp. pepper
- Fresh parsley, for garnish (optional)

Instructions:

1. Preheat the oven to 400°F (200°C).
2. In a small bowl, whisk together the orange marmalade, soy sauce, olive oil, orange zest, minced garlic, dried thyme, salt, and pepper.
3. Place the chicken thighs in a baking dish, skin side up. Brush the glaze mixture evenly over the chicken thighs, reserving a small amount for later.
4. Bake the chicken thighs in the preheated oven for 20-25 minutes, or until the chicken is cooked through and the skin is crispy and golden brown. Baste the chicken with the reserved glaze mixture halfway through the cooking time.
5. Once cooked, remove the chicken thighs from the oven and let them rest for a few minutes.
6. Garnish with fresh parsley, if desired, and serve the orange glazed chicken thighs with your favorite side dishes such as steamed vegetables, brown rice, or a green salad.

Nutritional Information (per serving):
Cal: 283 | Fat: 17g | Chol: 141mg | Sod: 241mg | Carbs: 9g | Fiber: 0g | Sugars: 8g | Pro: 23g

18. Curry Lime Turkey Skewers

Preparation time: 10 minutes
Marinating time: 30 minutes
Cooking time: 15 minutes
Servings: 4

Ingredients:

- 1 pound turkey breast, cut into 1-inch cubes
- 2 tablespoons fresh lime juice
- 1 tbsp. olive oil
- 1 tbsp. curry powder
- 1 tsp. ground cumin
- 1 tsp. ground coriander
- 1/2 tsp. turmeric
- 1/2 tsp. paprika
- 1/4 tsp. salt
- 1/4 tsp. pepper
- Skewers, soaked in water if using wooden skewers
- Fresh cilantro, for garnish (optional)
- Lime wedges, for serving (optional)

Instructions:

1. In a bowl, combine the lime juice, olive oil, curry powder, cumin, coriander, turmeric, paprika, salt, and pepper to make the marinade.
2. Add the turkey cubes to the marinade and toss to coat. Let the turkey marinate in the refrigerator for at least 30 minutes.
3. Preheat the grill or grill pan over medium heat.
4. Thread the marinated turkey cubes onto the skewers.
5. Grill the turkey skewers for about 12-15 minutes, turning occasionally, until the turkey is cooked through and slightly charred on the edges.
6. Remove the skewers from the grill and let them rest for a few minutes.
7. Garnish with fresh cilantro, if desired, and serve the curry lime turkey skewers with lime wedges on the side for squeezing over the meat.

Nutritional Information (per serving):
Cal: 189 | Fat: 5g | Chol: 77mg | Sod: 177mg | Carbs: 3g | Fiber: 1g | Sugars: 0g | Pro: 33g

19. Garlic Parmesan Meatballs

Preparation time: 15 minutes
Cooking time: 20 minutes
Servings: 4

Ingredients:

- 1 pound ground turkey
- 1/4 cup grated Parmesan cheese
- 1/4 cup whole wheat bread crumbs
- 2 cloves garlic, minced
- 1/4 cup chopped fresh parsley
- 1 tsp. dried oregano
- 1/2 tsp. salt
- 1/4 tsp. pepper
- 1 large egg, lightly beaten
- Olive oil, for greasing the baking sheet

Instructions:

1. Preheat the oven to 400°F (200°C). Grease a baking sheet with olive oil.
2. In a large bowl, combine the ground turkey, grated Parmesan cheese, bread crumbs, minced garlic, chopped parsley, dried oregano, salt, pepper, and beaten egg. Mix well until all the ingredients are evenly incorporated.
3. Shape the mixture into meatballs, about 1 inch in diameter, and place them on the greased baking sheet.
4. Bake the turkey meatballs in the preheated oven for about 18-20 minutes, or until they are cooked through and golden brown on the outside.
5. Remove the meatballs from the oven and let them cool for a few minutes before serving.

Nutritional Information (per serving):
Cal: 248 | Fat: 11g | Chol: 125mg | Sod: 358mg | Carbs: 7g | Fiber: 1g | Sugars: 1g | Pro: 30g

20. Greek Lemon Chicken Skewers

Preparation time: 15 minutes
Marinating time: 1 hour
Cooking time: 10 minutes
Servings: 4

Ingredients:

- 1.5 pounds boneless, skinless chicken breasts, cut into 1-inch cubes
- 2 tablespoons fresh lemon juice
- 2 tablespoons olive oil
- 2 cloves garlic, minced
- 1 tsp. dried oregano
- 1/2 tsp. salt
- 1/4 tsp. pepper
- 1 medium red onion, cut into wedges
- Wooden skewers, soaked in water for 30 minutes

Instructions:

1. In a bowl, whisk together the lemon juice, olive oil, minced garlic, dried oregano, salt, and pepper to make the marinade.
2. Place the chicken cubes in a resealable plastic bag or a shallow dish. Pour the marinade over the chicken and toss to coat evenly. Marinate in the refrigerator for at least 1 hour.

3. Preheat the grill or grill pan over medium-high heat.
4. Thread the marinated chicken cubes onto the soaked wooden skewers, alternating with the onion wedges.
5. Grill the skewers for about 4-5 minutes per side, or until the chicken is cooked through and has grill marks. Make sure to turn the skewers occasionally for even cooking.
6. Once cooked, remove the skewers from the grill and let them rest for a few minutes before serving.

Nutritional Information (per serving):
Cal: 260 | Fat: 10g | Chol: 99mg | Sod: 315mg | Carbs: 6g | Fiber: 1g | Sugars: 3g | Pro: 35g

21. Paprika Baked Chicken Wings

Preparation time: 10 minutes
Cooking time: 45 minutes
Servings: 4

Ingredients:

- 2 pounds chicken wings
- 1 tbsp. olive oil
- 1 tsp. paprika
- 1/2 tsp. garlic powder
- 1/2 tsp. onion powder
- 1/2 tsp. dried oregano
- 1/2 tsp. salt
- 1/4 tsp. pepper
- Fresh parsley, for garnish (optional)

Instructions:

1. Preheat the oven to 425°F (220°C) and line a baking sheet with parchment paper.
2. In a bowl, combine the paprika, garlic powder, onion powder, dried oregano, salt, and pepper to make the seasoning mixture.
3. Pat dry the chicken wings using paper towels to remove any excess moisture.
4. Place the chicken wings in a large bowl, drizzle with olive oil, and toss to coat evenly.
5. Sprinkle the seasoning mixture over the chicken wings and toss again to ensure they are coated evenly.
6. Arrange the seasoned chicken wings in a single layer on the prepared baking sheet.
7. Bake in the preheated oven for 40-45 minutes, or until the chicken wings are cooked through and crispy, flipping them halfway through.
8. Once cooked, remove the chicken wings from the oven and let them cool for a few minutes.
9. Garnish with fresh parsley, if desired, before serving.

Nutritional Information (per serving):
Cal: 265 | Fat: 18g | Chol: 94mg | Sod: 316mg | Carbs: 0g | Fiber: 0g | Sugars: 0g | Pro: 25g

22. Tangy BBQ Turkey Meatloaf

Preparation time: 15 minutes
Cooking time: 1 hour
Servings: 6

Ingredients:

- 1.5 pounds ground turkey
- 1/2 cup whole wheat breadcrumbs
- 1/4 cup finely chopped onion
- 1/4 cup finely chopped bell pepper
- 1/4 cup grated Parmesan cheese
- 2 tablespoons Worcestershire sauce
- 2 tablespoons low-sodium ketchup
- 1 tbsp. Dijon mustard
- 1 tsp. dried oregano
- 1/2 tsp. garlic powder
- 1/2 tsp. onion powder
- 1/4 tsp. pepper
- 1/4 tsp. salt
- 1/4 cup low-sodium BBQ sauce

Instructions:

1. Preheat the oven to 375°F (190°C) and lightly grease a loaf pan.
2. In a large bowl, combine the ground turkey, breadcrumbs, onion, bell pepper, Parmesan cheese, Worcestershire sauce, ketchup, Dijon mustard, dried oregano, garlic powder, onion powder, pepper, and salt. Mix well until all ingredients are evenly incorporated.
3. Transfer the mixture to the greased loaf pan and shape it into a loaf.
4. Spread the BBQ sauce evenly over the top of the meatloaf.
5. Place the loaf pan in the preheated oven and bake for 50-60 minutes, or until the meatloaf is cooked through and the internal temperature reaches 165°F (74°C).
6. Remove the meatloaf from the oven and let it rest for a few minutes before slicing.
7. Slice the meatloaf and serve with additional BBQ sauce, if desired.

Nutritional Information (per serving):
Cal: 230 | Fat: 10g | Chol: 77mg | Sod: 333mg | Carbs: 10g | Fiber: 1g | Sugars: 3g | Pro: 25g

23. Spinach and Feta Stuffed Chicken

Preparation time: 15 minutes
Cooking time: 25 minutes
Servings: 4

Ingredients:

- 4 boneless, skinless chicken breasts
- 2 cups fresh spinach leaves
- 1/2 cup crumbled feta cheese
- 2 tablespoons chopped sun-dried tomatoes (optional)
- 1 tsp. dried oregano
- 1/2 tsp. garlic powder
- 1/2 tsp. pepper
- 1/4 tsp. salt
- 1 tbsp. olive oil

Instructions:

1. Preheat the oven to 400°F (200°C) and lightly grease a baking dish.
2. Using a sharp knife, make a horizontal slit in each chicken breast to create a pocket for stuffing. Be careful not to cut all the way through.
3. In a bowl, combine the spinach, feta cheese, sun-dried tomatoes (if using), dried oregano, garlic powder, pepper, and salt.
4. Stuff each chicken breast with the spinach and feta mixture, pressing it gently to fill the pocket.
5. Heat olive oil in a skillet over medium-high heat. Sear the stuffed chicken breasts for 2-3 minutes on each side, until lightly browned.
6. Transfer the seared chicken breasts to the prepared baking dish and bake in the preheated oven for 20-25 minutes, or until the chicken is cooked through and no longer pink in the center.
7. Remove from the oven and let the chicken rest for a few minutes before serving.

Nutritional Information (per serving):
Cal: 260 | Fat: 9g | Chol: 87mg | Sod: 328mg | Carbs: 2g | Fiber: 1g | Sugars: 1g | Pro: 39g

24. Cilantro Lime Turkey Breast

Preparation time: 10 minutes
Cooking time: 1 hour 30 minutes
Servings: 6

Ingredients:

- 1 bone-in turkey breast (about 4 pounds)
- 1/4 cup fresh cilantro, chopped
- 3 tablespoons lime juice
- 2 tablespoons olive oil
- 2 cloves garlic, minced
- 1 tsp. ground cumin
- 1/2 tsp. salt
- 1/4 tsp. pepper

Instructions:

1. Preheat the oven to 325°F (165°C).
2. In a small bowl, combine the chopped cilantro, lime juice, olive oil, minced garlic, ground cumin, salt, and pepper to make the marinade.
3. Place the turkey breast in a roasting pan or baking dish, and pour the marinade over the turkey. Make sure to coat it evenly on all sides.
4. Cover the roasting pan with aluminum foil and let the turkey marinate in the refrigerator for about 30 minutes.
5. Remove the foil and roast the turkey breast in the preheated oven for 1 hour and 30 minutes, or until a meat thermometer inserted into the thickest part of the breast registers 165°F (75°C).
6. Remove the turkey from the oven and let it rest for 10-15 minutes before slicing.
7. Slice the turkey breast and serve with your favorite side dishes.

Nutritional Information (per serving):
Cal: 345 | Fat: 12g | Chol: 161mg | Sod: 295mg | Carbs: 1g | Fiber: 0g | Sugars: 0g | Pro: 55g

25. Herbed Chicken Quinoa Bowl

Preparation time: 10 minutes
Cooking time: 25 minutes
Servings: 4

Ingredients:

- 1 cup quinoa, rinsed
- 2 cups low-sodium chicken broth
- 4 boneless, skinless chicken breasts
- 1 tbsp. olive oil
- 1 tsp. dried thyme
- 1 tsp. dried rosemary
- 1/2 tsp. dried oregano
- 1/2 tsp. garlic powder
- Salt and pepper, to taste
- 4 cups mixed salad greens
- 1 cup cherry tomatoes, halved
- 1/2 cup cucumber, diced
- 1/4 cup red onion, thinly sliced
- Lemon wedges, for serving

Instructions:

1. In a medium saucepan, bring the chicken broth to a boil. Add the quinoa, reduce heat to low, cover, and simmer for about 15-20 minutes, or until the quinoa is cooked and the liquid is absorbed. Fluff the quinoa with a fork and set aside.
2. Preheat the oven to 400°F (200°C). Season the chicken breasts with salt, pepper, dried thyme,

dried rosemary, dried oregano, and garlic powder.

3. Heat olive oil in a large oven-safe skillet over
   medium-high heat. Add the seasoned chicken
   breasts and sear for 2-3 minutes on each side,
   until browned.
4. Transfer the skillet to the preheated oven and
   bake for about 15 minutes or until the chicken is
   cooked through and reaches an internal temperature of 165°F (75°C).
5. Remove the chicken from the oven and let it rest
   for a few minutes. Slice the chicken into strips.
6. In a large bowl, combine the cooked quinoa,
   mixed salad greens, cherry tomatoes, cucumber,
   and red onion. Toss to mix well.
7. Divide the quinoa salad mixture into serving
   bowls. Top each bowl with sliced herbed chicken.
8. Serve the herbed chicken quinoa bowls with
   lemon wedges for squeezing over the top.

Nutritional Information (per serving):
Cal: 385 | Fat: 8g | Chol: 76mg | Sod: 172mg | Carbs:
42g | Fiber: 6g | Sugars: 4g | Pro: 37g

Beef and Pork

1. Beef and Veggie Stir Fry

Preparation time: 15 minutes
Cooking time: 15 minutes
Servings: 4

Ingredients:

- 1 pound lean beef (such as sirloin or flank steak), thinly sliced
- 2 tablespoons low-sodium soy sauce
- 2 tablespoons cornstarch
- 1 tbsp. vegetable oil
- 2 cloves garlic, minced
- 1 tsp. grated fresh ginger
- 1 medium onion, sliced
- 2 bell peppers (any color), sliced
- 2 cups broccoli florets
- 1 cup snap peas
- 1 cup sliced carrots
- 2 green onions, chopped (for garnish)

For the Sauce:

- 1/4 cup low-sodium soy sauce
- 2 tablespoons rice vinegar
- 1 tbsp. honey
- 1 tbsp. sesame oil
- 1/2 tsp. red pepper flakes (optional)

Instructions:

1. In a bowl, combine the thinly sliced beef, 2 tablespoons of low-sodium soy sauce, and 1 tbsp. of cornstarch. Toss until the beef is coated evenly. Set aside to marinate for about 10 minutes.
2. In a small bowl, whisk together the ingredients for the sauce: 1/4 cup low-sodium soy sauce, rice vinegar, honey, sesame oil, and red pepper flakes (if using). Set aside.
3. Heat the vegetable oil in a large skillet or wok over medium-high heat. Add the minced garlic and grated ginger, and sauté for about 1 minute until fragrant.
4. Add the marinated beef to the skillet and stir-fry for about 3-4 minutes until browned. Remove the beef from the skillet and set aside.
5. In the same skillet, add the sliced onion, bell peppers, broccoli florets, snap peas, and carrots. Stir-fry for about 4-5 minutes until the vegetables are crisp-tender.
6. Return the cooked beef to the skillet and pour the sauce over the beef and vegetables. Stir well to coat everything evenly.
7. In a small bowl, mix 1 tbsp. of cornstarch with 2 tablespoons of cold water until smooth. Add the cornstarch slurry to the skillet and stir well. Cook for an additional 1-2 minutes until the sauce thickens.
8. Remove the skillet from heat. Garnish the beef and veggie stir-fry with chopped green onions.
9. Serve the stir-fry hot over steamed brown rice or quinoa.

Nutritional Information (per serving):
Cal: 330 | Fat: 10g | Chol: 55mg | Sod: 380mg | Carbs: 31g | Fiber: 6g | Sugars: 11g | Pro: 30g

2. Pork Tenderloin Medallions

Preparation time: 15 minutes
Cooking time: 20 minutes
Servings: 4

Ingredients:

- 1 pound pork tenderloin, trimmed and cut into 1-inch thick medallions
- 1 tsp. dried thyme
- 1 tsp. paprika
- 1/2 tsp. garlic powder
- 1/2 tsp. onion powder
- 1/4 tsp. pepper
- 1 tbsp. olive oil
- 1 cup low-sodium chicken broth
- 1 tbsp. cornstarch
- 1 tbsp. water
- Fresh parsley, chopped (for garnish)

Instructions:

1. In a small bowl, combine the dried thyme, paprika, garlic powder, onion powder, and pepper. Mix well.
2. Season the pork tenderloin medallions on both sides with the spice mixture.
3. Heat the olive oil in a large skillet over medium-high heat.
4. Add the pork medallions to the skillet and cook for about 3-4 minutes per side until browned and cooked through. Transfer the cooked pork to a plate and cover to keep warm.
5. In the same skillet, add the low-sodium chicken broth and bring to a simmer.
6. In a separate small bowl, whisk together the cornstarch and water until smooth.
7. Slowly pour the cornstarch mixture into the simmering chicken broth, stirring constantly.
8. Cook for an additional 1-2 minutes until the sauce thickens.
9. Return the pork tenderloin medallions to the skillet and coat them with the sauce.
10. Remove the skillet from heat and garnish with fresh chopped parsley.
11. Serve the pork tenderloin medallions with your choice of steamed vegetables or a side salad.

Nutritional Information (per serving):
Cal: 230 | Fat: 9g | Chol: 75mg | Sod: 150mg | Carbs: 6g | Fiber: 0g | Sugars: 0g | Pro: 28g

3. Beef and Bean Chili

Preparation time: 15 minutes
Cooking time: 1 hour
Servings: 6

Ingredients:

- 1 pound lean ground beef
- 1 medium onion, diced
- 2 cloves garlic, minced
- 1 red bell pepper, diced
- 1 can (14.5 ounces) diced tomatoes, low sodium
- 1 can (15 ounces) kidney beans, rinsed and drained
- 1 can (15 ounces) black beans, rinsed and drained
- 1 cup low-sodium beef broth
- 2 tablespoons chili powder
- 1 tsp. ground cumin
- 1/2 tsp. paprika
- 1/4 tsp. cayenne pepper (optional for spice)
- Salt and pepper to taste
- Chopped fresh cilantro (for garnish)
- Optional toppings: shredded cheese, diced avocado, sour cream

Instructions:

1. In a large pot or Dutch oven, brown the ground beef over medium heat, breaking it up into crumbles. Drain any excess fat.
2. Add the diced onion, minced garlic, and diced red bell pepper to the pot. Cook for 5 minutes until the vegetables are softened.
3. Add the diced tomatoes, kidney beans, black beans, beef broth, chili powder, ground cumin, paprika, cayenne pepper (if using), salt, and pepper. Stir well to combine.
4. Bring the chili to a boil, then reduce the heat to low. Cover the pot and simmer for 45 minutes to 1 hour, stirring occasionally.
5. Taste and adjust the seasoning if needed.
6. Serve the beef and bean chili hot, garnished with chopped fresh cilantro. You can also add optional toppings like shredded cheese, diced avocado, or sour cream.

Nutritional Information (per serving):
Cal: 270 | Fat: 7g | Chol: 40mg | Sod: 300mg | Carbs: 32g | Fiber: 10g | Sugars: 5g | Pro: 23g

4. BBQ Pork Lettuce Wraps

Preparation time: 15 minutes
Cooking time: 30 minutes
Servings: 4

Ingredients:

- 1 pound lean pork tenderloin, thinly sliced
- 1/2 cup low-sodium BBQ sauce
- 2 tablespoons low-sodium soy sauce
- 1 tbsp. honey
- 1 tbsp. apple cider vinegar
- 1 tsp. smoked paprika
- 1/2 tsp. garlic powder
- 1/2 tsp. onion powder
- 1/4 tsp. pepper
- 8 large lettuce leaves (such as iceberg or butter lettuce)
- Optional toppings: diced tomatoes, sliced red onion, shredded carrots, chopped cilantro

Instructions:

1. In a bowl, whisk together the BBQ sauce, soy sauce, honey, apple cider vinegar, smoked paprika, garlic powder, onion powder, and pepper.
2. Place the pork tenderloin slices in a zip-top bag and pour the marinade over the pork. Seal the bag and marinate in the refrigerator for at least 1 hour or overnight.
3. Preheat a grill or grill pan over medium-high heat.
4. Remove the pork from the marinade, allowing any excess marinade to drip off.
5. Grill the pork slices for 3-4 minutes per side until cooked through and slightly charred.
6. Remove the pork from the grill and let it rest for a few minutes. Then, slice it into thin strips.
7. Arrange the lettuce leaves on a serving platter.
8. Fill each lettuce leaf with a few slices of grilled pork.
9. Top with optional toppings such as diced tomatoes, sliced red onion, shredded carrots, and chopped cilantro.
10. Serve the BBQ pork lettuce wraps immediately.

Nutritional Information (per serving):
Cal: 230 | Fat: 5g | Chol: 75mg | Sod: 280mg | Carbs: 16g | Fiber: 2g | Sugars: 12g | Pro: 29g

5. Greek Beef Skewers

Preparation time: 15 minutes
Marinating time: 1 hour
Cooking time: 10 minutes
Servings: 4

Ingredients:

- 1 pound lean beef, cut into 1-inch cubes
- 2 tablespoons extra-virgin olive oil
- 2 tablespoons lemon juice
- 2 garlic cloves, minced
- 1 tsp. dried oregano
- 1/2 tsp. dried thyme
- 1/2 tsp. dried rosemary
- 1/2 tsp. pepper
- 1/4 tsp. salt
- 1 large red bell pepper, cut into chunks
- 1 large yellow bell pepper, cut into chunks
- 1 red onion, cut into chunks
- 8 wooden skewers, soaked in water for 30 minutes

Instructions:

1. In a bowl, whisk together the olive oil, lemon juice, minced garlic, dried oregano, dried thyme, dried rosemary, pepper, and salt to make the marinade.
2. Place the beef cubes in a zip-top bag and pour the marinade over the beef. Seal the bag and marinate in the refrigerator for at least 1 hour.
3. Preheat a grill or grill pan over medium-high heat.
4. Thread the marinated beef cubes, red bell pepper chunks, yellow bell pepper chunks, and red onion chunks onto the soaked wooden skewers, alternating between the ingredients.
5. Grill the skewers for about 10 minutes, turning occasionally, until the beef is cooked to your desired doneness and the vegetables are tender-crisp.
6. Remove the skewers from the grill and let them rest for a few minutes before serving.
7. Serve the Greek beef skewers hot with a side salad or whole grain pita bread.

Nutritional Information (per serving):
Cal: 250 | Fat: 12g | Chol: 75mg | Sod: 180mg | Carbs: 8g | Fiber: 2g | Sugars: 4g | Pro: 28g

6. Honey Glazed Pork Chops

Preparation time: 10 minutes
Cooking time: 15 minutes
Servings: 4

Ingredients:

- 4 boneless pork chops
- 2 tablespoons honey
- 2 tablespoons low-sodium soy sauce
- 1 tbsp. Dijon mustard
- 1 tbsp. olive oil
- 2 cloves garlic, minced

- 1/2 tsp. dried thyme
- 1/2 tsp. paprika
- 1/4 tsp. pepper
- Fresh parsley, chopped (for garnish)

Instructions:

1. In a small bowl, whisk together the honey, soy sauce, Dijon mustard, olive oil, minced garlic, dried thyme, paprika, and pepper to make the glaze.
2. Heat a large skillet over medium-high heat.
3. Season the pork chops with a pinch of salt and pepper on both sides.
4. Place the pork chops in the skillet and cook for about 4-5 minutes on each side until browned and cooked through.
5. Pour the glaze over the pork chops in the skillet, turning the chops to coat them evenly.
6. Reduce the heat to low and simmer for an additional 2-3 minutes, allowing the glaze to thicken slightly.
7. Remove the pork chops from the skillet and let them rest for a few minutes.
8. Garnish with chopped parsley before serving.

Nutritional Information (per serving):
Cal: 240 | Fat: 9g | Chol: 75mg | Sod: 220mg | Carbs: 10g | Fiber: 0g | Sugars: 9g | Pro: 27g

7. Beef and Mushroom Stir Fry

Preparation time: 15 minutes
Cooking time: 10 minutes
Servings: 4

Ingredients:

- 1 pound lean beef steak, thinly sliced
- 2 tablespoons low-sodium soy sauce
- 1 tbsp. cornstarch
- 1 tbsp. olive oil
- 2 cloves garlic, minced
- 1 tsp. grated ginger
- 8 ounces mushrooms, sliced
- 1 red bell pepper, sliced
- 1 medium onion, sliced
- 2 cups broccoli florets
- 2 tablespoons low-sodium beef broth
- 1 tbsp. oyster sauce (optional)
- 1/4 tsp. pepper
- Fresh cilantro, chopped (for garnish)

Instructions:

1. In a bowl, combine the sliced beef, soy sauce, and cornstarch. Toss until the beef is coated evenly and set aside.
2. Heat the olive oil in a large skillet or wok over medium-high heat.

3. Add the minced garlic and grated ginger to the skillet and sauté for about 1 minute until fragrant.
4. Add the sliced mushrooms, bell pepper, onion, and broccoli florets to the skillet. Stir-fry for about 5 minutes until the vegetables are tender-crisp.
5. Push the vegetables to one side of the skillet and add the beef slices to the other side. Cook for about 3-4 minutes until the beef is browned and cooked to your desired doneness.
6. In a small bowl, whisk together the beef broth, oyster sauce (if using), and pepper. Pour the mixture over the beef and vegetables in the skillet.
7. Stir everything together to coat the beef and vegetables with the sauce. Cook for an additional 1-2 minutes until the sauce thickens slightly.
8. Remove from heat and garnish with chopped cilantro before serving.

Nutritional Information (per serving):
Cal: 250 | Fat: 9g | Chol: 50mg | Sod: 220mg | Carbs: 16g | Fiber: 4g | Sugars: 6g | Pro: 26g

8. Teriyaki Pork Tenderloin

Preparation time: 15 minutes
Marinating time: 30 minutes
Cooking time: 20 minutes
Servings: 4

Ingredients:

- 1 pound pork tenderloin
- 3 tablespoons low-sodium soy sauce
- 2 tablespoons honey
- 2 tablespoons rice vinegar
- 1 tbsp. sesame oil
- 2 cloves garlic, minced
- 1 tsp. grated ginger
- 1/4 tsp. pepper
- 1 tbsp. cornstarch
- 2 tablespoons water
- Sesame seeds (for garnish, optional)
- Sliced green onions (for garnish, optional)

Instructions:

1. Preheat the oven to 400°F (200°C).
2. In a small bowl, whisk together the soy sauce, honey, rice vinegar, sesame oil, minced garlic, grated ginger, and pepper.
3. Place the pork tenderloin in a shallow dish or resealable plastic bag. Pour half of the teriyaki sauce mixture over the pork, reserving the other half for later. Ensure the pork is well coated with the marinade. Let it marinate in the refrigerator for at least 30 minutes.
4. Heat a large oven-safe skillet or grill pan over medium-high heat. Add a small amount of oil to the pan.
5. Remove the pork tenderloin from the marinade,

allowing any excess marinade to drip off. Place the pork in the hot skillet and sear for about 2-3 minutes on each side until browned.
6. Transfer the skillet to the preheated oven and bake for about 12-15 minutes or until the internal temperature of the pork reaches 145°F (63°C). Cooking time may vary depending on the thickness of the tenderloin.
7. While the pork is cooking, pour the reserved teriyaki sauce into a small saucepan. In a separate small bowl, whisk together the cornstarch and water to create a slurry. Add the slurry to the saucepan with the teriyaki sauce.
8. Cook the sauce over medium heat, stirring constantly, until it thickens to your desired consistency.
9. Once the pork is cooked, remove it from the oven and let it rest for a few minutes before slicing it into medallions.
10. Serve the sliced pork tenderloin drizzled with the thickened teriyaki sauce. Garnish with sesame seeds and sliced green onions, if desired.

Nutritional Information (per serving):
Cal: 240 | Fat: 6g | Chol: 75mg | Sod: 220mg | Carbs: 15g | Fiber: 0g | Sugars: 12g | Pro: 30g

9. Beef and Lentil Soup

Preparation time: 10 minutes
Cooking time: 1 hour 30 minutes
Servings: 6

Ingredients:

- 1 pound pork tenderloin
- 1 pound lean beef stew meat, cut into small cubes
- 1 tbsp. olive oil
- 1 onion, chopped
- 2 carrots, diced
- 2 celery stalks, diced
- 2 cloves garlic, minced
- 1 cup dried lentils, rinsed and drained
- 6 cups low-sodium beef broth
- 2 cups water
- 1 bay leaf
- 1 tsp. dried thyme
- 1/2 tsp. paprika
- Salt and pepper to taste
- Fresh parsley for garnish (optional)

Instructions:

1. Heat the olive oil in a large pot or Dutch oven over medium heat.
2. Add the beef cubes to the pot and cook until browned on all sides. Remove the beef from the pot and set it aside.

3. In the same pot, add the chopped onion, carrots, celery, and minced garlic. Sauté for about 5 minutes until the vegetables are slightly softened.
4. Return the browned beef to the pot. Add the rinsed lentils, beef broth, water, bay leaf, dried thyme, and paprika. Stir to combine.
5. Bring the soup to a boil, then reduce the heat to low. Cover the pot and simmer for about 1 hour and 30 minutes, or until the beef is tender and the lentils are cooked through. Stir occasionally.
6. Season the soup with salt and pepper to taste. Remove the bay leaf before serving.
7. Ladle the soup into bowls and garnish with fresh parsley, if desired.

Nutritional Information (per serving):
Cal: 280 | Fat: 7g | Chol: 45mg | Sod: 230mg | Carbs: 28g | Fiber: 10g | Sugars: 4g | Pro: 27g

10. Garlic Rosemary Pork Roast

Preparation time: 10 minutes
Cooking time: 1 hour 30 minutes
Servings: 6

Ingredients:

- 2 pounds boneless pork loin roast
- 4 cloves garlic, minced
- 2 tablespoons fresh rosemary, chopped
- 1 tbsp. olive oil
- 1 tsp. lemon zest
- 1/2 tsp. salt
- 1/4 tsp. pepper
- Cooking spray

Instructions:

1. Preheat the oven to 350°F (175°C).
2. In a small bowl, combine the minced garlic, chopped rosemary, olive oil, lemon zest, salt, and pepper.
3. Place the pork roast on a cutting board and pat it dry with paper towels.
4. Rub the garlic rosemary mixture all over the pork roast, making sure to coat it evenly.
5. Place the pork roast on a rack in a roasting pan sprayed with cooking spray.
6. Roast the pork in the preheated oven for about 1 hour and 30 minutes, or until the internal temperature reaches 145°F (63°C).
7. Remove the pork roast from the oven and let it rest for 5-10 minutes before slicing.
8. Slice the pork roast into thin slices and serve.

Nutritional Information (per serving):
Cal: 240 | Fat: 9g | Chol: 95mg | Sod: 210mg | Carbs: 1g | Fiber: 0g | Sugars: 0g | Pro: 36g

11. Spicy Pork Lettuce Wraps

Preparation time: 15 minutes
Cooking time: 10 minutes
Servings: 4

Ingredients:

- 1 pound lean ground pork
- 2 tablespoons low-sodium soy sauce
- 1 tbsp. rice vinegar
- 1 tbsp. Sriracha sauce (adjust to taste)
- 1 tbsp. sesame oil
- 2 cloves garlic, minced
- 1 tsp. fresh ginger, grated
- 1/2 cup diced red bell pepper
- 1/2 cup diced water chestnuts
- 1/4 cup sliced green onions
- 8 large lettuce leaves (such as butter lettuce or iceberg lettuce)

Instructions:

1. In a small bowl, whisk together the low-sodium soy sauce, rice vinegar, Sriracha sauce, and sesame oil. Set aside.
2. Heat a large skillet or wok over medium-high heat. Add the ground pork and cook until browned and cooked through, breaking it up with a spoon or spatula.
3. Add the minced garlic and grated ginger to the skillet with the cooked pork. Stir-fry for 1 minute until fragrant.
4. Add the diced red bell pepper and water chestnuts to the skillet and continue to stir-fry for an additional 2 minutes.
5. Pour the sauce mixture over the pork and vegetables in the skillet. Stir to combine and cook for another 2-3 minutes until heated through.
6. Remove from heat and stir in the sliced green onions.
7. To serve, spoon the pork mixture onto the lettuce leaves. Roll up the leaves to form wraps and secure with toothpicks if desired.
8. Enjoy the spicy pork lettuce wraps as a flavorful and low-sodium meal.

Nutritional Information (per serving):
Cal: 250 | Fat: 16g | Chol: 55mg | Sod: 320mg | Carbs: 7g | Fiber: 2g | Sugars: 2g | Pro: 20g

12. Asian Beef Noodle Bowl

Preparation time: 15 minutes
Cooking time: 15 minutes
Servings: 4

Ingredients:

- 8 ounces whole wheat spaghetti or rice noodles
- 1 pound lean beef sirloin, thinly sliced
- 2 tablespoons reduced-sodium soy sauce
- 2 tablespoons hoisin sauce
- 1 tbsp. rice vinegar
- 1 tbsp. sesame oil
- 2 cloves garlic, minced
- 1 tsp. grated fresh ginger
- 2 cups chopped broccoli florets
- 1 red bell pepper, thinly sliced
- 1 carrot, thinly sliced
- 2 green onions, sliced
- 1 tbsp. sesame seeds (optional)

Instructions:

1. Cook the noodles according to the package instructions. Drain and set aside.
2. In a small bowl, whisk together the reduced-sodium soy sauce, hoisin sauce, rice vinegar, sesame oil, minced garlic, and grated ginger. Set aside.
3. Heat a large skillet or wok over medium-high heat. Add the beef slices and cook for 2-3 minutes until browned and cooked to your desired level of doneness. Remove the beef from the skillet and set aside.
4. In the same skillet, add the broccoli florets, red bell pepper, and carrot slices. Stir-fry for 3-4 minutes until the vegetables are crisp-tender.
5. Return the cooked beef to the skillet with the vegetables. Pour the sauce mixture over the beef and vegetables. Stir to coat everything evenly and cook for an additional 1-2 minutes until heated through.
6. Divide the cooked noodles among four bowls. Top with the beef and vegetable mixture. Garnish with sliced green onions and sesame seeds, if desired.
7. Serve the Asian Beef Noodle Bowl immediately as a delicious and low-sodium meal.

Nutritional Information (per serving):
Cal: 400 | Fat: 9g | Chol: 60mg | Sod: 350mg | Carbs: 54g | Fiber: 7g | Sugars: 6g | Pro: 29g

13. Paprika Rubbed Pork Chops

Preparation time: 10 minutes
Cooking time: 15 minutes
Servings: 4

Ingredients:

- 4 boneless pork chops, about 1 inch thick
- 1 tbsp. paprika
- 1 tsp. garlic powder

- 1 tsp. onion powder
- 1/2 tsp. ground pepper
- 1/2 tsp. dried thyme
- 1/2 tsp. dried oregano
- 1/4 tsp. cayenne pepper (optional)
- 1 tbsp. olive oil

Instructions:

1. Preheat your grill or stovetop grill pan to medium-high heat.
2. In a small bowl, combine the paprika, garlic powder, onion powder, pepper, dried thyme, dried oregano, and cayenne pepper (if using). Mix well to create the spice rub.
3. Pat dry the pork chops with a paper towel to remove any excess moisture. Rub both sides of each pork chop with the spice rub, pressing it gently into the meat.
4. Drizzle the olive oil over the seasoned pork chops and rub it in to coat them evenly.
5. Place the pork chops on the preheated grill or grill pan. Cook for about 6-7 minutes per side, or until the internal temperature reaches 145°F (63°C) for medium doneness.
6. Remove the pork chops from the grill and let them rest for a few minutes before serving.
7. Serve the Paprika Rubbed Pork Chops with your choice of side dishes, such as steamed vegetables or a green salad, for a delicious and low-sodium meal.

Nutritional Information (per serving):
Cal: 250 | Fat: 12g | Chol: 75mg | Sod: 65mg | Carbs: 2g | Fiber: 1g | Sugars: 0g | Pro: 32g

14. Paprika Rubbed Pork Chops

Preparation time: 15 minutes
Cooking time: 2 hours
Servings: 6

Ingredients:

- 1.5 pounds beef stew meat, cut into bite-sized pieces
- 1 onion, diced
- 3 cloves garlic, minced
- 2 carrots, peeled and chopped
- 2 celery stalks, chopped
- 1 red bell pepper, diced
- 1 can (14.5 ounces) diced tomatoes, undrained
- 2 cups low-sodium beef broth
- 1 tbsp. ground cumin
- 1 tbsp. ground coriander
- 1 tsp. ground cinnamon
- 1 tsp. ground ginger
- 1/2 tsp. ground turmeric
- 1/4 tsp. cayenne pepper (optional, for heat)
- Salt and pepper, to taste

- Fresh cilantro, chopped (for garnish)

Instructions:

1. In a large pot or Dutch oven, heat some olive oil over medium heat. Add the diced onion and minced garlic, and sauté until they become fragrant and translucent.
2. Add the beef stew meat to the pot and cook until browned on all sides.
3. Add the chopped carrots, celery, red bell pepper, diced tomatoes (with their juice), and low-sodium beef broth to the pot. Stir to combine.
4. Add the ground cumin, ground coriander, ground cinnamon, ground ginger, ground turmeric, and cayenne pepper (if using). Season with salt and pepper to taste.
5. Stir well to ensure the spices are evenly distributed. Bring the stew to a boil, then reduce the heat to low. Cover the pot and simmer for about 2 hours, or until the beef is tender and the flavors are well blended. Stir occasionally during cooking.
6. Taste and adjust the seasonings as needed. If desired, add more salt, pepper, or spices to suit your taste preferences.
7. Serve the Moroccan Spiced Beef Stew hot, garnished with fresh chopped cilantro. Enjoy it with some whole grain couscous or steamed vegetables for a complete meal.

Nutritional Information (per serving):
Cal: 290 | Fat: 10g | Chol: 75mg | Sod: 160mg | Carbs: 17g | Fiber: 4g | Sugars: 7g | Pro: 33g

15. Pork and Cabbage Stir Fry

Preparation time: 15 minutes
Cooking time: 15 minutes
Servings: 4

Ingredients:

- 1 pound pork tenderloin, thinly sliced
- 1 tbsp. low-sodium soy sauce
- 1 tbsp. rice vinegar
- 1 tbsp. cornstarch
- 2 tablespoons olive oil
- 2 cloves garlic, minced
- 1 tsp. grated ginger
- 1 small head of cabbage, thinly sliced
- 2 carrots, julienned
- 1 bell pepper, thinly sliced
- 2 green onions, sliced
- Salt and pepper, to taste
- Sesame seeds (for garnish)

Instructions:

1. In a small bowl, whisk together the low-sodium soy sauce, rice vinegar, and cornstarch. Add the sliced pork tenderloin and toss to coat. Let it marinate for 10 minutes.
2. Heat 1 tbsp. of olive oil in a large skillet or wok over medium-high heat. Add the marinated pork and stir-fry until cooked through. Remove the pork from the skillet and set it aside.
3. In the same skillet, heat the remaining tbsp. of olive oil. Add the minced garlic and grated ginger, and sauté for about 1 minute until fragrant.
4. Add the sliced cabbage, julienned carrots, and sliced bell pepper to the skillet. Stir-fry for about 5 minutes until the vegetables are tender-crisp.
5. Return the cooked pork to the skillet and toss everything together. Season with salt and pepper to taste.
6. Add the sliced green onions and stir-fry for another minute.
7. Remove from heat and garnish with sesame seeds.
8. Serve the Pork and Cabbage Stir-Fry hot as a main dish or with brown rice or quinoa as a side.

Nutritional Information (per serving):
Cal: 250 | Fat: 9g | Chol: 75mg | Sod: 220mg | Carbs: 15g | Fiber: 5g | Sugars: 7g | Pro: 27g

16. Beef n' Quinoa Stuffed Peppers

Preparation time: 15 minutes
Cooking time: 40 minutes
Servings: 4

Ingredients:

- 4 large bell peppers (any color), tops removed and seeds removed
- 1 pound lean ground beef
- 1 small onion, diced
- 2 cloves garlic, minced
- 1 cup cooked quinoa
- 1 cup diced tomatoes (canned or fresh)
- 1 tsp. dried basil
- 1 tsp. dried oregano
- Salt and pepper, to taste
- 1/4 cup grated Parmesan cheese

Instructions:

1. Preheat your oven to 375°F (190°C).
2. In a large pot, bring water to a boil. Add the bell peppers and cook for 5 minutes to slightly soften them. Remove the peppers from the pot and set them aside.
3. In a skillet over medium heat, cook the ground beef until browned. Add the diced onion and

minced garlic, and cook until the onion is translucent.

4. Add the cooked quinoa, diced tomatoes, dried basil, dried oregano, salt, and pepper to the skillet. Stir well to combine all the ingredients. Cook for an additional 2-3 minutes to heat through.
5. Place the bell peppers upright in a baking dish. Spoon the beef and quinoa mixture into each bell pepper until they are filled. Press the filling down gently to pack it.
6. Sprinkle the grated Parmesan cheese over the stuffed peppers.
7. Cover the baking dish with foil and bake in the preheated oven for 25 minutes.
8. Remove the foil and bake for an additional 10 minutes or until the peppers are tender and the cheese is golden brown.
9. Remove from the oven and let them cool slightly before serving.

Nutritional Information (per serving):
Cal: 300 | Fat: 12g | Chol: 60mg | Sod: 200mg | Carbs: 25g | Fiber: 5g | Sugars: 9g | Pro: 23g

17. Tangy BBQ Pork Ribs

Preparation time: 15 minutes
Cooking time: 2 hours 30 minutes
Servings: 4

Ingredients:

- 2 racks of pork baby back ribs
- 1 cup low-sodium barbecue sauce
- 2 tablespoons apple cider vinegar
- 1 tbsp. honey
- 1 tbsp. Dijon mustard
- 1 tsp. smoked paprika
- 1/2 tsp. garlic powder
- 1/2 tsp. onion powder
- Salt and pepper, to taste

Instructions:

1. Preheat your oven to 275°F (135°C).
2. Prepare the ribs by removing the thin membrane from the back of each rack. This can be done by sliding a knife under the membrane and then using a paper towel to grip and pull it off.
3. In a bowl, combine the barbecue sauce, apple cider vinegar, honey, Dijon mustard, smoked paprika, garlic powder, onion powder, salt, and pepper. Stir well to combine.
4. Place the ribs on a large baking sheet lined with foil. Brush the sauce mixture generously over both sides of the ribs, reserving some for later.
5. Cover the baking sheet with another sheet of foil, sealing the edges to create a packet. This will help keep the ribs moist during cooking.

6. Bake the ribs in the preheated oven for 2 hours, or until the meat is tender and starts to pull away from the bones.
7. Remove the foil from the baking sheet and brush the ribs with the reserved sauce mixture. Increase the oven temperature to 400°F (200°C).
8. Return the ribs to the oven, uncovered, and bake for an additional 20-30 minutes, or until the sauce is caramelized and sticky.
9. Remove the ribs from the oven and let them rest for a few minutes before slicing and serving.

Nutritional Information (per serving):
Cal: 500 | Fat: 30g | Chol: 120mg | Sod: 250mg | Carbs: 18g | Fiber: 1g | Sugars: 14g | Pro: 40g

18. Ginger Soy Beef Skewers

Preparation time: 15 minutes
Marinating time: 30 minutes
Cooking time: 10 minutes
Servings: 4

Ingredients:

- 1.5 lbs (680g) beef sirloin, cut into 1-inch cubes
- 2 tablespoons reduced-sodium soy sauce
- 2 tablespoons fresh lemon juice
- 1 tbsp. honey
- 1 tbsp. grated ginger
- 2 cloves garlic, minced
- 1 tbsp. sesame oil
- 1/4 tsp. pepper
- Bamboo skewers, soaked in water for 30 minutes

Instructions:

1. In a bowl, combine the soy sauce, lemon juice, honey, grated ginger, minced garlic, sesame oil, and pepper. Stir well to create the marinade.
2. Add the beef cubes to the marinade and toss to coat evenly. Cover the bowl and refrigerate for at least 30 minutes to allow the flavors to meld.
3. Preheat your grill or grill pan over medium-high heat.
4. Thread the marinated beef cubes onto the soaked bamboo skewers, dividing them evenly among the skewers.
5. Place the skewers on the preheated grill and cook for about 3-4 minutes per side, or until the beef reaches your desired level of doneness.
6. Remove the skewers from the grill and let them rest for a few minutes before serving.

Nutritional Information (per serving):
Cal: 250 | Fat: 10g | Chol: 70mg | Sod: 230mg | Carbs: 6g | Fiber: 0g | Sugars: 4g | Pro: 32g

19. Herb Roasted Pork Tenderloin

Preparation time: 10 minutes
Cooking time: 25-30 minutes
Servings: 4

Ingredients:

- 1 lb (450g) pork tenderloin
- 1 tbsp. olive oil
- 2 cloves garlic, minced
- 1 tsp. dried thyme
- 1 tsp. dried rosemary
- 1/2 tsp. dried oregano
- 1/2 tsp. dried basil
- 1/2 tsp. salt (optional)
- 1/4 tsp. pepper

Instructions:

1. Preheat the oven to 425°F (220°C).
2. Place the pork tenderloin on a baking sheet lined with parchment paper or foil.
3. In a small bowl, combine the olive oil, minced garlic, dried thyme, dried rosemary, dried oregano, dried basil, salt (if using), and pepper. Mix well to create the herb seasoning.
4. Rub the herb seasoning all over the pork tenderloin, ensuring it is evenly coated.
5. Place the seasoned pork tenderloin in the preheated oven and roast for 25-30 minutes, or until the internal temperature reaches 145°F (63°C).
6. Remove the pork tenderloin from the oven and let it rest for 5 minutes before slicing.
7. Slice the roasted pork tenderloin into thin slices and serve.

Nutritional Information (per serving):
Cal: 180 | Fat: 8g | Chol: 75mg | Sod: 240mg | Carbs: 0g | Fiber: 0g | Sugars: 0g | Pro: 26g

20. Greek Beef Pita Wraps

Preparation time: 15 minutes
Cooking time: 10 minutes
Servings: 4

Ingredients:

- 1 lb (450g) lean ground beef
- 1 small onion, finely chopped
- 2 cloves garlic, minced
- 1 tsp. dried oregano
- 1/2 tsp. dried basil
- 1/2 tsp. dried thyme
- 1/4 tsp. salt (optional)
- 1/4 tsp. pepper
- 4 whole wheat pita breads
- 1 cup Greek yogurt
- 1 cup diced tomatoes
- 1 cup diced cucumber
- 1/4 cup chopped fresh parsley
- 1/4 cup crumbled feta cheese

Instructions:

1. In a large skillet, cook the lean ground beef over medium heat until browned and cooked through. Drain any excess fat.
2. Add the chopped onion, minced garlic, dried oregano, dried basil, dried thyme, salt (if using), and pepper to the skillet. Cook for an additional 2-3 minutes until the onion is softened and the flavors are well combined.
3. Warm the whole wheat pita breads in a toaster or oven.
4. In a small bowl, combine the Greek yogurt, diced tomatoes, diced cucumber, and chopped fresh parsley to make the tzatziki sauce.
5. Assemble the wraps by spreading a generous amount of tzatziki sauce on each warm pita bread.
6. Divide the cooked ground beef mixture among the pita breads, placing it in the center.
7. Sprinkle crumbled feta cheese on top of the beef mixture in each wrap.
8. Fold the sides of the pita bread over the filling and roll it up tightly.
9. Serve the Greek Beef Pita Wraps immediately.

Nutritional Information (per serving):
Cal: 380 | Fat: 14g | Chol: 75mg | Sod: 360mg | Carbs: 31g | Fiber: 5g | Sugars: 6g | Pro: 31g

21. Citrus Glazed Pork Chops

Preparation time: 10 minutes
Cooking time: 15 minutes
Servings: 4

Ingredients:

- 4 boneless pork chops
- 2 tablespoons fresh lemon juice
- 2 tablespoons fresh orange juice
- 2 tablespoons honey
- 1 tbsp. low-sodium soy sauce
- 1 tsp. grated ginger
- 1 clove garlic, minced
- 1/2 tsp. dried thyme
- 1/4 tsp. pepper
- 1 tbsp. olive oil

Instructions:

1. In a small bowl, whisk together the lemon juice, orange juice, honey, soy sauce, grated ginger, minced garlic, dried thyme, and pepper to

make the citrus glaze.

2. Place the pork chops in a shallow dish or zip-top bag. Pour half of the citrus glaze over the pork chops, reserving the remaining glaze for later. Marinate the pork chops in the refrigerator for at least 30 minutes, or up to 2 hours.
3. Heat the olive oil in a skillet over medium-high heat.
4. Remove the pork chops from the marinade and shake off any excess. Discard the used marinade.
5. Add the pork chops to the hot skillet and cook for 4-5 minutes on each side, or until they reach an internal temperature of 145°F (63°C). Cooking time may vary depending on the thickness of the pork chops.
6. Pour the reserved citrus glaze over the pork chops in the skillet and cook for an additional 1-2 minutes, allowing the glaze to thicken and coat the chops.
7. Remove the pork chops from the skillet and let them rest for a few minutes before serving.
8. Serve the Citrus Glazed Pork Chops with your choice of sides, such as steamed vegetables or a salad.

Nutritional Information (per serving):
Cal: 230 | Fat: 8g | Chol: 65mg | Sod: 190mg | Carbs: 14g | Fiber: 0g | Sugars: 13g | Pro: 24g

22. Beef and Sweet Potato Hash

Preparation time: 10 minutes
Cooking time: 25 minutes
Servings: 4

Ingredients:

- 1 pound lean ground beef
- 2 medium sweet potatoes, peeled and diced
- 1 medium onion, diced
- 1 red bell pepper, diced
- 2 cloves garlic, minced
- 1 tsp. smoked paprika
- 1/2 tsp. ground cumin
- 1/4 tsp. chili powder
- Salt and pepper to taste
- 2 tablespoons olive oil
- Fresh parsley or cilantro for garnish (optional)

Instructions:

1. Heat the olive oil in a large skillet over medium heat.
2. Add the diced sweet potatoes and cook for 5-7 minutes, or until they start to soften.
3. Add the diced onion, red bell pepper, and minced garlic to the skillet. Cook for another 3-4 minutes, or until the vegetables are tender.

4. Push the vegetables to one side of the skillet and add the ground beef to the other side. Cook the ground beef, breaking it up with a spoon, until it is browned and cooked through.
5. Stir in the smoked paprika, ground cumin, chili powder, salt, and pepper. Mix well to combine all the ingredients.
6. Continue cooking for another 2-3 minutes, allowing the flavors to meld together.
7. Remove the skillet from heat and garnish with fresh parsley or cilantro, if desired.
8. Serve the Beef and Sweet Potato Hash hot and enjoy!

Nutritional Information (per serving):
Cal: 310 | Fat: 13g | Chol: 70mg | Sod: 80mg | Carbs: 25g | Fiber: 4g | Sugars: 7g | Pro: 24g

23. Italian Pork Meatballs

Preparation time: 15 minutes
Cooking time: 25 minutes
Servings: 4

Ingredients:

- 1 pound lean ground pork
- 1/2 cup whole wheat breadcrumbs
- 1/4 cup grated Parmesan cheese
- 1/4 cup chopped fresh parsley
- 1/4 cup chopped fresh basil
- 1/4 cup chopped fresh oregano
- 1 small onion, finely chopped
- 2 cloves garlic, minced
- 1 large egg
- 1/2 tsp. salt
- 1/4 tsp. pepper
- 2 cups low-sodium marinara sauce
- Cooking spray

Instructions:

1. Preheat the oven to 400°F (200°C). Line a baking sheet with aluminum foil and lightly coat it with cooking spray.
2. In a large mixing bowl, combine the ground pork, breadcrumbs, Parmesan cheese, parsley, basil, oregano, onion, garlic, egg, salt, and pepper. Mix well until all the ingredients are evenly incorporated.
3. Shape the mixture into meatballs, about 1 to 1.5 inches in diameter, and place them on the prepared baking sheet.
4. Bake the meatballs in the preheated oven for 20-25 minutes, or until they are cooked through and browned.
5. While the meatballs are baking, heat the marinara sauce in a saucepan over low heat until warmed.

6. Once the meatballs are cooked, transfer them to the saucepan with the marinara sauce. Gently stir to coat the meatballs with the sauce.
7. Simmer the meatballs in the sauce for an additional 5 minutes to allow the flavors to meld together.
8. Serve the Italian Pork Meatballs hot with your favorite side dish or over whole wheat pasta or zucchini noodles.

Nutritional Information (per serving):
Cal: 290 | Fat: 12g | Chol: 110mg | Sod: 460mg | Carbs: 18g | Fiber: 3g | Sugars: 7g | Pro: 27g

24. Beef and Cabbage Stir Fry

Preparation time: 15 minutes
Cooking time: 15 minutes
Servings: 4

Ingredients:

- 1 pound lean beef (such as sirloin or flank steak), thinly sliced
- 1 small head cabbage, shredded
- 1 medium carrot, julienned
- 1 red bell pepper, thinly sliced
- 1 yellow onion, thinly sliced
- 2 cloves garlic, minced
- 1 tbsp. low-sodium soy sauce
- 1 tbsp. rice vinegar
- 1 tbsp. sesame oil
- 1 tsp. grated fresh ginger
- 1/2 tsp. red pepper flakes (optional)
- Cooking spray
- Salt and pepper to taste
- Chopped green onions and sesame seeds for garnish

Instructions:

1. Heat a large skillet or wok over medium-high heat. Lightly coat it with cooking spray.
2. Add the sliced beef to the skillet and stir-fry for 3-4 minutes, or until browned. Remove the beef from the skillet and set aside.
3. In the same skillet, add the garlic, ginger, and red pepper flakes (if using). Stir-fry for 1 minute until fragrant.
4. Add the cabbage, carrot, bell pepper, and onion to the skillet. Stir-fry for 5-6 minutes, or until the vegetables are crisp-tender.
5. In a small bowl, whisk together the soy sauce, rice vinegar, and sesame oil. Pour the sauce over the vegetables in the skillet and stir to coat.
6. Return the cooked beef to the skillet and toss with the vegetables and sauce. Cook for an additional 2-3 minutes to heat through.
7. Season with salt and pepper to taste.

8. Serve the Beef and Cabbage Stir-Fry hot, garnished with chopped green onions and sesame seeds.

Nutritional Information (per serving):
Cal: 250 | Fat: 8g | Chol: 60mg | Sod: 180mg | Carbs: 17g | Fiber: 6g | Sugars: 9g | Pro: 28g

25. Honey Mustard Pork Loin

Preparation time: 10 minutes
Cooking time: 1 hour 30 minutes
Servings: 6

Ingredients:

- 2 pounds boneless pork loin
- 1/4 cup Dijon mustard
- 2 tablespoons honey
- 2 tablespoons low-sodium soy sauce
- 2 cloves garlic, minced
- 1 tbsp. olive oil
- 1 tsp. dried thyme
- 1/2 tsp. pepper
- Cooking spray
- Salt to taste

Instructions:

1. Preheat the oven to 350°F (175°C).
2. In a small bowl, whisk together the Dijon mustard, honey, soy sauce, minced garlic, olive oil, dried thyme, and pepper.
3. Place the pork loin in a baking dish coated with cooking spray. Season the pork loin with salt to taste.
4. Pour the honey mustard mixture over the pork loin, making sure it is evenly coated.
5. Cover the baking dish with aluminum foil and bake for 1 hour.
6. After 1 hour, remove the foil and continue baking for an additional 15-30 minutes, or until the internal temperature of the pork reaches 145°F (63°C).
7. Remove the pork loin from the oven and let it rest for 10 minutes before slicing.
8. Slice the pork loin into thin slices and serve warm.

Nutritional Information (per serving):
Cal: 250 | Fat: 8g | Chol: 80mg | Sod: 180mg | Carbs: 6g | Fiber: 0g | Sugars: 5g | Pro: 36g

Fish and Seafood

1. Grilled Salmon Skewers

Preparation time: 15 minutes
Marinating time: 30 minutes
Cooking time: 10 minutes
Servings: 4

Ingredients:

- 1 pound salmon fillets, skin removed, cut into 1-inch cubes
- 2 tablespoons olive oil
- 2 tablespoons lemon juice
- 2 cloves garlic, minced
- 1 tsp. dried dill
- 1/2 tsp. paprika
- 1/4 tsp. pepper
- 1 bell pepper, cut into 1-inch pieces
- 1 red onion, cut into 1-inch pieces
- 8 cherry tomatoes
- Cooking spray
- Salt to taste

Instructions:

1. In a bowl, whisk together the olive oil, lemon juice, minced garlic, dried dill, paprika, and pepper to make the marinade.
2. Place the salmon cubes in a shallow dish and pour the marinade over them. Gently toss to ensure the salmon is evenly coated. Cover the dish and let it marinate in the refrigerator for 30 minutes.
3. Preheat the grill to medium-high heat.
4. Thread the marinated salmon cubes onto skewers, alternating with bell pepper, red onion, and cherry tomatoes.
5. Lightly coat the grill grates with cooking spray to prevent sticking.
6. Place the skewers on the grill and cook for about 4-5 minutes per side, or until the salmon is cooked through and flakes easily with a fork.
7. Remove the skewers from the grill and season with salt to taste.
8. Serve the grilled salmon skewers hot with your choice of side dishes.

Nutritional Information (per serving):
Cal: 250 | Fat: 15g | Chol: 70mg | Sod: 100mg | Carbs: 7g | Fiber: 2g | Sugars: 3g | Pro: 23g

2. Lemon Herb Baked Cod

Preparation time: 10 minutes
Cooking time: 15 minutes
Servings: 4

Ingredients:

- 4 cod fillets (about 4-6 ounces each)
- 2 tablespoons olive oil
- 2 tablespoons fresh lemon juice
- 2 cloves garlic, minced
- 1 tsp. dried thyme
- 1 tsp. dried parsley
- 1/2 tsp. paprika
- 1/4 tsp. pepper
- Lemon wedges, for serving
- Fresh parsley, chopped, for garnish

Instructions:

1. Preheat the oven to 400°F (200°C) and lightly grease a baking dish.
2. In a small bowl, whisk together the olive oil, lemon juice, minced garlic, dried thyme, dried parsley, paprika, and pepper to make the marinade.
3. Place the cod fillets in the prepared baking dish. Pour the marinade over the cod, ensuring each fillet is coated evenly.
4. Let the cod marinate in the refrigerator for about 10 minutes to allow the flavors to develop.
5. Bake the cod in the preheated oven for 12-15 minutes, or until the fish is opaque and flakes easily with a fork.
6. Remove the baked cod from the oven and let it rest for a few minutes.
7. Serve the Lemon Herb Baked Cod hot, garnished with fresh parsley and accompanied by lemon wedges for squeezing over the fish.

Nutritional Information (per serving):
Cal: 180 | Fat: 8g | Chol: 65mg | Sod: 90mg | Carbs: 2g | Fiber: 0g | Sugars: 0g | Pro: 25g

3. Teriyaki Glazed Tuna Steaks

Preparation time: 10 minutes
Marinating time: 30 minutes
Cooking time: 6-8 minutes
Servings: 4

Ingredients:

- 4 tuna steaks (about 6 ounces each)
- 1/4 cup reduced-sodium soy sauce
- 2 tablespoons honey
- 2 tablespoons rice vinegar
- 1 tbsp. grated fresh ginger
- 2 cloves garlic, minced
- 1 tbsp. sesame oil
- 1/4 tsp. pepper
- 1 tbsp. sesame seeds, for garnish
- Green onions, sliced, for garnish

Instructions:

1. In a small bowl, whisk together the reduced-sodium soy sauce, honey, rice vinegar, grated ginger, minced garlic, sesame oil, and pepper to make the teriyaki marinade.
2. Place the tuna steaks in a shallow dish or a resealable plastic bag. Pour the marinade over the tuna steaks, making sure they are coated evenly. Marinate in the refrigerator for at least 30 minutes, turning the steaks occasionally.
3. Preheat the grill or a grill pan over medium-high heat.
4. Remove the tuna steaks from the marinade, reserving the marinade for later use.
5. Grill the tuna steaks for 3-4 minutes per side, or until they reach the desired level of doneness. Baste the steaks with the reserved marinade while grilling.
6. Remove the grilled tuna steaks from the heat and let them rest for a few minutes.
7. Sprinkle the tuna steaks with sesame seeds and sliced green onions for garnish.
8. Serve the Teriyaki Glazed Tuna Steaks hot with steamed vegetables or a side salad.

Nutritional Information (per serving):
Cal: 245 | Fat: 7g | Chol: 65mg | Sod: 300mg | Carbs: 11g | Fiber: 0g | Sugars: 9g | Pro: 34g

4. Garlic Butter Shrimp Scampi

Preparation time: 10 minutes
Cooking time: 10 minutes
Servings: 4

Ingredients:

- 1 pound large shrimp, peeled and deveined
- 4 tablespoons unsalted butter
- 4 cloves garlic, minced
- 1/4 cup low-sodium chicken broth
- 2 tablespoons fresh lemon juice
- 1/4 tsp. red pepper flakes (optional)
- Salt and pepper to taste
- 2 tablespoons fresh parsley, chopped
- Lemon wedges, for garnish

Instructions:

1. In a large skillet, melt the butter over medium heat. Add the minced garlic and cook for 1-2 minutes until fragrant.
2. Add the shrimp to the skillet and cook for 2-3 minutes on each side until they turn pink and opaque.
3. Remove the shrimp from the skillet and set aside.
4. In the same skillet, add the chicken broth, lemon juice, and red pepper flakes (if using). Stir well to combine.

5. Cook the sauce for 2-3 minutes, allowing it to reduce slightly.
6. Season the sauce with salt and pepper to taste.
7. Return the cooked shrimp to the skillet and toss them in the sauce to coat evenly.
8. Cook for an additional 1-2 minutes to warm the shrimp.
9. Sprinkle the chopped parsley over the shrimp scampi and stir gently.
10. Remove from heat and serve the Garlic Butter Shrimp Scampi immediately, garnished with lemon wedges.

Nutritional Information (per serving):
Cal: 200 | Fat: 11g | Chol: 230mg | Sod: 120mg | Carbs: 2g | Fiber: 0g | Sugars: 0g | Pro: 23g

5. Citrus Grilled Tilapia Fillets

Preparation time: 10 minutes
Marinating time: 30 minutes
Cooking time: 8 minutes
Servings: 4

Ingredients:

- 4 tilapia fillets
- 2 tablespoons fresh lemon juice
- 2 tablespoons fresh lime juice
- 2 tablespoons fresh orange juice
- 2 tablespoons olive oil
- 2 cloves garlic, minced
- 1 tsp. ground cumin
- 1/2 tsp. paprika
- Salt and pepper to taste
- Fresh cilantro, chopped, for garnish

Instructions:

1. In a small bowl, whisk together the lemon juice, lime juice, orange juice, olive oil, minced garlic, cumin, paprika, salt, and pepper.
2. Place the tilapia fillets in a shallow dish and pour the marinade over them, making sure they are well coated. Marinate in the refrigerator for 30 minutes.
3. Preheat the grill to medium-high heat.
4. Remove the tilapia fillets from the marinade and discard the excess marinade.
5. Place the fillets on the preheated grill and cook for about 4 minutes on each side until the fish is opaque and easily flakes with a fork.
6. Remove the grilled tilapia fillets from the grill and transfer them to a serving plate.
7. Garnish with fresh chopped cilantro.
8. Serve the Citrus Grilled Tilapia Fillets immediately with your choice of side dishes.

Nutritional Information (per serving):
Cal: 150 | Fat: 6g | Chol: 50mg | Sod: 80mg | Carbs: 2g | Fiber: 0g | Sugars: 1g | Pro: 23g

6. Mediterranean Baked Sea Bass

Preparation time: 10 minutes
Cooking time: 20 minutes
Servings: 4

Ingredients:

- 4 sea bass fillets (about 6 ounces each)
- 2 tablespoons extra-virgin olive oil
- 2 cloves garlic, minced
- 1 tsp. dried oregano
- 1 tsp. dried thyme
- 1/2 tsp. paprika
- 1/4 tsp. salt
- 1/4 tsp. pepper
- Juice of 1 lemon
- Fresh parsley, chopped, for garnish
- Lemon wedges, for serving

Instructions:

1. Preheat the oven to 400°F (200°C). Line a baking sheet with parchment paper.
2. Place the sea bass fillets on the prepared baking sheet.
3. In a small bowl, whisk together the olive oil, minced garlic, dried oregano, dried thyme, paprika, salt, and pepper.
4. Drizzle the olive oil mixture over the sea bass fillets, making sure they are evenly coated.
5. Squeeze the lemon juice over the fillets.
6. Bake the sea bass in the preheated oven for about 20 minutes or until the fish is cooked through and flakes easily with a fork.
7. Remove the baked sea bass from the oven and garnish with fresh chopped parsley.
8. Serve the Mediterranean Baked Sea Bass with lemon wedges on the side.

Nutritional Information (per serving):
Cal: 230 | Fat: 12g | Chol: 65mg | Sod: 170mg | Carbs: 2g | Fiber: 0g | Sugars: 0g | Pro: 26g

7. Spicy Cajun Blackened Catfish

Preparation time: 10 minutes
Cooking time: 10 minutes
Servings: 4

Ingredients:

- 4 catfish fillets (about 6 ounces each)
- 2 teaspoons paprika
- 1 tsp. dried thyme
- 1 tsp. dried oregano
- 1 tsp. garlic powder
- 1 tsp. onion powder
- 1/2 tsp. cayenne pepper
- 1/2 tsp. pepper
- 1/2 tsp. salt
- 2 tablespoons olive oil

Instructions:

1. In a small bowl, mix together the paprika, dried thyme, dried oregano, garlic powder, onion powder, cayenne pepper, pepper, and salt.
2. Pat the catfish fillets dry with a paper towel.
3. Rub the spice mixture evenly onto both sides of each catfish fillet.
4. Heat the olive oil in a large skillet over medium-high heat.
5. Once the oil is hot, carefully add the catfish fillets to the skillet.
6. Cook the catfish for about 3-4 minutes on each side or until they are blackened and cooked through.
7. Remove the catfish from the skillet and let them rest for a few minutes before serving.

Nutritional Information (per serving):
Cal: 230 | Fat: 10g | Chol: 70mg | Sod: 300mg | Carbs: 2g | Fiber: 1g | Sugars: 0g | Pro: 31g

8. Herb Crusted Halibut Fillets

Preparation time: 10 minutes
Cooking time: 12 minutes
Servings: 4

Ingredients:

- 4 halibut fillets (about 6 ounces each)
- 2 tablespoons chopped fresh parsley
- 2 tablespoons chopped fresh dill
- 2 tablespoons chopped fresh chives
- 2 cloves garlic, minced
- 1 tbsp. lemon zest
- 1 tbsp. olive oil
- 1/4 tsp. salt
- 1/4 tsp. pepper

Instructions:

1. Preheat the oven to 400°F (200°C).
2. In a small bowl, combine the chopped fresh parsley, dill, chives, minced garlic, and lemon zest.
3. Place the halibut fillets on a baking sheet lined with parchment paper.
4. Brush the top of each fillet with olive oil.
5. Sprinkle the herb mixture evenly over the top of each fillet, pressing gently to adhere.

6. Season the fillets with salt and pepper.
7. Bake the halibut fillets in the preheated oven for about 10-12 minutes or until they are opaque and flake easily with a fork.
8. Remove the halibut from the oven and let them rest for a few minutes before serving.

Nutritional Information (per serving):
Cal: 190 | Fat: 6g | Chol: 75mg | Sod: 190mg | Carbs: 2g | Fiber: 0g | Sugars: 0g | Pro: 32g

9. Sesame Crusted Ahi Tuna

Preparation time: 15 minutes
Cooking time: 2 minutes
Servings: 4

Ingredients:

- 4 ahi tuna steaks (about 6 ounces each)
- 2 tablespoons low-sodium soy sauce
- 2 tablespoons toasted sesame oil
- 2 tablespoons sesame seeds
- 1 tbsp. minced fresh ginger
- 1 tbsp. minced garlic
- 1/4 tsp. pepper
- 1 tbsp. vegetable oil (for cooking)

Instructions:

1. In a shallow dish, combine the low-sodium soy sauce, toasted sesame oil, minced ginger, minced garlic, and pepper.
2. Place the ahi tuna steaks in the marinade and let them marinate for about 10 minutes, flipping them halfway through.
3. Heat the vegetable oil in a skillet or grill pan over high heat.
4. While the oil is heating, spread the sesame seeds on a plate.
5. Remove the ahi tuna steaks from the marinade and press both sides into the sesame seeds, coating them evenly.
6. Carefully place the coated tuna steaks in the hot skillet or grill pan.
7. Cook the tuna steaks for about 1 minute on each side for medium-rare, or adjust the cooking time to your desired level of doneness.
8. Remove the tuna steaks from the heat and let them rest for a few minutes before slicing.

Nutritional Information (per serving):
Cal: 220 | Fat: 10g | Chol: 65mg | Sod: 150mg | Carbs: 2g | Fiber: 1g | Sugars: 0g | Pro: 30g

10. Lemon Pepper Swordfish

Preparation time: 10 minutes
Marinating time: 30 minutes
Cooking time: 10 minutes
Servings: 4

Ingredients:

- 4 swordfish steaks (about 6 ounces each)
- 2 tablespoons fresh lemon juice
- 2 tablespoons olive oil
- 1 tsp. lemon zest
- 1 tsp. freshly ground pepper
- 1/2 tsp. dried thyme
- 1/2 tsp. garlic powder
- 1/4 tsp. salt
- Lemon wedges (for serving)

Instructions:

1. In a shallow dish, whisk together the fresh lemon juice, olive oil, lemon zest, pepper, dried thyme, garlic powder, and salt.
2. Add the swordfish steaks to the marinade and turn them to coat evenly. Let them marinate in the refrigerator for about 30 minutes.
3. Preheat the grill to medium-high heat.
4. Remove the swordfish steaks from the marinade and discard the remaining marinade.
5. Place the swordfish steaks on the preheated grill and cook for about 4-5 minutes per side, or until the fish is opaque and easily flakes with a fork.
6. Remove the swordfish steaks from the grill and let them rest for a few minutes.
7. Serve the grilled swordfish with lemon wedges for squeezing over the top.

Nutritional Information (per serving):
Cal: 260 | Fat: 14g | Chol: 110mg | Sod: 170mg | Carbs: 1g | Fiber: 0g | Sugars: 0g | Pro: 31g

11. Dijon Mustard Baked Trout

Preparation time: 10 minutes
Cooking time: 15 minutes
Servings: 4

Ingredients:

- 4 trout fillets (about 6 ounces each)
- 2 tablespoons Dijon mustard
- 1 tbsp. olive oil
- 1 tbsp. fresh lemon juice
- 1 tsp. dried dill
- 1/2 tsp. garlic powder
- 1/4 tsp. salt
- 1/4 tsp. pepper

- Lemon wedges (for serving)
- Fresh dill sprigs (for garnish)

Instructions:

1. Preheat the oven to 400°F (200°C) and line a baking sheet with parchment paper.
2. In a small bowl, whisk together the Dijon mustard, olive oil, lemon juice, dried dill, garlic powder, salt, and pepper.
3. Place the trout fillets on the prepared baking sheet and brush the mustard mixture over the top of each fillet, coating them evenly.
4. Bake the trout in the preheated oven for about 12-15 minutes, or until the fish is cooked through and flakes easily with a fork.
5. Remove the trout from the oven and let it rest for a few minutes.
6. Serve the Dijon Mustard Baked Trout with lemon wedges and garnish with fresh dill sprigs.

Nutritional Information (per serving):
Cal: 200 | Fat: 8g | Chol: 70mg | Sod: 220mg | Carbs: 1g | Fiber: 0g | Sugars: 0g | Pro: 30g

12. Cilantro Lime Shrimp Skewers

Preparation time: 15 minutes
Marinating time: 30 minutes
Cooking time: 6 minutes
Servings: 4

Ingredients:

- 1 pound large shrimp, peeled and deveined
- 2 tablespoons fresh lime juice
- 2 tablespoons olive oil
- 2 tablespoons chopped fresh cilantro
- 2 cloves garlic, minced
- 1/2 tsp. ground cumin
- 1/4 tsp. salt
- 1/4 tsp. pepper
- 4 skewers (if using wooden skewers, soak them in water for 30 minutes)

Instructions:

1. In a bowl, combine the lime juice, olive oil, chopped cilantro, minced garlic, ground cumin, salt, and pepper. Mix well.
2. Add the shrimp to the bowl and toss to coat them evenly with the marinade. Let the shrimp marinate in the refrigerator for 30 minutes.
3. Preheat the grill to medium-high heat.
4. Thread the marinated shrimp onto the skewers, dividing them equally.
5. Place the shrimp skewers on the preheated grill and cook for about 2-3 minutes per side, or until the shrimp are pink and cooked through.

6. Remove the shrimp skewers from the grill and let them rest for a minute before serving.
7. Serve the Cilantro Lime Shrimp Skewers as a main dish or as a delicious addition to salads or rice.

Nutritional Information (per serving):
Cal: 160 | Fat: 7g | Chol: 190mg | Sod: 190mg | Carbs: 1g | Fiber: 0g | Sugars: 0g | Pro: 23g

13. Italian Herb Roasted Salmon

Preparation time: 10 minutes
Cooking time: 15 minutes
Servings: 4

Ingredients:

- 4 salmon fillets (4-6 ounces each), skin-on
- 1 tbsp. olive oil
- 2 teaspoons dried Italian herbs (such as basil, oregano, and thyme)
- 1/2 tsp. garlic powder
- 1/2 tsp. onion powder
- 1/2 tsp. salt
- 1/4 tsp. pepper
- Lemon wedges, for serving (optional)

Instructions:

1. Preheat the oven to 425°F (220°C). Line a baking sheet with parchment paper or foil for easy cleanup.
2. Place the salmon fillets on the prepared baking sheet, skin-side down.
3. Drizzle the olive oil evenly over the salmon fillets.
4. In a small bowl, combine the dried Italian herbs, garlic powder, onion powder, salt, and pepper. Mix well.
5. Sprinkle the herb mixture evenly over the salmon fillets, pressing lightly to adhere.
6. Place the baking sheet with the salmon in the preheated oven and roast for about 12-15 minutes, or until the salmon is cooked through and flakes easily with a fork.
7. Remove the salmon from the oven and let it rest for a minute before serving.
8. Serve the Italian Herb Roasted Salmon with lemon wedges, if desired, and pair it with your favorite roasted vegetables or a fresh salad.

Nutritional Information (per serving):
Cal: 280 | Fat: 17g | Chol: 80mg | Sod: 310mg | Carbs: 0g | Fiber: 0g | Sugars: 0g | Pro: 30g

14. Greek Style Stuffed Sole

Preparation time: 20 minutes
Cooking time: 25 minutes
Servings: 4

Ingredients:

- 4 sole fillets (about 6 ounces each)
- 1/2 cup cooked quinoa
- 1/4 cup crumbled feta cheese
- 2 tablespoons chopped Kalamata olives
- 2 tablespoons chopped sun-dried tomatoes
- 1 tbsp. chopped fresh parsley
- 1 tbsp. lemon juice
- 1 tbsp. olive oil
- 1/2 tsp. dried oregano
- 1/4 tsp. garlic powder
- 1/4 tsp. pepper
- Lemon wedges, for serving (optional)

Instructions:

1. Preheat the oven to 375°F (190°C). Lightly grease a baking dish with olive oil or coat it with cooking spray.
2. In a medium bowl, combine the cooked quinoa, feta cheese, Kalamata olives, sun-dried tomatoes, parsley, lemon juice, olive oil, dried oregano, garlic powder, and pepper. Mix well.
3. Lay the sole fillets flat on a clean work surface. Spoon the quinoa mixture onto each fillet, dividing it equally among them.
4. Roll up the fillets, enclosing the stuffing. Secure the rolls with toothpicks if needed.
5. Place the stuffed sole fillets in the prepared baking dish and drizzle with a little olive oil.
6. Bake in the preheated oven for about 20-25 minutes, or until the fish is cooked through and flakes easily with a fork.
7. Remove the toothpicks, if used, before serving.
8. Serve the Greek Style Stuffed Sole with lemon wedges, if desired, and accompany it with a side of steamed vegetables or a Greek salad.

Nutritional Information (per serving):
Cal: 220 | Fat: 9g | Chol: 60mg | Sod: 250mg | Carbs: 8g | Fiber: 1g | Sugars: 1g | Pro: 26g

15. Honey Soy Glazed Salmon

Preparation time: 10 minutes
Cooking time: 15 minutes
Servings: 4

Ingredients:

- 4 salmon fillets (about 6 ounces each)
- 3 tablespoons reduced-sodium soy sauce
- 2 tablespoons honey
- 1 tbsp. rice vinegar
- 1 tbsp. fresh lemon juice
- 1 tbsp. minced garlic
- 1 tsp. grated ginger
- 1/2 tsp. sesame oil
- 1/4 tsp. pepper
- Chopped green onions and sesame seeds for garnish (optional)

Instructions:

1. Preheat the oven to 400°F (200°C). Line a baking sheet with parchment paper or foil and lightly grease it with olive oil or coat it with cooking spray.
2. In a small bowl, whisk together the reduced-sodium soy sauce, honey, rice vinegar, lemon juice, minced garlic, grated ginger, sesame oil, and pepper to make the glaze.
3. Place the salmon fillets on the prepared baking sheet. Brush the glaze generously over the salmon, reserving some for later.
4. Bake in the preheated oven for about 12-15 minutes, or until the salmon is cooked through and flakes easily with a fork. Baste the salmon with the reserved glaze halfway through cooking.
5. Remove the salmon from the oven and let it rest for a few minutes.
6. Serve the Honey Soy Glazed Salmon hot, garnished with chopped green onions and sesame seeds, if desired. You can accompany it with steamed vegetables and brown rice or quinoa.

Nutritional Information (per serving):
Cal: 280 | Fat: 13g | Chol: 70mg | Sod: 320mg | Carbs: 12g | Fiber: 0g | Sugars: 11g | Pro: 27g

16. Pesto Grilled Mahi Mahi

Preparation time: 15 minutes
Marinating time: 30 minutes
Cooking time: 10 minutes
Servings: 4

Ingredients:

- 4 mahi-mahi fillets (about 6 ounces each)
- 1/4 cup fresh basil leaves
- 1/4 cup fresh parsley leaves
- 2 tablespoons pine nuts
- 2 cloves garlic
- 2 tablespoons grated Parmesan cheese
- 2 tablespoons extra-virgin olive oil
- 1 tbsp. fresh lemon juice
- 1/4 tsp. pepper
- Lemon wedges, for serving (optional)

Instructions:

1. In a food processor or blender, combine the fresh basil leaves, parsley leaves, pine nuts, garlic, grated Parmesan cheese, extra-virgin olive oil, fresh lemon juice, and pepper. Process until well blended and a smooth pesto sauce forms.
2. Place the mahi-mahi fillets in a shallow dish or zip-top bag. Spoon the pesto sauce over the fish, coating each fillet evenly. Cover the dish or seal the bag and let the fish marinate in the refrigerator for at least 30 minutes.
3. Preheat the grill to medium-high heat.
4. Remove the mahi-mahi fillets from the marinade and discard any excess marinade.
5. Grill the mahi-mahi fillets for about 4-5 minutes per side, or until the fish is cooked through and flakes easily with a fork.
6. Remove the grilled mahi-mahi from the grill and let it rest for a few minutes.
7. Serve the Pesto Grilled Mahi-Mahi hot, accompanied by lemon wedges if desired. You can serve it with a side of roasted vegetables or a fresh salad.

Nutritional Information (per serving):
Cal: 250 | Fat: 13g | Chol: 125mg | Sod: 180mg | Carbs: 2g | Fiber: 1g | Sugars: 0g | Pro: 30g

17. Coconut Curry Shrimp Stir Fry

Preparation time: 15 minutes
Cooking time: 15 minutes
Servings: 4

Ingredients:

- 1 pound shrimp, peeled and deveined
- 1 tbsp. coconut oil
- 1 onion, thinly sliced
- 2 cloves garlic, minced
- 1 red bell pepper, thinly sliced
- 1 yellow bell pepper, thinly sliced
- 1 cup snow peas
- 1 can (13.5 ounces) coconut milk (light)
- 2 tablespoons red curry paste
- 1 tbsp. low-sodium soy sauce
- 1 tbsp. lime juice
- Fresh cilantro, for garnish
- Cooked brown rice, for serving

Instructions:

1. In a large skillet or wok, heat the coconut oil over medium heat.
2. Add the onion and garlic to the skillet and sauté for 2-3 minutes, until the onion becomes translucent.
3. Add the red and yellow bell peppers and snow peas to the skillet. Stir-fry for another 2-3 minutes until the vegetables are crisp-tender.
3. Push the vegetables to one side of the skillet and add the shrimp to the other side. Cook the shrimp for about 2 minutes on each side until they turn pink and opaque.
4. In a small bowl, whisk together the coconut milk, red curry paste, low-sodium soy sauce, and lime juice. Pour the sauce over the shrimp and vegetables in the skillet.
5. Stir everything together to coat the shrimp and vegetables in the coconut curry sauce. Simmer for 2-3 minutes until heated through.
6. Remove the skillet from heat. Garnish with fresh cilantro.
7. Serve the Coconut Curry Shrimp Stir-Fry over cooked brown rice.

Nutritional Information (per serving):
Cal: 240 | Fat: 12g | Chol: 170mg | Sod: 230mg | Carbs: 11g | Fiber: 3g | Sugars: 5g | Pro: 23g

18. Oven Baked Orange Roughy

Preparation time: 10 minutes
Cooking time: 15 minutes
Servings: 4

Ingredients:

- 4 orange roughy fillets
- 2 tablespoons olive oil
- 2 cloves garlic, minced
- 1 tsp. dried thyme
- 1 tsp. dried oregano
- 1/2 tsp. paprika
- 1/2 tsp. salt
- 1/4 tsp. pepper
- Fresh lemon wedges, for serving
- Fresh parsley, for garnish

Instructions:

1. Preheat your oven to 400°F (200°C). Line a baking sheet with parchment paper or lightly grease it.
2. Place the orange roughy fillets on the prepared baking sheet.
3. In a small bowl, combine the olive oil, minced garlic, dried thyme, dried oregano, paprika, salt, and pepper. Stir well to create a paste.
4. Spread the herb and spice mixture evenly over both sides of the orange roughy fillets.
5. Bake the fillets in the preheated oven for about 12-15 minutes, or until the fish is cooked through and flakes easily with a fork.
6. Remove the baking sheet from the oven and let the fish rest for a few minutes.
7. Serve the Oven-Baked Orange Roughy with fresh

lemon wedges and garnish with fresh parsley.

Nutritional Information (per serving):
Cal: 180 | Fat: 9g | Chol: 55mg | Sod: 300mg | Carbs: 1g | Fiber: 0g | Sugars: 0g | Pro: 23g

19. Herbed Baked Haddock Fillets

Preparation time: 10 minutes
Cooking time: 15 minutes
Servings: 4

Ingredients:

- 4 haddock fillets (about 6 ounces each)
- 2 tablespoons olive oil
- 2 cloves garlic, minced
- 1 tbsp. fresh lemon juice
- 1 tsp. dried thyme
- 1 tsp. dried basil
- 1/2 tsp. dried oregano
- 1/2 tsp. paprika
- 1/2 tsp. salt
- 1/4 tsp. pepper
- Fresh parsley, for garnish

Instructions:

1. Preheat your oven to 400°F (200°C). Line a baking sheet with parchment paper or lightly grease it.
2. Place the haddock fillets on the prepared baking sheet.
3. In a small bowl, combine the olive oil, minced garlic, lemon juice, dried thyme, dried basil, dried oregano, paprika, salt, and pepper. Stir well to create a paste.
4. Spread the herb and spice mixture evenly over both sides of the haddock fillets.
5. Bake the fillets in the preheated oven for about 12-15 minutes, or until the fish is cooked through and flakes easily with a fork.
6. Remove the baking sheet from the oven and let the fish rest for a few minutes.
7. Serve the Herbed Baked Haddock Fillets garnished with fresh parsley.

Nutritional Information (per serving):
Cal: 180 | Fat: 7g | Chol: 85mg | Sod: 250mg | Carbs: 2g | Fiber: 0g | Sugars: 0g | Pro: 26g

20. Lemon Garlic Shrimp Skewers

Preparation time: 10 minutes
Marinating time: 30 minutes
Cooking time: 5 minutes
Servings: 4

Ingredients:

- 1 pound large shrimp, peeled and deveined
- 2 tablespoons olive oil
- 2 cloves garlic, minced
- 2 tablespoons fresh lemon juice
- 1 tsp. lemon zest
- 1 tsp. dried oregano
- 1/2 tsp. salt
- 1/4 tsp. pepper
- Wooden or metal skewers
- Lemon wedges, for serving
- Fresh parsley, for garnish

Instructions:

1. In a bowl, combine the olive oil, minced garlic, lemon juice, lemon zest, dried oregano, salt, and pepper. Mix well to make the marinade.
2. Add the peeled and deveined shrimp to the marinade. Toss to coat the shrimp evenly. Cover the bowl and refrigerate for 30 minutes to allow the flavors to meld.
3. If using wooden skewers, soak them in water for about 30 minutes to prevent burning.
4. Preheat your grill or grill pan over medium heat.
5. Thread the marinated shrimp onto the skewers, about 4-5 shrimp per skewer.
6. Grill the shrimp skewers for about 2-3 minutes on each side, or until the shrimp are cooked through and opaque.
7. Remove the skewers from the grill and let them rest for a minute.
8. Serve the Lemon Garlic Shrimp Skewers with lemon wedges and garnish with fresh parsley.

Nutritional Information (per serving):
Cal: 160 | Fat: 8g | Chol: 190mg | Sod: 300mg | Carbs: 2g | Fiber: 0g | Sugars: 0g | Pro: 21g

21. Balsamic Glazed Salmon

Preparation time: 10 minutes
Cooking time: 15 minutes
Servings: 4

Ingredients:

- 4 salmon fillets (about 6 ounces each)
- 1/4 cup balsamic vinegar
- 2 tablespoons honey
- 1 tbsp. Dijon mustard
- 2 cloves garlic, minced
- 1 tbsp. olive oil
- Salt and pepper, to taste
- Fresh parsley, for garnish (optional)

Instructions:

1. Preheat your oven to 400°F (200°C).
2. In a small bowl, whisk together the balsamic vinegar, honey, Dijon mustard, minced garlic, olive oil, salt, and pepper.
3. Place the salmon fillets on a baking sheet lined with parchment paper or foil.
4. Brush the balsamic glaze mixture evenly over the salmon fillets, reserving a little for later.
5. Bake the salmon in the preheated oven for about 12-15 minutes, or until the fish is cooked through and flakes easily with a fork.
6. Remove the salmon from the oven and brush with the remaining balsamic glaze.
7. Garnish with fresh parsley, if desired, and serve hot.

Nutritional Information (per serving):
Cal: 320 | Fat: 16g | Chol: 80mg | Sod: 150mg | Carbs: 12g | Fiber: 0g | Sugars: 10g | Pro: 30g

22. Mediterranean Tuna Salad

Preparation time: 15 minutes
Servings: 4

Ingredients:

- 2 cans (5 ounces each) tuna in water, drained
- 1 cup cherry tomatoes, halved
- 1/2 English cucumber, diced
- 1/4 red onion, thinly sliced
- 1/4 cup Kalamata olives, pitted and halved
- 1/4 cup feta cheese, crumbled
- 2 tablespoons fresh lemon juice
- 2 tablespoons extra virgin olive oil
- 1 tbsp. chopped fresh parsley
- 1 tbsp. chopped fresh dill (optional)
- Salt and pepper, to taste
- Mixed greens, for serving

Instructions:

1. In a large bowl, flake the drained tuna using a fork.
2. Add the cherry tomatoes, cucumber, red onion, Kalamata olives, and feta cheese to the bowl with the tuna.
3. In a small bowl, whisk together the lemon juice, olive oil, chopped parsley, chopped dill (if using), salt, and pepper.
4. Pour the dressing over the tuna mixture and toss gently to combine.
5. Taste and adjust the seasoning as needed.
6. Serve the Mediterranean tuna salad over a bed of mixed greens.

Nutritional Information (per serving):
Cal: 190 | Fat: 10g | Chol: 25mg | Sod: 300mg | Carbs: 7g | Fiber: 2g | Sugars: 3g | Pro: 19g

23. Spicy Blackened Red Snapper

Preparation time: 15 minutes
Cooking time: 10 minutes
Servings: 4

Ingredients:

- 4 red snapper fillets (4-6 ounces each)
- 2 teaspoons paprika
- 1 tsp. dried thyme
- 1 tsp. garlic powder
- 1/2 tsp. onion powder
- 1/2 tsp. cayenne pepper (adjust according to spice preference)
- 1/2 tsp. pepper
- 1/2 tsp. salt
- 2 tablespoons olive oil

Instructions:

1. Preheat the oven to 400°F (200°C).
2. In a small bowl, combine the paprika, dried thyme, garlic powder, onion powder, cayenne pepper, pepper, and salt.
3. Pat the red snapper fillets dry with paper towels.
4. Rub the spice mixture evenly over both sides of the fillets.
5. Heat the olive oil in a large oven-safe skillet over medium-high heat.
6. Once the oil is hot, add the red snapper fillets to the skillet, skin side down.
7. Cook for 2-3 minutes until the skin is crispy and blackened.
8. Carefully flip the fillets using a spatula and transfer the skillet to the preheated oven.
9. Bake for 5-7 minutes, or until the fish is cooked through and flakes easily with a fork.
10. Remove the skillet from the oven and let the fish rest for a few minutes before serving.

Nutritional Information (per serving):
Cal: 200 | Fat: 8g | Chol: 60mg | Sod: 300mg | Carbs: 1g | Fiber: 0g | Sugars: 0g | Pro: 31g

24. Ginger Soy Glazed Sea Bass

Preparation time: 10 minutes
Cooking time: 10 minutes
Servings: 4

Ingredients:

- 4 sea bass fillets (4-6 ounces each)

- 2 tablespoons reduced-sodium soy sauce
- 1 tbsp. fresh ginger, grated
- 1 tbsp. honey
- 1 tbsp. rice vinegar
- 1 tbsp. olive oil
- 1 tbsp. sesame seeds
- 2 green onions, thinly sliced (for garnish)

Instructions:

1. Preheat the oven to 400°F (200°C).
2. In a small bowl, whisk together the soy sauce, grated ginger, honey, rice vinegar, and olive oil to make the glaze.
3. Place the sea bass fillets in a shallow baking dish or on a baking sheet lined with parchment paper.
4. Brush the glaze mixture evenly over both sides of the fillets.
5. Sprinkle the sesame seeds over the top of the fillets.
6. Bake in the preheated oven for 10 minutes or until the fish is cooked through and flakes easily with a fork.
7. Remove from the oven and garnish with sliced green onions.
8. Serve the Ginger Soy Glazed Sea Bass with steamed vegetables or a side salad.

Nutritional Information (per serving):
Cal: 180 | Fat: 6g | Chol: 70mg | Sod: 250mg | Carbs: 6g | Fiber: 1g | Sugars: 4g | Pro: 25g

25. Cajun Seasoned Grilled Trout

Preparation time: 10 minutes
Cooking time: 10 minutes
Servings: 4

Ingredients:

- 4 trout fillets (4-6 ounces each)
- 1 tbsp. paprika
- 1 tsp. garlic powder
- 1 tsp. onion powder
- 1 tsp. dried thyme
- 1 tsp. dried oregano
- 1/2 tsp. cayenne pepper (adjust to taste)
- 1/2 tsp. pepper
- 1/2 tsp. salt
- 1 tbsp. olive oil

Instructions:

1. Preheat the grill to medium-high heat.
2. In a small bowl, combine the paprika, garlic powder, onion powder, dried thyme, dried oregano, cayenne pepper, pepper, and salt to make the Cajun seasoning.
3. Rub the trout fillets with olive oil on both sides.
4. Sprinkle the Cajun seasoning evenly over both sides of the trout fillets, pressing it gently to adhere.
5. Place the seasoned trout fillets on the preheated grill.
6. Grill for about 4-5 minutes per side, or until the fish is cooked through and flakes easily with a fork.
7. Remove from the grill and let rest for a few minutes before serving.
8. Serve the Cajun Seasoned Grilled Trout with a squeeze of fresh lemon juice and your choice of steamed vegetables or a side salad.

Nutritional Information (per serving):
Cal: 180 | Fat: 6g | Chol: 70mg | Sod: 220mg | Carbs: 2g | Fiber: 1g | Sugars: 0g | Pro: 28g

Vegetables and Grains

1. Quinoa Veggie Stir Fry

Preparation time: 15 minutes
Cooking time: 20 minutes
Servings: 4

Ingredients:

- 1 cup quinoa
- 2 cups water
- 2 tablespoons low-sodium soy sauce
- 1 tbsp. sesame oil
- 1 tbsp. olive oil
- 2 cloves garlic, minced
- 1 small onion, diced
- 1 bell pepper, thinly sliced
- 1 carrot, thinly sliced
- 1 zucchini, thinly sliced
- 1 cup broccoli florets
- 1 cup snap peas
- 1 cup mushrooms, sliced
- Salt and pepper to taste
- Optional toppings: sliced green onions, sesame seeds

Instructions:

1. Rinse the quinoa under cold water. In a medium saucepan, bring the water to a boil. Add the rinsed quinoa and reduce the heat to low. Cover and simmer for about 15 minutes or until the quinoa is tender and the water is absorbed. Remove from heat and let it sit, covered, for 5 minutes. Fluff with a fork.
2. In a small bowl, whisk together the low-sodium soy sauce and sesame oil. Set aside.
3. In a large skillet or wok, heat the olive oil over medium heat. Add the minced garlic and diced onion. Sauté for 2-3 minutes until the onion becomes translucent.
4. Add the bell pepper, carrot, zucchini, broccoli florets, snap peas, and mushrooms to the skillet. Stir-fry for about 5-7 minutes until the vegetables are crisp-tender.
5. Pour the soy sauce and sesame oil mixture over the vegetables. Stir to coat evenly. Cook for an additional 2 minutes to heat through.
6. Season with salt and pepper to taste.
7. Serve the quinoa on a plate or bowl and top it with the stir-fried vegetables. Garnish with sliced green onions and sesame seeds if desired.

Nutritional Information (per serving):
Cal: 280 | Fat: 8g | Chol: 0mg | Sod: 200mg | Carbs: 44g | Fiber: 7g | Sugars: 6g | Pro: 10g

2. Mediterranean Couscous Salad

Preparation time: 15 minutes
Cooking time: 10 minutes
Chilling time: 1 hour (optional)
Servings: 4

Ingredients:

- 1 cup whole wheat couscous
- 1 ¼ cups low-sodium vegetable broth
- 1 cup cherry tomatoes, halved
- 1 cucumber, diced
- ½ red onion, finely chopped
- ½ cup Kalamata olives, pitted and halved
- ½ cup crumbled feta cheese
- ¼ cup fresh parsley, chopped
- 2 tablespoons fresh lemon juice
- 2 tablespoons extra-virgin olive oil
- 1 clove garlic, minced
- Salt and pepper to taste

Instructions:

1. In a medium saucepan, bring the vegetable broth to a boil. Remove from heat and stir in the couscous. Cover and let it sit for 5 minutes.
2. Fluff the couscous with a fork to separate the grains. Allow it to cool completely.
3. In a large bowl, combine the cooked and cooled couscous, cherry tomatoes, cucumber, red onion, Kalamata olives, feta cheese, and parsley.
4. In a small bowl, whisk together the fresh lemon juice, extra-virgin olive oil, minced garlic, salt, and pepper.
5. Pour the dressing over the couscous salad and toss gently to combine all the ingredients.
6. Taste and adjust the seasoning if needed.
7. If desired, cover the bowl and refrigerate for at least 1 hour to allow the flavors to meld together.
8. Serve chilled and enjoy!

Nutritional Information (per serving):
Cal: 280 | Fat: 11g | Chol: 15mg | Sod: 250mg | Carbs: 37g | Fiber: 6g | Sugars: 5g | Pro: 9g

3. Roasted Vegetable Quinoa Bowl

Preparation time: 10 minutes
Cooking time: 30 minutes
Servings: 4

Ingredients:

- 1 cup quinoa
- 2 cups low-sodium vegetable broth
- 2 cups mixed vegetables (e.g., bell peppers, zucchini, broccoli), chopped

- 1 red onion, sliced
- 2 tablespoons olive oil
- 1 tsp. dried herbs (such as thyme, oregano, or rosemary)
- Salt and pepper to taste
- ¼ cup chopped fresh parsley (optional)
- 2 tablespoons lemon juice
- 2 tablespoons balsamic vinegar
- ¼ cup crumbled feta cheese (optional)

Instructions:

1. Preheat the oven to 400°F (200°C).
2. Rinse the quinoa thoroughly under cold water.
3. In a medium saucepan, bring the vegetable broth to a boil. Add the rinsed quinoa, reduce the heat, cover, and simmer for about 15 minutes or until the liquid is absorbed. Remove from heat and let it sit, covered, for 5 minutes. Fluff with a fork.
4. Meanwhile, spread the chopped vegetables and sliced red onion on a baking sheet. Drizzle with olive oil, sprinkle with dried herbs, salt, and pepper. Toss to coat evenly.
5. Roast the vegetables in the preheated oven for about 20 minutes or until they are tender and lightly browned, stirring once halfway through.
6. In a small bowl, whisk together the lemon juice and balsamic vinegar.
7. In a large bowl, combine the cooked quinoa, roasted vegetables, and the lemon-balsamic dressing. Toss gently to combine.
8. Taste and adjust the seasoning if needed. Sprinkle with fresh parsley and crumbled feta cheese if desired.
9. Serve warm or at room temperature.

Nutritional Information (per serving):
Cal: 290 | Fat: 10g | Chol: 5mg | Sod: 150mg | Carbs: 42g | Fiber: 7g | Sugars: 6g | Pro: 9g

4. Garlic Parmesan Cauliflower

Preparation time: 10 minutes
Cooking time: 25 minutes
Servings: 4

Ingredients:

- 1 large head of cauliflower, cut into florets
- 2 tablespoons olive oil
- 3 cloves garlic, minced
- 1/4 cup grated Parmesan cheese
- 1/2 tsp. dried oregano
- 1/2 tsp. dried basil
- Salt and pepper to taste
- Fresh parsley, chopped (for garnish)

Instructions:

1. Preheat the oven to 425°F (220°C).
2. Place the cauliflower florets in a large bowl.
3. In a small bowl, combine the olive oil, minced garlic, grated Parmesan cheese, dried oregano, dried basil, salt, and pepper. Mix well.
4. Pour the garlic Parmesan mixture over the cauliflower florets. Toss until the florets are evenly coated.
5. Spread the cauliflower florets in a single layer on a baking sheet.
6. Roast in the preheated oven for 20-25 minutes, or until the cauliflower is tender and golden brown, stirring once halfway through.
7. Remove from the oven and garnish with freshly chopped parsley.
8. Serve hot as a side dish or a healthy snack.

Nutritional Information (per serving):
Cal: 280 | Fat: 11g | Chol: 15mg | Sod: 250mg | Carbs:
Cal: 120 | Fat: 8g | Chol: 4mg | Sod: 180mg | Carbs: 9g | Fiber: 3g | Sugars: 3g | Pro: 5g

5. Spinach n' Feta Stuffed Peppers

Preparation time: 15 minutes
Cooking time: 25 minutes
Servings: 4

Ingredients:

- 4 large bell peppers (any color)
- 1 tbsp. olive oil
- 1 small onion, diced
- 2 cloves garlic, minced
- 4 cups fresh spinach, chopped
- 1 cup cooked quinoa
- 1/2 cup crumbled feta cheese
- 1/4 cup chopped fresh parsley
- Salt and pepper to taste

Instructions:

1. Preheat the oven to 375°F (190°C).
2. Cut off the tops of the bell peppers and remove the seeds and membranes.
3. In a large skillet, heat the olive oil over medium heat. Add the diced onion and minced garlic. Sauté until the onion is translucent and fragrant, about 2-3 minutes.
4. Add the chopped spinach to the skillet and cook until wilted, stirring occasionally.
5. In a mixing bowl, combine the cooked spinach, quinoa, crumbled feta cheese, chopped parsley, salt, and pepper. Mix well.
6. Stuff each bell pepper with the spinach and quinoa mixture, pressing it down gently.
7. Place the stuffed peppers in a baking dish and cover with foil.
8. Bake in the preheated oven for 20 minutes. Then

remove the foil and bake for an additional 5
minutes to lightly brown the tops of the peppers.

9. Remove from the oven and let cool for a few
minutes before serving.

Nutritional Information (per serving):
Cal: 210 | Fat: 8g | Chol: 13mg | Sod: 220mg | Carbs:
28g | Fiber: 6g | Sugars: 9g | Pro: 10g

6. Tomato Basil Quinoa Salad

Preparation time: 15 minutes
Cooking time: 20 minutes
Servings: 4

Ingredients:

- 1 cup quinoa
- 2 cups water
- 2 cups cherry tomatoes, halved
- 1/2 cup fresh basil leaves, thinly sliced
- 2 tablespoons extra-virgin olive oil
- 2 tablespoons balsamic vinegar
- 1 clove garlic, minced
- Salt and pepper to taste

Instructions:

1. Rinse the quinoa thoroughly under cold water.
2. In a medium saucepan, bring the water to a boil.
   Add the rinsed quinoa and reduce the heat to
   low. Cover and simmer for about 15-20 minutes,
   or until the quinoa is cooked and the water is
   absorbed. Remove from heat and let it cool.
3. In a large bowl, combine the cooked quinoa,
   cherry tomatoes, and basil leaves.
4. In a separate small bowl, whisk together the olive
   oil, balsamic vinegar, minced garlic, salt, and
   pepper.
5. Pour the dressing over the quinoa mixture and
   toss gently to coat all the ingredients.
6. Adjust the seasoning according to your taste.
7. Let the salad sit for about 10 minutes to allow the
   flavors to meld together.
8. Serve the Tomato Basil Quinoa Salad at room
   temperature or chilled.

Nutritional Information (per serving):
Cal: 230 | Fat: 9g | Chol: 0mg | Sod: 40mg | Carbs:
32g | Fiber: 5g | Sugars: 3g | Pro: 6g

7. Grilled Vegetable Skewers

Preparation time: 15 minutes
Cooking time: 10 minutes
Servings: 4

Ingredients:

- 2 zucchinis, cut into thick slices
- 1 red bell pepper, cut into chunks
- 1 yellow bell pepper, cut into chunks
- 1 red onion, cut into wedges
- 8 cherry tomatoes
- 8 button mushrooms
- 2 tablespoons extra-virgin olive oil
- 1 tbsp. balsamic vinegar
- 1 tsp. dried oregano
- Salt and pepper to taste

Instructions:

1. Preheat the grill to medium-high heat.
2. In a large bowl, combine the zucchinis, bell peppers, red onion, cherry tomatoes, and mushrooms.
3. In a small bowl, whisk together the olive oil, balsamic vinegar, dried oregano, salt, and pepper
   to make the marinade.
4. Pour the marinade over the vegetables and toss
   gently to coat them evenly.
5. Thread the vegetables onto skewers, alternating
   between different types of vegetables.
6. Place the skewers on the preheated grill and
   cook for about 8-10 minutes, turning occasionally, until the vegetables are tender and lightly
   charred.
7. Remove the skewers from the grill and let them
   cool slightly before serving.

Nutritional Information (per serving):
Cal: 110 | Fat: 7g | Chol: 0mg | Sod: 15mg | Carbs:
11g | Fiber: 3g | Sugars: 6g | Pro: 3g

8. Caprese Quinoa Stuffed Tomatoes

Preparation time: 20 minutes
Cooking time: 20 minutes
Servings: 4

Ingredients:

- 4 large tomatoes
- 1 cup cooked quinoa
- 1/2 cup fresh mozzarella balls, halved
- 1/2 cup cherry tomatoes, halved
- 1/4 cup fresh basil leaves, chopped
- 1 tbsp. extra-virgin olive oil
- 1 tbsp. balsamic vinegar
- Salt and pepper to taste

Instructions:

1. Preheat the oven to 375°F (190°C).
2. Cut off the tops of the tomatoes and scoop out
   the seeds and pulp using a spoon. Set the tomato shells aside.
3. In a large bowl, combine the cooked quinoa,

mozzarella balls, cherry tomatoes, and fresh basil.

4. Drizzle the olive oil and balsamic vinegar over the quinoa mixture. Season with salt and pepper to taste. Toss gently to combine.
5. Spoon the quinoa mixture into the hollowed-out tomato shells, pressing gently to fill them.
6. Place the stuffed tomatoes on a baking sheet and bake in the preheated oven for 15-20 minutes, or until the tomatoes are tender and the filling is heated through.
7. Remove from the oven and let them cool slightly before serving.

Nutritional Information (per serving):
Cal: 180 | Fat: 9g | Chol: 10mg | Sod: 50mg | Carbs: 18g | Fiber: 3g | Sugars: 4g | Pro: 8g

9. Butternut Squash Risotto Delight

Preparation time: 10 minutes
Cooking time: 40 minutes
Servings: 4

Ingredients:

- 1 butternut squash, peeled, seeded, and cut into small cubes
- 1 tbsp. olive oil
- 1 small onion, finely chopped
- 2 cloves garlic, minced
- 1 cup Arborio rice
- 4 cups low-sodium vegetable broth
- 1/2 cup grated Parmesan cheese
- 1 tbsp. fresh sage leaves, chopped
- Salt and pepper to taste

Instructions:

1. In a large skillet, heat the olive oil over medium heat. Add the chopped onion and minced garlic. Sauté until the onion is translucent and fragrant.
2. Add the Arborio rice to the skillet and stir to coat the rice with the oil. Cook for 1-2 minutes, stirring constantly.
3. Add the butternut squash cubes to the skillet and stir to combine with the rice.
4. Begin adding the vegetable broth to the skillet, one ladleful at a time, stirring constantly. Allow the rice to absorb the broth before adding more. Continue this process until the rice is cooked al dente and the butternut squash is tender.
5. Stir in the grated Parmesan cheese and fresh sage. Season with salt and pepper to taste.
6. Remove from heat and let it sit for a few minutes before serving.

Nutritional Information (per serving):
Cal: 280 | Fat: 6g | Chol: 7mg | Sod: 150mg | Carbs: 51g | Fiber: 4g | Sugars: 4g | Pro: 8g

10. Veggie Fried Rice

Preparation time: 15 minutes
Cooking time: 15 minutes
Servings: 4

Ingredients:

- 2 cups cooked brown rice
- 1 tbsp. vegetable oil
- 1 small onion, finely chopped
- 2 cloves garlic, minced
- 1 cup mixed vegetables (such as carrots, peas, bell peppers), chopped
- 2 green onions, chopped
- 2 tablespoons low-sodium soy sauce
- 1 tbsp. sesame oil
- 2 eggs, beaten (optional)
- Salt and pepper to taste

Instructions:

1. Heat the vegetable oil in a large skillet or wok over medium heat. Add the chopped onion and minced garlic. Sauté until the onion is translucent and fragrant.
2. Add the mixed vegetables to the skillet and stir-fry for 3-4 minutes until they are tender-crisp.
3. Push the vegetables to one side of the skillet and pour the beaten eggs into the empty space. Scramble the eggs until cooked through.
4. Add the cooked brown rice to the skillet and stir to combine with the vegetables and eggs. Cook for an additional 2-3 minutes, stirring occasionally.
5. Stir in the low-sodium soy sauce and sesame oil. Season with salt and pepper to taste.
6. Remove from heat and garnish with chopped green onions before serving.

Nutritional Information (per serving):
Cal: 230 | Fat: 8g | Chol: 62mg | Sod: 170mg | Carbs: 32g | Fiber: 4g | Sugars: 3g | Pro: 7g

11. Roasted Sprouts Medley

Preparation time: 10 minutes
Cooking time: 25 minutes
Servings: 4

Ingredients:

- 1 pound Brussels sprouts, trimmed and halved
- 1 medium sweet potato, peeled and diced
- 1 red bell pepper, seeded and diced

- 1 tbsp. olive oil
- 1 tsp. dried thyme
- 1/2 tsp. garlic powder
- 1/2 tsp. paprika
- Salt and pepper to taste

Instructions:

1. Preheat the oven to 425°F (220°C).
2. In a large mixing bowl, combine the Brussels sprouts, sweet potato, and red bell pepper.
3. Drizzle olive oil over the vegetables and toss to coat evenly.
4. Sprinkle dried thyme, garlic powder, paprika, salt, and pepper over the vegetables. Toss again to distribute the seasonings evenly.
5. Spread the vegetables in a single layer on a baking sheet.
6. Roast in the preheated oven for 20-25 minutes, or until the Brussels sprouts are tender and lightly browned, stirring once halfway through.
7. Remove from the oven and let cool for a few minutes before serving.

Nutritional Information (per serving):
Cal: 120 | Fat: 4g | Chol: 0mg | Sod: 35mg | Carbs: 19g | Fiber: 6g | Sugars: 4g | Pro: 4g

12. Greek Orzo Salad

Preparation time: 15 minutes
Cooking time: 10 minutes
Chilling time: 1 hour (optional)
Servings: 4

Ingredients:

- 1 cup orzo pasta
- 1 cup cherry tomatoes, halved
- 1 English cucumber, diced
- 1/2 red onion, thinly sliced
- 1/2 cup Kalamata olives, pitted and halved
- 1/2 cup crumbled feta cheese
- 1/4 cup chopped fresh parsley
- 2 tablespoons extra virgin olive oil
- 2 tablespoons lemon juice
- 1 tsp. dried oregano
- Salt and pepper to taste

Instructions:

1. Cook the orzo pasta according to the package instructions. Drain and rinse with cold water to cool it down.
2. In a large mixing bowl, combine the cooked orzo pasta, cherry tomatoes, cucumber, red onion, Kalamata olives, feta cheese, and parsley.
3. In a small bowl, whisk together the olive oil, lemon juice, dried oregano, salt, and pepper.

4. Pour the dressing over the orzo salad and toss well to combine.
5. Taste and adjust the seasonings if needed.
6. If time allows, refrigerate the salad for at least 1 hour to allow the flavors to meld together.
7. Serve chilled and enjoy!

Nutritional Information (per serving):
Cal: 280 | Fat: 11g | Chol: 15mg | Sod: 240mg | Carbs: 37g | Fiber: 3g | Sugars: 4g | Pro: 9g

13. Spicy Cauliflower Rice Stir Fry

Preparation time: 15 minutes
Cooking time: 15 minutes
Servings: 4

Ingredients:

- 1 medium head cauliflower
- 1 tbsp. olive oil
- 1 small onion, diced
- 2 cloves garlic, minced
- 1 red bell pepper, diced
- 1 cup broccoli florets
- 1 medium carrot, sliced
- 1 cup snap peas, trimmed
- 2 tablespoons low-sodium soy sauce
- 1 tsp. sriracha sauce (adjust to taste)
- 1/2 tsp. ground ginger
- 1/4 tsp. red pepper flakes (adjust to taste)
- Salt and pepper to taste
- 2 green onions, chopped (for garnish)

Instructions:

1. Cut the cauliflower into florets and pulse them in a food processor until they resemble rice. Set aside.
2. Heat the olive oil in a large skillet or wok over medium heat.
3. Add the diced onion and minced garlic to the skillet and sauté for 2-3 minutes until the onion becomes translucent.
4. Add the red bell pepper, broccoli florets, carrot slices, and snap peas to the skillet. Stir-fry for 4-5 minutes until the vegetables are tender-crisp.
5. Push the vegetables to one side of the skillet and add the cauliflower rice to the empty space. Stir-fry for 2-3 minutes until the cauliflower is cooked but still slightly crisp.
6. In a small bowl, whisk together the low-sodium soy sauce, sriracha sauce, ground ginger, red pepper flakes, salt, and pepper.
7. Pour the sauce over the cauliflower rice and vegetables. Stir well to coat everything evenly.
8. Cook for an additional 1-2 minutes, allowing the flavors to meld together.
9. Remove from heat and garnish with chopped

green onions.
10. Serve the spicy cauliflower rice stir-fry as a main dish or as a side dish with your favorite Pro.

Nutritional Information (per serving):
Cal: 95 | Fat: 4g | Chol: 0mg | Sod: 195mg | Carbs: 13g | Fiber: 5g | Sugars: 5g | Pro: 4g

14. Ratatouille with Brown Rice

Preparation time: 15 minutes
Cooking time: 40 minutes
Servings: 4

Ingredients:

- 1 cup brown rice
- 2 tablespoons olive oil
- 1 medium onion, diced
- 2 cloves garlic, minced
- 1 medium eggplant, diced
- 1 medium zucchini, diced
- 1 red bell pepper, diced
- 1 yellow bell pepper, diced
- 1 can (14 oz) diced tomatoes
- 2 tablespoons tomato paste
- 1 tsp. dried basil
- 1 tsp. dried oregano
- 1/2 tsp. dried thyme
- Salt and pepper to taste
- Fresh basil leaves, for garnish (optional)

Instructions:

1. Cook the brown rice according to the package instructions. Set aside.
2. Heat the olive oil in a large pot or skillet over medium heat.
3. Add the diced onion and minced garlic to the pot and sauté for 2-3 minutes until the onion becomes translucent.
4. Add the diced eggplant, zucchini, and bell peppers to the pot. Sauté for 5-7 minutes until the vegetables start to soften.
5. Stir in the diced tomatoes (including the juice) and tomato paste. Mix well.
6. Add the dried basil, dried oregano, dried thyme, salt, and pepper to the pot. Stir to combine all the ingredients.
7. Reduce the heat to low, cover the pot, and simmer for 25-30 minutes, stirring occasionally, until the vegetables are tender and the flavors have melded together.
8. Taste and adjust the seasoning if needed.
9. Serve the ratatouille over the cooked brown rice.
10. Garnish with fresh basil leaves if desired.

Nutritional Information (per serving):
Cal: 235 | Fat: 8g | Chol: 0mg | Sod: 180mg | Carbs: 38g | Fiber: 8g | Sugars: 10g | Pro: 5g

15. Zucchini Noodle Primavera

Preparation time: 15 minutes
Cooking time: 15 minutes
Servings: 4

Ingredients:

- 4 medium zucchini
- 2 tablespoons olive oil
- 1 small onion, thinly sliced
- 2 cloves garlic, minced
- 1 red bell pepper, thinly sliced
- 1 yellow bell pepper, thinly sliced
- 1 cup cherry tomatoes, halved
- 1 cup broccoli florets
- 1 cup sliced mushrooms
- 1/2 cup low-sodium vegetable broth
- 1 tsp. dried basil
- 1 tsp. dried oregano
- Salt and pepper to taste
- Grated Parmesan cheese for serving (optional)

Instructions:

1. Use a spiralizer or a julienne peeler to create zucchini noodles (zoodles). Set aside.
2. Heat the olive oil in a large skillet over medium heat.
3. Add the sliced onion and minced garlic to the skillet and sauté for 2-3 minutes until the onion becomes translucent.
4. Add the sliced bell peppers, cherry tomatoes, broccoli florets, and mushrooms to the skillet. Sauté for 5-7 minutes until the vegetables start to soften.
5. Pour in the vegetable broth and season with dried basil, dried oregano, salt, and pepper. Stir well.
6. Add the zucchini noodles to the skillet and cook for an additional 3-4 minutes until the noodles are just tender.
7. Taste and adjust the seasoning if needed.
8. Remove from heat and serve the Zucchini Noodle Primavera immediately.
9. Optional: Sprinkle with grated Parmesan cheese for added flavor.

Nutritional Information (per serving):
Cal: 110 | Fat: 7g | Chol: 0mg | Sod: 75mg | Carbs: 11g | Fiber: 4g | Sugars: 6g | Pro: 3g

16. Tomato and Mozzarella Farro

Preparation time: 10 minutes
Cooking time: 20 minutes
Servings: 4

Ingredients:

- 1 cup farro
- 2 cups low-sodium vegetable broth
- 2 cups cherry tomatoes, halved
- 1 cup fresh mozzarella cheese, diced
- 1/4 cup fresh basil leaves, chopped
- 2 tablespoons extra-virgin olive oil
- 2 tablespoons balsamic vinegar
- Salt and pepper to taste

Instructions:

1. Rinse the farro under cold water. In a saucepan, bring the vegetable broth to a boil. Add the rinsed farro and reduce the heat to low. Cover and simmer for about 20 minutes or until the farro is tender. Drain any excess liquid and let it cool.
2. In a large bowl, combine the cooked and cooled farro, cherry tomatoes, fresh mozzarella, and chopped basil leaves.
3. In a small bowl, whisk together the olive oil and balsamic vinegar. Season with salt and pepper to taste.
4. Drizzle the dressing over the farro salad and toss gently to coat all the ingredients.
5. Serve the Tomato and Mozzarella Farro Salad immediately or refrigerate for later use.

Nutritional Information (per serving):
Cal: 320 | Fat: 15g | Chol: 20mg | Sod: 100mg | Carbs: 36g | Fiber: 6g | Sugars: 4g | Pro: 13g

17. Cauliflower Rice Sushi Rolls

Preparation time: 30 minutes
Servings: 4

Ingredients:

- 2 cups cauliflower rice
- 4 nori seaweed sheets
- 1 small avocado, sliced
- 1 small cucumber, julienned
- 1 small carrot, julienned
- 4 cooked shrimp, peeled and sliced in half lengthwise
- Low-sodium soy sauce or tamari, for serving
- Pickled ginger, for serving
- Wasabi, for serving

Instructions:

1. Place the cauliflower rice in a microwave-safe bowl and microwave for 2-3 minutes until tender. Let it cool slightly.
2. Lay a bamboo sushi mat on a clean surface and place a nori sheet on top.
3. Wet your hands with water to prevent sticking, and spread about 1/2 cup of cauliflower rice evenly over the nori, leaving a 1-inch border at the top.
4. Arrange a few slices of avocado, cucumber, carrot, and shrimp in a line across the center of the rice.
5. Using the bamboo mat, roll the nori tightly, applying gentle pressure. Wet the border with water to seal the roll.
6. Repeat the process with the remaining ingredients to make the remaining rolls.
7. Using a sharp knife, slice each roll into bite-sized pieces.
8. Serve the Cauliflower Rice Sushi Rolls with low-sodium soy sauce or tamari, pickled ginger, and wasabi.

Nutritional Information (per serving):
Cal: 120 | Fat: 4g | Chol: 40mg | Sod: 160mg | Carbs: 12g | Fiber: 6g | Sugars: 4g | Pro: 10g

18. Spinach and Mushroom Quiche

Preparation time: 15 minutes
Cooking time: 45 minutes
Servings: 6

Ingredients:

- 1 pre-made pie crust (whole wheat or gluten-free, if preferred)
- 1 tbsp. olive oil
- 1 small onion, diced
- 2 cups fresh spinach, chopped
- 1 cup sliced mushrooms
- 4 eggs
- 1 cup low-fat milk
- 1/2 cup shredded low-fat cheese (such as Swiss or cheddar)
- Salt and pepper to taste

Instructions:

1. Preheat the oven to 375°F (190°C).
2. In a skillet, heat the olive oil over medium heat. Add the diced onion and cook until translucent.
3. Add the chopped spinach and sliced mushrooms to the skillet. Sauté until the spinach wilts and the mushrooms are tender. Remove from heat and let cool slightly.
4. In a mixing bowl, whisk together the eggs and

low-fat milk. Season with salt and pepper.

5. Place the pre-made pie crust in a pie dish and crimp the edges.
6. Spread the cooked spinach and mushroom mixture evenly over the pie crust.
7. Pour the egg and milk mixture over the vegetables.
8. Sprinkle the shredded low-fat cheese on top.
9. Place the quiche in the preheated oven and bake for 40-45 minutes, or until the center is set and the top is golden brown.
10. Remove from the oven and let cool for a few minutes before slicing.
11. Serve warm or at room temperature.

Nutritional Information (per serving):
Cal: 220 | Fat: 12g | Chol: 140mg | Sod: 240mg | Carbs: 17g | Fiber: 2g | Sugars: 3g | Pro: 11g

19. Quinoa Stuffed Bell Peppers

Preparation time: 20 minutes
Cooking time: 30 minutes
Servings: 4

Ingredients:

- 4 large bell peppers (any color)
- 1 cup quinoa, rinsed
- 1 tbsp. olive oil
- 1 small onion, diced
- 2 cloves garlic, minced
- 1 cup diced tomatoes (fresh or canned)
- 1 cup black beans, rinsed and drained
- 1 cup corn kernels (fresh or frozen)
- 1 tbsp. chili powder
- 1 tsp. cumin
- 1/2 tsp. paprika
- Salt and pepper to taste
- Optional toppings: chopped fresh cilantro, sliced avocado, salsa

Instructions:

1. Preheat the oven to 375°F (190°C).
2. Cut off the tops of the bell peppers and remove the seeds and membranes. Set aside.
3. In a saucepan, bring 2 cups of water to a boil. Add the rinsed quinoa, reduce heat to low, cover, and simmer for about 15 minutes or until the quinoa is cooked and the water is absorbed.
4. In a large skillet, heat the olive oil over medium heat. Add the diced onion and minced garlic. Sauté until the onion becomes translucent.
5. Add the diced tomatoes, black beans, and corn kernels to the skillet. Stir in the chili powder, cumin, paprika, salt, and pepper. Cook for about 5 minutes to heat through and combine the flavors.

6. Remove the skillet from heat and add the cooked quinoa. Mix well to combine.
7. Stuff each bell pepper with the quinoa and vegetable mixture. Place the stuffed peppers in a baking dish.
8. Cover the baking dish with foil and bake for 20-25 minutes, or until the peppers are tender.
9. Remove from the oven and let cool for a few minutes.
10. Serve the Mexican Quinoa Stuffed Bell Peppers with optional toppings such as chopped fresh cilantro, sliced avocado, and salsa.

Nutritional Information (per serving):
Cal: 280 | Fat: 6g | Chol: 0mg | Sod: 230mg | Carbs: 50g | Fiber: 11g | Sugars: 9g | Pro: 10g

20. Sweet Potato and Bean Tacos

Preparation time: 25 minutes
Cooking time: 25 minutes
Servings: 4

Ingredients:

- 2 medium sweet potatoes, peeled and diced
- 1 tbsp. olive oil
- 1 tsp. chili powder
- 1/2 tsp. cumin
- 1/2 tsp. paprika
- Salt and pepper to taste
- 1 can (15 ounces) black beans, rinsed and drained
- 1/2 cup diced red onion
- 1/4 cup chopped fresh cilantro
- 8 small corn tortillas
- Optional toppings: avocado slices, salsa, lime wedges

Instructions:

1. Preheat the oven to 425°F (220°C).
2. Place the diced sweet potatoes on a baking sheet. Drizzle with olive oil and sprinkle with chili powder, cumin, paprika, salt, and pepper. Toss to coat the sweet potatoes evenly with the spices.
3. Roast the sweet potatoes in the preheated oven for about 20-25 minutes or until they are tender and slightly caramelized.
4. In a bowl, combine the black beans, diced red onion, and chopped cilantro. Mix well.
5. Warm the corn tortillas in a dry skillet over medium heat or in the oven for a few minutes until pliable.
6. To assemble the tacos, place a spoonful of the black bean mixture on each tortilla. Top with roasted sweet potatoes and any desired optional toppings.

7. Serve the Sweet Potato and Black Bean Tacos warm.

Nutritional Information (per serving):
Cal: 270 | Fat: 5g | Chol: 0mg | Sod: 160mg | Carbs: 51g | Fiber: 12g | Sugars: 6g | Pro: 9g

21. Veggie Packed Brown Rice Pilaf

Preparation time: 10 minutes
Cooking time: 35 minutes
Servings: 4

Ingredients:

- 1 cup brown rice
- 2 cups low-sodium vegetable broth
- 1 tbsp. olive oil
- 1 small onion, diced
- 2 cloves garlic, minced
- 1 carrot, diced
- 1 zucchini, diced
- 1 red bell pepper, diced
- 1 cup frozen peas
- 1 tsp. dried thyme
- Salt and pepper to taste
- Optional garnish: chopped fresh parsley

Instructions:

1. Rinse the brown rice under cold water and drain.
2. In a medium saucepan, bring the vegetable broth to a boil. Add the brown rice, reduce the heat to low, cover, and simmer for about 30-35 minutes or until the rice is tender and the liquid is absorbed.
3. In a large skillet, heat the olive oil over medium heat. Add the diced onion and minced garlic and sauté for 2-3 minutes until fragrant and slightly translucent.
4. Add the diced carrot, zucchini, and red bell pepper to the skillet. Cook for about 5 minutes or until the vegetables are tender-crisp.
5. Stir in the frozen peas, dried thyme, salt, and pepper. Cook for an additional 2 minutes until the peas are heated through.
6. Once the brown rice is cooked, add it to the skillet with the cooked vegetables. Stir well to combine and heat through for a few minutes.
7. Taste and adjust the seasoning if needed.
8. Garnish with chopped fresh parsley if desired.
9. Serve the Veggie-Packed Brown Rice Pilaf as a side dish or a light main course.

Nutritional Information (per serving):
Cal: 230 | Fat: 5g | Chol: 0mg | Sod: 100mg | Carbs: 42g | Fiber: 7g | Sugars: 7g | Pro: 6g

22. Eggplant Parmesan Casserole

Preparation time: 20 minutes
Cooking time: 40 minutes
Servings: 4

Ingredients:

- 1 large eggplant
- 2 cups marinara sauce (look for low-sodium options)
- 1 cup shredded mozzarella cheese
- 1/4 cup grated Parmesan cheese
- 1/4 cup whole wheat bread crumbs
- 1 tbsp. olive oil
- 2 cloves garlic, minced
- 1/2 tsp. dried basil
- 1/2 tsp. dried oregano
- Salt and pepper to taste
- Optional garnish: fresh basil leaves

Instructions:

1. Preheat the oven to 375°F (190°C). Lightly grease a baking dish.
2. Slice the eggplant into 1/4-inch thick rounds. Sprinkle salt over the eggplant slices and let them sit for about 15 minutes. This helps remove excess moisture.
3. Rinse the eggplant slices under cold water and pat them dry with paper towels.
4. In a small bowl, combine the bread crumbs, grated Parmesan cheese, dried basil, dried oregano, minced garlic, salt, and pepper.
5. Dip each eggplant slice into the olive oil, ensuring both sides are coated, then press into the breadcrumb mixture to coat evenly. Place the coated slices on the prepared baking dish.
6. Bake the eggplant slices in the preheated oven for about 20 minutes or until they are golden and tender.
7. Remove the baking dish from the oven and spread marinara sauce over the eggplant slices. Sprinkle shredded mozzarella cheese on top.
8. Return the dish to the oven and bake for another 15-20 minutes or until the cheese is melted and bubbly.
9. Garnish with fresh basil leaves if desired.
10. Serve the Eggplant Parmesan Casserole hot as a main course or a side dish.

Nutritional Information (per serving):
Cal: 240 | Fat: 11g | Chol: 25mg | Sod: 400mg | Carbs: 25g | Fiber: 7g | Sugars: 12g | Pro: 12g

23. Quinoa Stuffed Mushrooms

Preparation time: 15 minutes
Cooking time: 25 minutes
Servings: 4

Ingredients:

- 4 large portobello mushrooms
- 1 cup cooked quinoa
- 1/2 cup diced red bell pepper
- 1/2 cup diced zucchini
- 1/4 cup diced red onion
- 2 cloves garlic, minced
- 2 tablespoons chopped fresh parsley
- 2 tablespoons grated Parmesan cheese
- 1 tbsp. olive oil
- 1/2 tsp. dried oregano
- Salt and pepper to taste

Instructions:

1. Preheat the oven to 375°F (190°C). Line a baking sheet with parchment paper.
2. Remove the stems from the portobello mushrooms and gently scrape out the gills using a spoon. Place the mushrooms on the prepared baking sheet.
3. In a large bowl, combine the cooked quinoa, diced red bell pepper, diced zucchini, diced red onion, minced garlic, chopped parsley, grated Parmesan cheese, olive oil, dried oregano, salt, and pepper. Mix well to combine.
4. Divide the quinoa mixture evenly among the portobello mushrooms, pressing it down gently.
5. Bake the stuffed mushrooms in the preheated oven for about 20-25 minutes or until the mushrooms are tender and the filling is heated through.
6. Remove from the oven and let the mushrooms cool for a few minutes before serving.
7. Serve the Quinoa Stuffed Portobello Mushrooms as a main course or a side dish.

Nutritional Information (per serving):
Cal: 170 | Fat: 5g | Chol: 2mg | Sod: 80mg | Carbs: 25g | Fiber: 4g | Sugars: 4g | Pro: 7g

24. Mediterranean Chickpea Salad

Preparation time: 15 minutes
Servings: 4

Ingredients:

- 2 cups cooked chickpeas (canned or soaked and cooked)
- 1 cup cherry tomatoes, halved
- 1 cucumber, diced
- 1/2 red onion, thinly sliced
- 1/4 cup Kalamata olives, pitted and halved
- 1/4 cup crumbled feta cheese
- 2 tablespoons chopped fresh parsley
- 2 tablespoons extra-virgin olive oil
- 2 tablespoons lemon juice
- 1 clove garlic, minced
- 1/2 tsp. dried oregano
- Salt and pepper to taste

Instructions:

1. In a large bowl, combine the cooked chickpeas, cherry tomatoes, cucumber, red onion, Kalamata olives, crumbled feta cheese, and chopped parsley.
2. In a separate small bowl, whisk together the extra-virgin olive oil, lemon juice, minced garlic, dried oregano, salt, and pepper to make the dressing.
3. Pour the dressing over the chickpea mixture and toss gently to combine, ensuring all the ingredients are well-coated.
4. Let the salad sit at room temperature for about 10 minutes to allow the flavors to meld together.
5. Serve the Mediterranean Chickpea Salad as a light and refreshing main course or as a side dish with grilled chicken or fish.

Nutritional Information (per serving):
Cal: 260 | Fat: 12g | Chol: 8mg | Sod: 290mg | Carbs: 30g | Fiber: 8g | Sugars: 6g | Pro: 10g

25. Spaghetti Squash n' Marinara

Preparation time: 50 minutes
Servings: 4

Ingredients:

- 1 medium spaghetti squash
- 2 cups marinara sauce (look for a low-sodium option or make your own)
- 1 tbsp. olive oil
- 2 cloves garlic, minced
- 1/2 tsp. dried oregano
- 1/2 tsp. dried basil
- Salt and pepper to taste
- Fresh basil leaves for garnish (optional)

Instructions:

1. Preheat the oven to 400°F (200°C).
2. Cut the spaghetti squash in half lengthwise and scoop out the seeds and fibrous strands from the center.
3. Brush the cut sides of the spaghetti squash with olive oil and season with salt and pepper.
4. Place the spaghetti squash halves, cut side down, on a baking sheet and roast in the preheated oven for about 40 minutes, or until the flesh

is tender and easily separated into spaghetti-like strands with a fork.

5. While the spaghetti squash is roasting, heat the olive oil in a saucepan over medium heat. Add the minced garlic, dried oregano, and dried basil. Sauté for 1-2 minutes until the garlic is fragrant.

6. Pour in the marinara sauce and stir well. Reduce the heat to low and simmer for 10-15 minutes to allow the flavors to meld together.

7. Once the spaghetti squash is cooked, use a fork to scrape the flesh into spaghetti-like strands. Divide the strands among four plates.

8. Top each serving of spaghetti squash with the marinara sauce. Garnish with fresh basil leaves, if desired.

9. Serve the Spaghetti Squash with Marinara as a nutritious and low-carb alternative to traditional pasta dishes.

Nutritional Information (per serving):
Cal: 150 | Fat: 4g | Chol: 0mg | Sod: 200mg | Carbs: 29g | Fiber: 6g | Sugars: 12g | Pro: 3g

Salads

1. Greek Salad Delight

Preparation time: 15 minutes
Servings: 4

Ingredients:

*   4 cups mixed salad greens
*   1 cup cherry tomatoes, halved
*   1 cucumber, sliced
*   1/2 red onion, thinly sliced
*   1/2 cup Kalamata olives, pitted
*   1/2 cup crumbled feta cheese
*   2 tablespoons extra-virgin olive oil
*   1 tbsp. lemon juice
*   1 tsp. dried oregano
*   Salt and pepper to taste

Instructions:

1. In a large salad bowl, combine the mixed salad greens, cherry tomatoes, cucumber slices, red onion slices, Kalamata olives, and crumbled feta cheese.
2. In a small bowl, whisk together the extra-virgin olive oil, lemon juice, dried oregano, salt, and pepper to make the dressing.
3. Drizzle the dressing over the salad and toss gently to coat all the ingredients.
4. Taste and adjust the seasoning if needed.
5. Serve the Greek Salad Delight immediately as a refreshing and nutritious side dish or light meal.

Nutritional Information (per serving):
Cal: 150 | Fat: 12g | Chol: 10mg | Sod: 250mg | Carbs: 8g | Fiber: 2g | Sugars: 3g | Pro: 4g

2. Quinoa Avocado Salad Bowl

Preparation time: 20 minutes
Servings: 4

Ingredients:

*   1 cup cooked quinoa
*   1 large avocado, diced
*   1 cup cherry tomatoes, halved
*   1/2 cup cucumber, diced
*   1/4 cup red onion, finely chopped
*   1/4 cup fresh cilantro, chopped
*   Juice of 1 lime
*   2 tablespoons extra-virgin olive oil
*   Salt and pepper to taste

Instructions:

1. In a large mixing bowl, combine the cooked quinoa, diced avocado, cherry tomatoes, cucumber, red onion, and chopped cilantro.
2. In a small bowl, whisk together the lime juice, extra-virgin olive oil, salt, and pepper to create the dressing.
3. Drizzle the dressing over the quinoa salad and toss gently to combine all the ingredients.
4. Taste and adjust the seasoning if needed.
5. Divide the Quinoa Avocado Salad mixture into four serving bowls.
6. Serve immediately and enjoy the nutritious and flavorful Quinoa Avocado Salad Bowl.

Nutritional Information (per serving):
Cal: 260 | Fat: 15g | Chol: 0mg | Sod: 10mg | Carbs: 28g | Fiber: 7g | Sugars: 3g | Pro: 6g

3. Caprese Salad Skewers

Preparation time: 15 minutes
Servings: 4

Ingredients:

*   2 cups cherry tomatoes
*   8 small fresh mozzarella balls
*   16 fresh basil leaves
*   1 tbsp. balsamic glaze
*   Freshly ground pepper to taste

Instructions:

1. Rinse the cherry tomatoes and pat them dry. Set aside.
2. Drain the mozzarella balls if they are stored in liquid, and pat them dry with a paper towel.
3. Take a skewer and thread on a cherry tomato, followed by a fresh mozzarella ball, and then a basil leaf. Repeat the process for each skewer.
4. Arrange the Caprese salad skewers on a serving platter.
5. Drizzle the balsamic glaze over the skewers.
6. Sprinkle freshly ground pepper over the skewers to taste.
7. Serve immediately as an appetizer or side dish.

Nutritional Information (per serving):
Cal: 110 | Fat: 8g | Chol: 20mg | Sod: 80mg | Carbs: 3g | Fiber: 0g | Sugars: 2g | Pro: 6g

4. Asian Cucumber Salad

Preparation time: 10 minutes
Servings: 4

Ingredients:

*   2 large cucumbers
*   1/4 cup rice vinegar
*   1 tbsp. low-sodium soy sauce
*   1 tbsp. sesame oil

- 1 tsp. honey or maple syrup
- 1 tbsp. toasted sesame seeds
- 2 green onions, thinly sliced
- Optional toppings: chopped cilantro, sliced red chili, or crushed peanuts

Instructions:

1. Rinse the cucumbers and pat them dry. Cut off the ends and thinly slice the cucumbers into rounds or semi-circles.
2. In a small bowl, whisk together the rice vinegar, low-sodium soy sauce, sesame oil, and honey (or maple syrup) until well combined.
3. In a large mixing bowl, add the cucumber slices, dressing mixture, toasted sesame seeds, and sliced green onions. Toss gently to coat the cucumbers evenly with the dressing.
4. Let the salad marinate for about 5 minutes to allow the flavors to meld together.
5. Serve the Asian Cucumber Salad in individual bowls or as a side dish, garnished with optional toppings like chopped cilantro, sliced red chili, or crushed peanuts.

Nutritional Information (per serving):
Cal: 60 | Fat: 4g | Chol: 0mg | Sod: 110mg | Carbs: 5g | Fiber: 1g | Sugars: 3g | Pro: 1g

5. Spinach Berry Salad Medley

Preparation time: 10 minutes
Servings: 4

Ingredients:

- 6 cups baby spinach leaves
- 1 cup mixed berries (such as strawberries, blueberries, and raspberries)
- 1/4 cup sliced almonds
- 2 tablespoons crumbled feta cheese (optional)
- Dressing:
- 2 tablespoons extra-virgin olive oil
- 1 tbsp. balsamic vinegar
- 1 tsp. honey or maple syrup
- Dash of salt and pepper

Instructions:

1. In a large salad bowl, add the baby spinach leaves, mixed berries, sliced almonds, and crumbled feta cheese (if using).
2. In a small bowl, whisk together the extra-virgin olive oil, balsamic vinegar, honey (or maple syrup), salt, and pepper to make the dressing.
3. Drizzle the dressing over the salad ingredients in the bowl.
4. Toss gently to coat the salad ingredients evenly with the dressing.

5. Serve the Spinach Berry Salad Medley immediately as a refreshing and nutritious side dish or light meal.

Nutritional Information (per serving):
Cal: 120 | Fat: 9g | Chol: 0mg | Sod: 80mg | Carbs: 9g | Fiber: 3g | Sugars: 5g | Pro: 3g

6. Mediterranean Chickpea Salad

Preparation time: 15 minutes
Servings: 4

Ingredients:

- 2 cans (15 ounces each) chickpeas (garbanzo beans), rinsed and drained
- 1 cucumber, diced
- 1 cup cherry tomatoes, halved
- 1/2 red onion, finely chopped
- 1/2 cup Kalamata olives, pitted and halved
- 1/4 cup crumbled feta cheese (optional)
- 2 tablespoons chopped fresh parsley
- Dressing:
- 2 tablespoons extra-virgin olive oil
- 1 tbsp. lemon juice
- 1 clove garlic, minced
- 1 tsp. dried oregano
- Dash of salt and pepper

Instructions:

1. In a large bowl, combine the chickpeas, cucumber, cherry tomatoes, red onion, Kalamata olives, crumbled feta cheese (if using), and chopped fresh parsley.
2. In a small bowl, whisk together the extra-virgin olive oil, lemon juice, minced garlic, dried oregano, salt, and pepper to make the dressing.
3. Drizzle the dressing over the chickpea salad mixture in the bowl.
4. Toss gently to coat all the ingredients evenly with the dressing.
5. Allow the Mediterranean Chickpea Salad to marinate in the refrigerator for at least 30 minutes to allow the flavors to meld together.
6. Serve the salad chilled as a refreshing and satisfying main dish or side dish.

Nutritional Information (per serving):
Cal: 260 | Fat: 11g | Chol: 5mg | Sod: 310mg | Carbs: 33g | Fiber: 9g | Sugars: 6g | Pro: 10g

7. Tomato Basil Mozzarella Salad

Preparation time: 10 minutes
Servings: 4

Ingredients:

- 4 ripe tomatoes, sliced
- 8 ounces fresh mozzarella cheese, sliced
- 1/2 cup fresh basil leaves
- 2 tablespoons extra-virgin olive oil
- 1 tbsp. balsamic vinegar
- Dash of salt and pepper

Instructions:

1. Arrange the tomato slices, mozzarella slices, and fresh basil leaves on a serving platter or individual plates.
2. Drizzle the extra-virgin olive oil and balsamic vinegar over the tomato, mozzarella, and basil.
3. Sprinkle a dash of salt and pepper to taste.
4. Serve immediately as a refreshing and flavorful salad.

Nutritional Information (per serving):

Cal: 220 | Fat: 17g | Chol: 35mg | Sod: 150mg | Carbs: 5g | Fiber: 1g | Sugars: 3g | Pro: 13g

8. Shrimp and Avocado Salad

Preparation time: 15 minutes
Servings: 4

Ingredients:

- 1 pound cooked shrimp, peeled and deveined
- 2 ripe avocados, diced
- 1 cup cherry tomatoes, halved
- 1/4 cup red onion, finely chopped
- 1/4 cup fresh cilantro, chopped
- 2 tablespoons lime juice
- 1 tbsp. extra-virgin olive oil
- Dash of salt and pepper

Instructions:

1. In a large bowl, combine the cooked shrimp, diced avocados, cherry tomatoes, red onion, and chopped cilantro.
2. In a small bowl, whisk together the lime juice, extra-virgin olive oil, salt, and pepper.
3. Pour the dressing over the shrimp and avocado mixture, and gently toss to coat.
4. Serve immediately as a refreshing and Pro-rich salad.

Nutritional Information (per serving):

Cal: 250 | Fat: 14g | Chol: 180mg | Sod: 160mg | Carbs: 9g | Fiber: 6g | Sugars: 2g | Pro: 23g

9. Zesty Kale Caesar Salad

Preparation time: 15 minutes
Servings: 4

Ingredients:

- 1 bunch kale, stems removed and leaves torn into bite-sized pieces
- 1/4 cup grated Parmesan cheese
- 1/4 cup whole wheat croutons
- 2 tablespoons lemon juice
- 2 tablespoons extra-virgin olive oil
- 1 tbsp. Dijon mustard
- 1 clove garlic, minced
- Dash of salt and pepper

Instructions:

1. In a large bowl, combine the kale, Parmesan cheese, and croutons.
2. In a small bowl, whisk together the lemon juice, extra-virgin olive oil, Dijon mustard, minced garlic, salt, and pepper.
3. Pour the dressing over the kale mixture, and toss to coat the leaves evenly.
4. Let the salad sit for 5 minutes to allow the flavors to meld.
5. Serve the zesty kale Caesar salad as a healthy and flavorful side dish or add grilled chicken or shrimp for a complete meal.

Nutritional Information (per serving):

Cal: 140 | Fat: 10g | Chol: 5mg | Sod: 170mg | Carbs: 9g | Fiber: 2g | Sugars: 1g | Pro: 5g

10. Zesty Kale Caesar Salad

Preparation time: 45 minutes
Servings: 4

Ingredients:

- 4 medium beets, trimmed and peeled
- 4 cups mixed salad greens
- 1/4 cup crumbled feta cheese
- 1/4 cup chopped walnuts
- 2 tablespoons balsamic vinegar
- 1 tbsp. extra-virgin olive oil
- 1 tsp. Dijon mustard
- Dash of salt and pepper

Instructions:

1. Preheat the oven to 400°F (200°C).
2. Wrap each beet tightly in aluminum foil and place them on a baking sheet.

3. Roast the beets in the oven for about 40 minutes, or until they are tender when pierced with a fork.
4. Remove the beets from the oven and let them cool. Once cooled, cut the beets into bite-sized cubes.
5. In a large bowl, combine the mixed salad greens, roasted beet cubes, crumbled feta cheese, and chopped walnuts.
6. In a small bowl, whisk together the balsamic vinegar, extra-virgin olive oil, Dijon mustard, salt, and pepper to make the dressing.
7. Pour the dressing over the salad and toss gently to coat all the ingredients.
8. Serve the roasted beet salad delight as a refreshing and nutritious side dish or add grilled chicken or tofu for a complete meal.

Nutritional Information (per serving):
Cal: 150 | Fat: 9g | Chol: 5mg | Sod: 140mg | Carbs: 13g | Fiber: 3g | Sugars: 9g | Pro: 5g

11. Black Bean Corn Salad

Preparation time: 15 minutes
Servings: 4

Ingredients:

- 1 can (15 ounces) black beans, rinsed and drained
- 1 cup frozen corn, thawed
- 1 small red bell pepper, diced
- 1/4 cup diced red onion
- 1/4 cup chopped fresh cilantro
- 2 tablespoons fresh lime juice
- 1 tbsp. extra-virgin olive oil
- 1 tsp. ground cumin
- 1/2 tsp. chili powder
- Dash of salt and pepper

Instructions:

1. In a large bowl, combine the black beans, corn, red bell pepper, red onion, and cilantro.
2. In a small bowl, whisk together the lime juice, olive oil, cumin, chili powder, salt, and pepper to make the dressing.
3. Pour the dressing over the black bean and corn mixture. Toss gently to coat all the ingredients.
4. Let the salad sit for a few minutes to allow the flavors to blend.
5. Serve the black bean corn salad as a refreshing side dish or as a topping for tacos, grilled chicken, or fish.

Nutritional Information (per serving):
Cal: 180 | Fat: 4g | Chol: 0mg | Sod: 100mg | Carbs: 30g | Fiber: 8g | Sugars: 3g | Pro: 9g

12. Greek Yogurt Chicken Salad

Preparation time: 20 minutes
Servings: 4

Ingredients:

- 2 cups cooked chicken breast, diced
- 1/2 cup plain Greek yogurt
- 1/4 cup diced cucumber
- 1/4 cup diced red bell pepper
- 1/4 cup diced red onion
- 2 tablespoons chopped fresh dill
- 1 tbsp. fresh lemon juice
- 1 tbsp. extra-virgin olive oil
- 1/2 tsp. garlic powder
- Dash of salt and pepper

Instructions:

1. In a large bowl, combine the diced chicken breast, Greek yogurt, cucumber, red bell pepper, red onion, dill, lemon juice, olive oil, garlic powder, salt, and pepper.
2. Stir well until all the ingredients are evenly coated with the yogurt mixture.
3. Taste and adjust the seasoning as desired.
4. Cover the bowl and refrigerate the chicken salad for at least 30 minutes to allow the flavors to meld together.
5. Serve the Greek Yogurt Chicken Salad as a filling for sandwiches, wraps, or on a bed of lettuce as a salad.

Nutritional Information (per serving):
Cal: 180 | Fat: 6g | Chol: 60mg | Sod: 80mg | Carbs: 5g | Fiber: 1g | Sugars: 2g | Pro: 25g

13. Watermelon Feta Salad

Preparation time: 15 minutes
Servings: 4

Ingredients:

- 4 cups cubed watermelon
- 1 cup crumbled feta cheese
- 1/4 cup fresh mint leaves, chopped
- 2 tablespoons extra-virgin olive oil
- 1 tbsp. balsamic vinegar
- Dash of pepper

Instructions:

1. In a large bowl, combine the cubed watermelon, crumbled feta cheese, and chopped mint leaves.
2. In a small bowl, whisk together the olive oil and balsamic vinegar.

3. Drizzle the dressing over the watermelon mixture.
4. Gently toss the salad to ensure all the ingredients are coated with the dressing.
5. Season with a dash of pepper.
6. Serve the Watermelon Feta Salad immediately as a refreshing side dish or as a light summer appetizer.

Nutritional Information (per serving):
Cal: 140 | Fat: 10g | Chol: 20mg | Sod: 200mg | Carbs: 10g | Fiber: 1g | Sugars: 8g | Pro: 5g

14. Tangy Coleslaw with Apple

Preparation time: 15 minutes
Servings: 4

Ingredients:

- 4 cups shredded cabbage (green or purple)
- 1 medium apple, thinly sliced
- 1/4 cup plain Greek yogurt
- 2 tablespoons apple cider vinegar
- 1 tbsp. honey
- 1 tbsp. Dijon mustard
- 1/4 tsp. pepper
- 2 tablespoons chopped fresh parsley (optional)

Instructions:

1. In a large bowl, combine the shredded cabbage and apple slices.
2. In a separate bowl, whisk together the Greek yogurt, apple cider vinegar, honey, Dijon mustard, and pepper until well combined.
3. Pour the dressing over the cabbage and apple mixture.
4. Toss everything together until the cabbage and apple are coated evenly with the dressing.
5. If desired, sprinkle with chopped fresh parsley for added flavor and garnish.
6. Let the coleslaw sit in the refrigerator for at least 10 minutes to allow the flavors to meld together.
7. Serve the Tangy Coleslaw with Apple as a side dish or a light and refreshing salad.

Nutritional Information (per serving):
Cal: 80 | Fat: 0g | Chol: 0mg | Sod: 60mg | Carbs: 20g | Fiber: 3g | Sugars: 15g | Pro: 2g

15. Cucumber Tomato Salad

Preparation time: 10 minutes
Servings: 4

Ingredients:

- 2 large cucumbers, diced
- 2 cups cherry tomatoes, halved
- 1/4 cup red onion, thinly sliced
- 2 tablespoons fresh lemon juice
- 1 tbsp. extra-virgin olive oil
- 1 tbsp. chopped fresh dill
- 1/4 tsp. pepper
- Optional: crumbled feta cheese for garnish (adjust amount based on preference)

Instructions:

1. In a large bowl, combine the diced cucumbers, cherry tomatoes, and sliced red onion.
2. In a small bowl, whisk together the lemon juice, olive oil, chopped fresh dill, and pepper.
3. Pour the dressing over the cucumber and tomato mixture.
4. Gently toss everything together until well coated.
5. Let the salad sit in the refrigerator for a few minutes to allow the flavors to meld together.
6. If desired, sprinkle crumbled feta cheese on top for added flavor and garnish.
7. Serve the Cucumber Tomato Salad as a refreshing side dish or light salad.

Nutritional Information (per serving):
Cal: 60 | Fat: 4g | Chol: 0mg | Sod: 10mg | Carbs: 6g | Fiber: 1g | Sugars: 3g | Pro: 1g

16. Quinoa Black Bean Salad

Preparation time: 20 minutes
Servings: 4

Ingredients:

- 1 cup cooked quinoa
- 1 can (15 oz) black beans, rinsed and drained
- 1 cup cherry tomatoes, halved
- 1/2 cup diced red bell pepper
- 1/2 cup diced yellow bell pepper
- 1/4 cup chopped red onion
- 1/4 cup chopped fresh cilantro
- 2 tablespoons fresh lime juice
- 1 tbsp. extra-virgin olive oil
- 1 clove garlic, minced
- 1/2 tsp. ground cumin
- 1/4 tsp. salt (optional)
- 1/4 tsp. pepper

Instructions:

1. In a large bowl, combine the cooked quinoa, black beans, cherry tomatoes, red bell pepper, yellow bell pepper, red onion, and cilantro.
2. In a small bowl, whisk together the lime juice, olive oil, minced garlic, ground cumin, salt (optional), and pepper.
3. Pour the dressing over the quinoa and black bean mixture.
4. Gently toss everything together until well combi

ned and evenly coated.

5. Adjust the seasoning according to taste preference.
6. Let the salad sit in the refrigerator for at least 15 minutes to allow the flavors to meld together.
7. Serve the Quinoa Black Bean Salad as a light and nutritious meal or side dish.

Nutritional Information (per serving):
Cal: 235 | Fat: 6g | Chol: 0mg | Sod: 240mg | Carbs: 37g | Fiber: 9g | Sugars: 3g | Pro: 10g

17. Broccoli Cranberry Salad

Preparation time: 15 minutes
Servings: 4

Ingredients:

- 4 cups broccoli florets
- 1/2 cup dried cranberries
- 1/4 cup chopped red onion
- 1/4 cup chopped walnuts
- 2 tablespoons apple cider vinegar
- 2 tablespoons plain Greek yogurt
- 1 tbsp. honey
- 1/2 tbsp. Dijon mustard
- 1/4 tsp. salt (optional)
- 1/4 tsp. pepper

Instructions:

1. In a large mixing bowl, combine the broccoli florets, dried cranberries, chopped red onion, and chopped walnuts.
2. In a separate small bowl, whisk together the apple cider vinegar, Greek yogurt, honey, Dijon mustard, salt (optional), and pepper until well combined.
3. Pour the dressing over the broccoli mixture and toss gently until all the ingredients are evenly coated.
4. Adjust the seasoning according to taste preference.
5. Let the salad sit in the refrigerator for at least 10 minutes to allow the flavors to meld together.
6. Serve the Broccoli Cranberry Salad as a refreshing and nutritious side dish.

Nutritional Information (per serving):
Cal: 125 | Fat: 5g | Chol: 0mg | Sod: 100mg | Carbs: 20g | Fiber: 4g | Sugars: 12g | Pro: 4g

18. Tuna Salad Lettuce Wraps

Preparation time: 10 minutes
Servings: 4

Ingredients:

- 2 cans (5 oz each) tuna, packed in water, drained
- 1/4 cup diced celery
- 1/4 cup diced red onion
- 1/4 cup diced cucumber
- 2 tablespoons plain Greek yogurt
- 2 tablespoons lemon juice
- 1 tbsp. Dijon mustard
- 1/2 tsp. dried dill
- Salt and pepper to taste
- 8 large lettuce leaves (such as romaine or butter lettuce)

Instructions:

1. In a medium-sized bowl, combine the drained tuna, diced celery, diced red onion, and diced cucumber.
2. In a separate small bowl, whisk together the Greek yogurt, lemon juice, Dijon mustard, dried dill, salt, and pepper until well combined.
3. Pour the dressing over the tuna mixture and stir gently until all the ingredients are evenly coated.
4. Taste and adjust the seasoning as desired.
5. Take a lettuce leaf and spoon a portion of the tuna salad onto the center.
6. Roll the lettuce leaf around the filling, tucking in the sides as you go, to create a wrap.
7. Repeat with the remaining lettuce leaves and tuna salad.
8. Serve the Tuna Salad Lettuce Wraps as a light and flavorful meal or snack.

Nutritional Information (per serving):
Cal: 120 | Fat: 2g | Chol: 25mg | Sod: 150mg | Carbs: 5g | Fiber: 1g | Sugars: 2g | Pro: 20g

19. Roasted Vegetable Salad Bowl

Preparation time: 30 minutes
Servings: 4

Ingredients:

- 2 cups mixed salad greens
- 1 medium zucchini, sliced
- 1 medium yellow squash, sliced
- 1 red bell pepper, sliced
- 1 yellow bell pepper, sliced
- 1 small red onion, sliced
- 1 tbsp. olive oil
- 1 tsp. dried Italian seasoning
- Salt and pepper to taste
- 1/4 cup crumbled feta cheese
- 2 tablespoons chopped fresh parsley
- 2 tablespoons balsamic vinegar
- 1 tbsp. extra-virgin olive oil

Instructions:

1. Preheat your oven to 425°F (220°C).
2. In a large mixing bowl, combine the sliced zucchini, yellow squash, red bell pepper, yellow bell pepper, and red onion.
3. Drizzle the vegetables with olive oil, sprinkle with dried Italian seasoning, salt, and pepper. Toss well to coat evenly.
4. Spread the vegetables in a single layer on a baking sheet.
5. Roast the vegetables in the preheated oven for about 20 minutes or until they are tender and slightly browned, stirring once halfway through.
6. While the vegetables are roasting, prepare the salad base. Divide the mixed salad greens among four serving bowls.
7. Once the vegetables are done, remove them from the oven and let them cool for a few minutes.
8. Place the roasted vegetables on top of the salad greens in each bowl.
9. Sprinkle the crumbled feta cheese and chopped parsley over the vegetables.
10. In a small bowl, whisk together the balsamic vinegar and extra-virgin olive oil. Drizzle the dressing over the salad bowls.
11. Toss gently to combine all the ingredients.
12. Serve the Roasted Vegetable Salad Bowls as a nutritious and satisfying meal.

Nutritional Information (per serving):
Cal: 150 | Fat: 10g | Chol: 5mg | Sod: 120mg | Carbs: 14g | Fiber: 4g | Sugars: 8g | Pro: 5g

20. Mango Spinach Salad

Preparation time: 15 minutes
Servings: 4

Ingredients:

- 6 cups fresh spinach leaves
- 1 ripe mango, peeled and diced
- 1/2 cup sliced red onion
- 1/4 cup chopped walnuts
- 2 tablespoons dried cranberries
- 2 tablespoons crumbled feta cheese
- 2 tablespoons balsamic vinegar
- 1 tbsp. extra-virgin olive oil
- 1 tsp. honey (optional)
- Salt and pepper to taste

Instructions:

1. In a large salad bowl, combine the fresh spinach leaves, diced mango, sliced red onion, chopped walnuts, dried cranberries, and crumbled feta cheese.
2. In a small bowl, whisk together the balsamic

vinegar, extra-virgin olive oil, honey (if desired), salt, and pepper to make the dressing.
3. Drizzle the dressing over the salad ingredients.
4. Toss gently to coat all the ingredients with the dressing.
5. Serve the Mango Spinach Salad immediately as a refreshing and nutritious meal.

Nutritional Information (per serving):
Cal: 150 | Fat: 8g | Chol: 2mg | Sod: 80mg | Carbs: 18g | Fiber: 3g | Sugars: 13g | Pro: 3g

21. Orzo Pasta Salad Delight

Preparation time: 20 minutes
Servings: 4

Ingredients:

- 1 cup uncooked orzo pasta
- 1 cup cherry tomatoes, halved
- 1 cup cucumber, diced
- 1/2 cup red onion, thinly sliced
- 1/4 cup Kalamata olives, pitted and halved
- 2 tablespoons fresh parsley, chopped
- 2 tablespoons extra-virgin olive oil
- 1 tbsp. lemon juice
- 1 clove garlic, minced
- Salt and pepper to taste

Instructions:

1. Cook the orzo pasta according to the package instructions. Drain and set aside to cool.
2. In a large bowl, combine the cooked orzo pasta, cherry tomatoes, cucumber, red onion, Kalamata olives, and fresh parsley.
3. In a small bowl, whisk together the extra-virgin olive oil, lemon juice, minced garlic, salt, and pepper to make the dressing.
4. Drizzle the dressing over the pasta salad and toss gently to coat all the ingredients.
5. Taste and adjust the seasoning if needed.
6. Serve the Orzo Pasta Salad Delight chilled or at room temperature as a refreshing and flavorful side dish or light meal.

Nutritional Information (per serving):
Cal: 230 | Fat: 8g | Chol: 0mg | Sod: 120mg | Carbs: 35g | Fiber: 3g | Sugars: 4g | Pro: 5g

22. Berry Walnut Salad Medley

Preparation time: 15 minutes
Servings: 4

Ingredients:

- 6 cups mixed salad greens

- 1 cup fresh strawberries, sliced
- 1 cup fresh blueberries
- 1/2 cup walnuts, chopped
- 1/4 cup crumbled feta cheese
- 2 tablespoons balsamic vinegar
- 1 tbsp. extra-virgin olive oil
- 1 tsp. honey
- Salt and pepper to taste

Instructions:

1. In a large salad bowl, combine the mixed salad greens, sliced strawberries, fresh blueberries, chopped walnuts, and crumbled feta cheese.
2. In a small bowl, whisk together the balsamic vinegar, extra-virgin olive oil, honey, salt, and pepper to make the dressing.
3. Drizzle the dressing over the salad ingredients and toss gently to coat everything evenly.
4. Taste and adjust the seasoning if needed.
5. Serve the Berry Walnut Salad Medley immediately as a refreshing and nutritious salad.

Nutritional Information (per serving):
Cal: 150 | Fat: 11g | Chol: 5mg | Sod: 140mg | Carbs: 12g | Fiber: 4g | Sugars: 6g | Pro: 4g

23. Mediterranean Pasta Salad

Preparation time: 20 minutes
Servings: 4

Ingredients:

- 8 ounces whole wheat or gluten-free pasta (penne, rotini, or your choice)
- 1 cup cherry tomatoes, halved
- 1 cup cucumber, diced
- 1/2 cup Kalamata olives, pitted and halved
- 1/2 cup crumbled feta cheese
- 1/4 cup red onion, thinly sliced
- 2 tablespoons extra-virgin olive oil
- 2 tablespoons lemon juice
- 1 tbsp. red wine vinegar
- 1 clove garlic, minced
- 1 tsp. dried oregano
- Salt and pepper to taste
- Fresh parsley, chopped (for garnish)

Instructions:

1. Cook the pasta according to the package instructions until al dente. Drain and rinse with cold water to cool.
2. In a large bowl, combine the cooked pasta, cherry tomatoes, cucumber, Kalamata olives, crumbled feta cheese, and red onion.
3. In a small bowl, whisk together the extra-virgin olive oil, lemon juice, red wine vinegar, minced

1. garlic, dried oregano, salt, and pepper to make the dressing.
2. Drizzle the dressing over the pasta salad and toss gently to coat everything evenly.
3. Taste and adjust the seasoning if needed.
4. Let the Mediterranean Pasta Salad sit in the refrigerator for about 30 minutes to allow the flavors to meld together.
5. Before serving, garnish with fresh chopped parsley.

Nutritional Information (per serving):
Cal: 250 | Fat: 10g | Chol: 10mg | Sod: 240mg | Carbs: 33g | Fiber: 5g | Sugars: 2g | Pro: 9g

24. Cauliflower "Potato" Salad

Preparation time: 15 minutes
Servings: 4

Ingredients:

- 1 medium head of cauliflower, cut into small florets
- 2 hard-boiled eggs, chopped
- 2 celery stalks, diced
- 2 green onions, thinly sliced
- 1/4 cup plain Greek yogurt
- 1 tbsp. Dijon mustard
- 1 tbsp. apple cider vinegar
- 1 tbsp. fresh dill, chopped
- 1 tbsp. fresh parsley, chopped
- Salt and pepper to taste

Instructions:

1. Bring a pot of salted water to a boil. Add the cauliflower florets and cook for about 5 minutes until tender but still slightly crisp. Drain and rinse with cold water to cool.
2. In a large bowl, combine the cooked cauliflower, chopped hard-boiled eggs, diced celery, and sliced green onions.
3. In a small bowl, whisk together the plain Greek yogurt, Dijon mustard, apple cider vinegar, chopped dill, chopped parsley, salt, and pepper to make the dressing.
4. Pour the dressing over the cauliflower mixture and gently toss to coat everything evenly.
5. Taste and adjust the seasoning if needed.
6. Cover the Cauliflower "Potato" Salad and refrigerate for at least 1 hour to allow the flavors to blend together.
7. Serve chilled and enjoy!

Nutritional Information (per serving):
Cal: 250 | Fat: 10g | Chol: 10mg | Sod: 240mg | Carbs: 33g | Fiber: 5g | Sugars: 2g | Pro: 9g

25. Cilantro Lime Quinoa Salad

Preparation time: 20 minutes
Servings: 4

Ingredients:

- 1 cup quinoa
- 2 cups water
- 1 can black beans, rinsed and drained
- 1 cup corn kernels (fresh or frozen)
- 1 red bell pepper, diced
- 1/4 cup red onion, finely chopped
- 1/4 cup fresh cilantro, chopped
- 2 tablespoons lime juice
- 2 tablespoons extra-virgin olive oil
- 1 tsp. ground cumin
- Salt and pepper to taste

Instructions:

1. Rinse the quinoa under cold water and drain.
2. In a medium saucepan, bring 2 cups of water to a boil. Add the quinoa and reduce the heat to low. Cover and simmer for about 15 minutes or until the water is absorbed and the quinoa is cooked.
3. Remove the quinoa from heat and let it cool for a few minutes.
4. In a large bowl, combine the cooked quinoa, black beans, corn kernels, diced red bell pepper, finely chopped red onion, and fresh cilantro.
5. In a small bowl, whisk together the lime juice, extra-virgin olive oil, ground cumin, salt, and pepper to make the dressing.
6. Pour the dressing over the quinoa mixture and toss gently to coat everything evenly.
7. Taste and adjust the seasoning if needed.
8. Cover the Cilantro Lime Quinoa Salad and refrigerate for at least 1 hour to allow the flavors to meld together.
9. Serve chilled and enjoy!

Nutritional Information (per serving):
Cal: 295 | Fat: 9g | Chol: 0mg | Sod: 80mg | Carbs: 46g | Fiber: 10g | Sugars: 4g | Pro: 11g

1. Whole Wheat Flatbread Pizza

Preparation time: 20 minutes
Cooking time: 15 minutes
Servings: 4

Ingredients:

- 4 whole wheat flatbreads
- 1 cup low-sodium tomato sauce
- 1 cup shredded part-skim mozzarella cheese
- 1 cup sliced bell peppers
- 1 cup sliced mushrooms
- 1 cup cherry tomatoes, halved
- 1/4 cup sliced black olives
- 1 tbsp. dried oregano
- Fresh basil leaves for garnish (optional)

Instructions:

1. Preheat the oven to 400°F (200°C).
2. Place the whole wheat flatbreads on a baking sheet lined with parchment paper.
3. Spread a thin layer of tomato sauce evenly on each flatbread.
4. Sprinkle the shredded mozzarella cheese over the tomato sauce.
5. Arrange the sliced bell peppers, mushrooms, cherry tomatoes, and black olives on top of the cheese.
6. Sprinkle dried oregano over the vegetables.
7. Place the baking sheet with the flatbreads in the preheated oven and bake for about 15 minutes, or until the cheese is melted and bubbly, and the crust is crispy.
8. Remove from the oven and let the pizzas cool for a few minutes.
9. Garnish with fresh basil leaves, if desired.
10. Cut each flatbread pizza into slices and serve.

Nutritional Information (per serving):
Cal: 250 | Fat: 6g | Chol: 10mg | Sod: 200mg | Carbs: 37g | Fiber: 7g | Sugars: 5g | Pro: 12g

2. Veggie Pita Pocket Delight

Preparation time: 15 minutes
Servings: 4

Ingredients:

- 4 whole wheat pita pockets
- 1 cup diced cucumber
- 1 cup diced tomatoes
- 1 cup shredded lettuce
- 1/2 cup sliced red onions
- 1/2 cup sliced bell peppers
- 1/4 cup chopped fresh parsley
- 1/4 cup crumbled feta cheese
- 2 tablespoons lemon juice
- 2 tablespoons extra-virgin olive oil
- Salt and pepper to taste

Instructions:

1. In a large bowl, combine the diced cucumber, tomatoes, shredded lettuce, red onions, bell peppers, and fresh parsley.
2. In a small bowl, whisk together the lemon juice, olive oil, salt, and pepper to make the dressing.
3. Pour the dressing over the vegetable mixture and toss well to combine.
4. Warm the whole wheat pita pockets in a toaster or microwave for a few seconds to make them more pliable.
5. Cut each pita pocket in half to create pockets.
6. Stuff each pita pocket with the vegetable mixture, dividing it equally among the pockets.
7. Sprinkle crumbled feta cheese on top of each pocket.
8. Serve immediately and enjoy!

Nutritional Information (per serving):
Cal: 200 | Fat: 7g | Chol: 5mg | Sod: 160mg | Carbs: 30g | Fiber: 5g | Sugars: 4g | Pro: 7g

3. Quinoa Pizza Bites

Preparation time: 25 minutes
Servings: 4

Ingredients:

- 1 cup cooked quinoa
- 1/2 cup shredded mozzarella cheese
- 1/4 cup grated Parmesan cheese
- 1/4 cup tomato sauce
- 1/4 cup diced bell peppers
- 1/4 cup diced tomatoes
- 1/4 cup sliced black olives
- 1/4 tsp. dried oregano
- 1/4 tsp. garlic powder
- Salt and pepper to taste
- Optional toppings: sliced mushrooms, diced onions, chopped basil

Instructions:

1. Preheat the oven to 375°F (190°C) and line a baking sheet with parchment paper.
2. In a mixing bowl, combine the cooked quinoa, shredded mozzarella cheese, grated Parmesan cheese, tomato sauce, diced bell peppers, diced tomatoes, sliced black olives, dried oregano, garlic powder, salt, and pepper. Mix well to combine.
3. Scoop about 1 tbsp. of the quinoa mixture and shape it into a small bite-sized ball. Place it on the prepared baking sheet. Repeat with the

remaining mixture, spacing the bites apart.

4. Bake in the preheated oven for 15-18 minutes, or until the edges are golden and crispy.
5. Remove from the oven and let the quinoa pizza bites cool for a few minutes before serving.
6. Serve the quinoa pizza bites as a delicious and nutritious appetizer or snack. You can also serve them with additional tomato sauce for dipping and your favorite optional toppings, if desired.

Nutritional Information (per serving):
Cal: 180 | Fat: 8g | Chol: 20mg | Sod: 230mg | Carbs: 16g | Fiber: 3g | Sugars: 2g | Pro: 11g

4. Zucchini Breaded Chicken Strips

Preparation time: 30 minutes
Servings: 4

Ingredients:

- 2 medium zucchini
- 2 boneless, skinless chicken breasts
- 1/2 cup whole wheat bread crumbs
- 1/4 cup grated Parmesan cheese
- 1 tsp. dried Italian seasoning
- 1/4 tsp. garlic powder
- Salt and pepper to taste
- 2 eggs, beaten
- Cooking spray

Instructions:

1. Preheat the oven to 425°F (220°C) and line a baking sheet with parchment paper. Set aside.
2. Trim the ends of the zucchini and cut them into long, thin strips resembling French fries.
3. Cut the chicken breasts into long, thin strips similar in size to the zucchini.
4. In a shallow bowl, combine the whole wheat bread crumbs, grated Parmesan cheese, dried Italian seasoning, garlic powder, salt, and pepper. Mix well.
5. Dip each zucchini strip and chicken strip into the beaten eggs, then coat them with the bread crumb mixture, pressing gently to adhere the coating.
6. Place the coated zucchini and chicken strips on the prepared baking sheet. Spray the strips with cooking spray to help them brown and crisp in the oven.
7. Bake in the preheated oven for 20-25 minutes, or until the zucchini and chicken are cooked through and the coating is golden and crispy.
8. Remove from the oven and let the zucchini breaded chicken strips cool for a few minutes before serving.
9. Serve the zucchini breaded chicken strips as a nutritious and delicious main dish or as a fun

appetizer. You can also serve them with your favorite dipping sauce or alongside a fresh salad.

Nutritional Information (per serving):
Cal: 220 | Fat: 7g | Chol: 135mg | Sod: 220mg | Carbs: 14g | Fiber: 3g | Sugars: 3g | Pro: 25g

5. Tomato Basil Bruschetta Toast

Preparation time: 15 minutes
Servings: 4

Ingredients:

- 4 slices whole grain bread
- 2 cups diced tomatoes
- 1/4 cup chopped fresh basil
- 2 cloves garlic, minced
- 1 tbsp. extra virgin olive oil
- 1 tbsp. balsamic vinegar
- Salt and pepper to taste

Instructions:

1. Preheat the oven to 375°F (190°C).
2. Place the bread slices on a baking sheet and toast them in the preheated oven for about 5 minutes, or until crispy.
3. In a medium bowl, combine the diced tomatoes, chopped basil, minced garlic, extra virgin olive oil, balsamic vinegar, salt, and pepper. Mix well to combine.
4. Remove the toasted bread from the oven and let it cool for a minute.
5. Spoon the tomato basil mixture onto each slice of bread, dividing it evenly.
6. Serve the tomato basil bruschetta toast immediately as an appetizer or a light meal.

Nutritional Information (per serving):
Cal: 150 | Fat: 5g | Chol: 0mg | Sod: 200mg | Carbs: 23g | Fiber: 4g | Sugars: 4g | Pro: 5g

6. Greek Yogurt Banana Bread

Preparation time: 10 minutes
Baking time: 50 minutes
Servings: 4

Ingredients:

- 2 cups whole wheat flour
- 1 tsp. baking soda
- 1/2 tsp. salt
- 1/2 tsp. ground cinnamon
- 1/4 tsp. ground nutmeg
- 3 ripe bananas, mashed
- 1/2 cup Greek yogurt
- 1/4 cup honey or maple syrup

- 1/4 cup unsweetened applesauce
- 2 eggs
- 1 tsp. vanilla extract

Instructions:

1. Preheat the oven to 350°F (175°C). Grease a 9x5-inch loaf pan and set aside.
2. In a large bowl, whisk together the whole wheat flour, baking soda, salt, cinnamon, and nutmeg.
3. In a separate bowl, mix together the mashed bananas, Greek yogurt, honey or maple syrup, applesauce, eggs, and vanilla extract until well combined.
4. Pour the wet ingredients into the dry ingredients and stir until just combined. Do not overmix.
5. Pour the batter into the prepared loaf pan and smooth the top.
6. Bake in the preheated oven for 45-50 minutes, or until a toothpick inserted into the center comes out clean.
7. Remove the banana bread from the oven and let it cool in the pan for 10 minutes. Then transfer it to a wire rack to cool completely before slicing.

Nutritional Information (per serving):
Cal: 170 | Fat: 2g | Chol: 35mg | Sod: 200mg | Carbs: 35g | Fiber: 4g | Sugars: 12g | Pro: 5g

7. Mediterranean Pita Pizza

Preparation time: 15 minutes
Cooking time: 10 minutes
Servings: 2

Ingredients:

- 2 whole wheat pita bread rounds
- 1/2 cup marinara sauce (low-sodium)
- 1/2 cup diced tomatoes
- 1/4 cup sliced black olives
- 1/4 cup crumbled feta cheese
- 2 tablespoons chopped red onion
- 2 tablespoons chopped fresh basil
- 1 tbsp. extra virgin olive oil
- Freshly ground pepper, to taste

Instructions:

1. Preheat the oven to 400°F (200°C). Place the pita bread rounds on a baking sheet.
2. Spread an equal amount of marinara sauce on each pita bread round, leaving a small border around the edges.
3. Top the sauce with diced tomatoes, black olives, feta cheese, red onion, and fresh basil.
4. Drizzle each pita with olive oil and season with pepper.

5. Place the baking sheet in the preheated oven and bake for 10 minutes, or until the edges of the pita bread are crispy and the cheese is melted.
6. Remove from the oven and let the pizzas cool for a few minutes before slicing.
7. Serve the Mediterranean pita pizzas as a delicious and healthy meal.

Nutritional Information (per serving):
Cal: 275 | Fat: 11g | Chol: 11mg | Sod: 329mg | Carbs: 35g | Fiber: 6g | Sugars: 6g | Pro: 9g

8. Spinach and Feta Stuffed Bread

Preparation time: 20 minutes
Cooking time: 25 minutes
Servings: 4

Ingredients:

- 1 large French bread loaf
- 1 tbsp. olive oil
- 2 cloves garlic, minced
- 4 cups fresh spinach leaves
- 1/2 cup crumbled feta cheese
- 1/4 cup chopped sun-dried tomatoes
- 2 tablespoons chopped fresh basil
- 1/2 tsp. dried oregano
- Freshly ground pepper, to taste

Instructions:

1. Preheat the oven to 375°F (190°C). Line a baking sheet with parchment paper.
2. Slice the French bread loaf in half lengthwise, creating two long halves. Place the halves on the prepared baking sheet.
3. In a large skillet, heat the olive oil over medium heat. Add the minced garlic and sauté for about 1 minute until fragrant.
4. Add the spinach leaves to the skillet and cook until wilted, stirring occasionally. Remove from heat.
5. In a bowl, combine the cooked spinach, crumbled feta cheese, sun-dried tomatoes, chopped basil, dried oregano, and pepper. Mix well.
6. Spread the spinach and feta mixture evenly onto one half of the French bread loaf. Place the other half on top, creating a sandwich.
7. Bake in the preheated oven for 20-25 minutes, or until the bread is crispy and the filling is heated through.
8. Remove from the oven and let it cool for a few minutes before slicing.
9. Serve the Spinach and Feta Stuffed Bread as a delicious and satisfying meal or appetizer.

Nutritional Information (per serving):
Cal: 352 | Fat: 11g | Chol: 17mg | Sod: 428mg | Carbs: 50g | Fiber: 4g | Sugars: 5g | Pro: 15g

9. Cauliflower Pizza Crust Delight

Preparation time: 20 minutes
Cooking time: 25 minutes
Servings: 4

Ingredients:

- 1 medium head of cauliflower
- 2 eggs
- 1/4 cup grated Parmesan cheese
- 1/4 cup almond flour
- 1/2 tsp. dried oregano
- 1/2 tsp. garlic powder
- 1/4 tsp. salt
- Freshly ground pepper, to taste
- Your choice of pizza toppings (e.g., tomato sauce, cheese, vegetables, lean meats)

Instructions:

1. Preheat the oven to 425°F (220°C). Line a baking sheet with parchment paper.
2. Cut the cauliflower into florets and place them in a food processor. Pulse until the cauliflower resembles rice-like grains.
3. Transfer the cauliflower rice to a microwave-safe bowl and microwave on high for 5-6 minutes until softened.
4. Let the cauliflower cool slightly, then transfer it to a clean kitchen towel or cheesecloth. Squeeze out as much liquid as possible.
5. In a large mixing bowl, combine the cauliflower rice, eggs, grated Parmesan cheese, almond flour, dried oregano, garlic powder, salt, and pepper. Mix well to form a dough-like consistency.
6. Place the cauliflower dough onto the prepared baking sheet. Use your hands to shape it into a round pizza crust, about 1/4 inch thick.
7. Bake in the preheated oven for 15-18 minutes until the crust is golden brown and firm.
8. Remove the crust from the oven and add your choice of pizza toppings. Spread tomato sauce, sprinkle cheese, and add vegetables or lean meats as desired.
9. Return the pizza to the oven and bake for an additional 8-10 minutes until the cheese is melted and toppings are cooked.
10. Remove from the oven and let it cool for a few minutes before slicing.
11. Serve the Cauliflower Pizza Crust Delight as a delicious and nutritious alternative to traditional pizza.

Nutritional Information (per serving):
Cal: 102 | Fat: 5g | Chol: 93mg | Sod: 208mg | Carbs: 8g | Fiber: 3g | Sugars: 2g | Pro: 7g

10. Sweet Potato Toasts Avocado

Preparation time: 10 minutes
Cooking time: 15 minutes
Servings: 2

Ingredients:

- 1 large sweet potato
- 1 ripe avocado
- Juice of 1/2 lemon
- 1 tbsp. extra-virgin olive oil
- Salt and pepper to taste
- Optional toppings: sliced cherry tomatoes, sprouts, crumbled feta cheese, chopped herbs

Instructions:

1. Preheat the oven to 400°F (200°C). Line a baking sheet with parchment paper.
2. Slice the sweet potato into 1/4-inch thick slices. You can leave the skin on or peel it, depending on your preference.
3. Place the sweet potato slices on the prepared baking sheet. Drizzle with a little olive oil and sprinkle with salt and pepper.
4. Bake in the preheated oven for about 15 minutes, or until the sweet potato slices are tender and slightly crisp around the edges.
5. While the sweet potato toasts are baking, prepare the avocado topping. In a small bowl, mash the ripe avocado with a fork. Add the lemon juice, extra-virgin olive oil, salt, and pepper. Mix well to combine.
6. Once the sweet potato toasts are ready, remove them from the oven and let them cool for a few minutes.
7. Spread a generous amount of the avocado mixture onto each sweet potato toast.
8. Top with your desired toppings, such as sliced cherry tomatoes, sprouts, crumbled feta cheese, or chopped herbs.
9. Serve the Sweet Potato Toasts with Avocado as a delicious and nutritious snack or light meal.

Nutritional Information (per serving):
Cal: 210 | Fat: 14g | Chol: 0mg | Sod: 47mg | Carbs: 21g | Fiber: 8g | Sugars: 4g | Pro: 3g

11. Caprese Garlic Bread Bites

Preparation time: 10 minutes
Cooking time: 10 minutes
Servings: 4

Ingredients:

- 1 baguette, sliced into bite-sized pieces
- 2 tablespoons extra-virgin olive oil

- 2 cloves garlic, minced
- 2 medium tomatoes, sliced
- 8 ounces fresh mozzarella cheese, sliced
- Fresh basil leaves
- Balsamic glaze (optional)
- Salt and pepper to taste

Instructions:

1. Preheat the oven to 400°F (200°C).
2. In a small bowl, mix the extra-virgin olive oil and minced garlic together.
3. Arrange the baguette slices on a baking sheet and brush one side of each slice with the garlic olive oil mixture.
4. Bake in the preheated oven for about 8-10 minutes, or until the bread is toasted and golden.
5. Once the bread is toasted, remove it from the oven and let it cool slightly.
6. Top each bread slice with a slice of tomato, a slice of mozzarella cheese, and a fresh basil leaf.
7. Season with salt and pepper to taste.
8. If desired, drizzle a little balsamic glaze over the Caprese bites for added flavor.
9. Serve the Caprese Garlic Bread Bites as an appetizer or snack.

Nutritional Information (per serving):
Cal: 257 | Fat: 12g | Chol: 20mg | Sod: 275mg | Carbs: 25g | Fiber: 2g | Sugars: 2g | Pro: 11g

12. Whole Grain Pita Wraps

Preparation time: 15 minutes
Servings: 2

Ingredients:

- 4 whole grain pita bread rounds
- 1 cup cooked quinoa
- 1 cup mixed salad greens
- 1 cup diced cucumbers
- 1 cup diced tomatoes
- 1/2 cup diced red onions
- 1/2 cup sliced olives
- 1/4 cup crumbled feta cheese
- 2 tablespoons extra-virgin olive oil
- 2 tablespoons lemon juice
- 1 tsp. dried oregano
- Salt and pepper to taste

Instructions:

1. In a large bowl, combine the cooked quinoa, salad greens, cucumbers, tomatoes, red onions, olives, feta cheese, extra-virgin olive oil, lemon juice, dried oregano, salt, and pepper. Toss well to coat all the ingredients.
2. Warm the pita bread rounds in a toaster or oven until slightly softened.

3. Cut each pita bread round in half to form two pockets.
4. Stuff each pita pocket with the quinoa salad mixture, pressing it gently to fill the pocket.
5. Serve the Whole Grain Pita Wraps immediately.

Nutritional Information (per serving):
Cal: 279 | Fat: 12g | Chol: 6mg | Sod: 245mg | Carbs: 35g | Fiber: 7g | Sugars: 4g | Pro: 9g

13. Quinoa Zucchini Bread

Preparation time: 15 minutes
Cooking time: 50 minutes
Servings: 12

Ingredients:

- 1 cup cooked quinoa
- 1 1/2 cups grated zucchini
- 1/2 cup unsweetened applesauce
- 1/4 cup honey or maple syrup
- 1/4 cup coconut oil, melted
- 2 eggs
- 1 tsp. vanilla extract
- 1 1/2 cups whole wheat flour
- 1 tsp. baking powder
- 1/2 tsp. baking soda
- 1/2 tsp. ground cinnamon
- 1/4 tsp. salt
- Optional toppings: chopped nuts, seeds, or dried fruit

Instructions:

1. Preheat your oven to 350°F (175°C). Grease a loaf pan or line it with parchment paper.
2. In a large bowl, combine the cooked quinoa, grated zucchini, applesauce, honey or maple syrup, melted coconut oil, eggs, and vanilla extract. Mix well.
3. In a separate bowl, whisk together the whole wheat flour, baking powder, baking soda, ground cinnamon, and salt.
4. Add the dry ingredients to the wet ingredients and stir until just combined. Be careful not to overmix.
5. Pour the batter into the prepared loaf pan and smooth the top with a spatula. Sprinkle with optional toppings if desired.
6. Bake in the preheated oven for about 45-50 minutes, or until a toothpick inserted into the center comes out clean.
7. Remove the bread from the oven and let it cool in the pan for 10 minutes. Then transfer it to a wire rack to cool completely.
8. Slice and serve the Quinoa Zucchini Bread.

Nutritional Information (per serving):
Cal: 173 | Fat: 6g | Chol: 31mg | Sod: 107mg | Carbs: 26g | Fiber: 3g | Sugars: 9g | Pro: 4g

14. Grilled Chicken Flatbread Pizza

Preparation time: 15 minutes
Cooking time: 10 minutes
Servings: 4

Ingredients:

- 4 whole wheat flatbreads
- 1 cup cooked and shredded chicken breast
- 1/2 cup low-sodium tomato sauce
- 1/2 cup shredded mozzarella cheese
- 1/4 cup sliced red onions
- 1/4 cup sliced bell peppers
- 1/4 cup sliced black olives
- 1 tbsp. chopped fresh basil
- Optional toppings: sliced mushrooms, diced tomatoes, spinach leaves

Instructions:

1. Preheat your grill or grill pan over medium heat.
2. Place the whole wheat flatbreads on a clean surface.
3. Spread an equal amount of tomato sauce over each flatbread, leaving a small border around the edges.
4. Sprinkle the shredded chicken evenly over the tomato sauce.
5. Top with shredded mozzarella cheese, sliced red onions, bell peppers, black olives, and any other desired toppings.
6. Transfer the flatbreads to the preheated grill and cook for about 8-10 minutes, or until the cheese is melted and the crust is crispy.
7. Remove the flatbreads from the grill and let them cool for a minute.
8. Sprinkle with chopped fresh basil.
9. Slice and serve the Grilled Chicken Flatbread Pizzas.

Nutritional Information (per serving):
Cal: 250 | Fat: 8g | Chol: 37mg | Sod: 240mg | Carbs: 26g | Fiber: 4g | Sugars: 4g | Pro: 19g

15. Roasted Pepper Hummus Toast

Preparation time: 10 minutes
Servings: 2

Ingredients:

- 4 slices of whole grain bread
- 1/2 cup roasted red pepper hummus
- 1 small cucumber, thinly sliced
- 1 small tomato, sliced
- 2 tablespoons chopped fresh parsley
- Optional toppings: sliced black olives, crumbled feta cheese, red pepper flakes

Instructions:

1. Toast the slices of whole grain bread until golden and crispy.
2. Spread a generous amount of roasted red pepper hummus on each slice of toast.
3. Top the hummus with a layer of thinly sliced cucumber and tomato slices.
4. Sprinkle chopped fresh parsley over the toppings.
5. If desired, add optional toppings such as sliced black olives, crumbled feta cheese, or a sprinkle of red pepper flakes.
6. Serve the Roasted Red Pepper Hummus Toast immediately.

Nutritional Information (per serving):
Cal: 180 | Fat: 7g | Chol: 0mg | Sod: 210mg | Carbs: 24g | Fiber: 6g | Sugars: 4g | Pro: 7g

16. Broccoli Cheddar Bread Rolls

Preparation time: 2 hours (includes rising time)
Servings: 12 rolls

Ingredients:

- 3 cups whole wheat flour
- 1 package (2 1/4 teaspoons) active dry yeast
- 1 tsp. salt
- 1/2 tsp. garlic powder
- 1/2 tsp. dried oregano
- 1 cup warm water
- 1 tbsp. olive oil
- 1 cup finely chopped broccoli florets
- 1 cup shredded reduced-fat cheddar cheese

Instructions:

1. In a large mixing bowl, combine the whole wheat flour, yeast, salt, garlic powder, and dried oregano.
2. Add the warm water and olive oil to the dry ingredients. Mix until a dough forms.
3. Turn the dough onto a floured surface and knead for about 5 minutes, until smooth and elastic.
4. Place the dough in a greased bowl, cover with a clean kitchen towel, and let it rise in a warm place for about 1 hour or until doubled in size.
5. Preheat the oven to 375°F (190°C). Line a baking sheet with parchment paper.
6. Punch down the dough and knead in the chopped broccoli and shredded cheddar cheese until evenly distributed.
7. Divide the dough into 12 equal portions. Shape

each portion into a ball and place them on the prepared baking sheet.

8. Cover the rolls with the kitchen towel and let them rise for an additional 30 minutes.
9. Bake the rolls in the preheated oven for 20-25 minutes, or until golden brown.
10. Remove from the oven and let the rolls cool on a wire rack before serving.

Nutritional Information (per serving):
Cal: 160 | Fat: 4g | Chol: 5mg | Sod: 200mg | Carbs: 26g | Fiber: 4g | Sugars: 1g | Pro: 7g

17. Turkey and Veggie Pita

Preparation time: 15 minutes
Servings: 2

Ingredients:

- 2 whole wheat pita breads
- 4 ounces sliced turkey breast
- 1/2 cup sliced cucumbers
- 1/2 cup sliced tomatoes
- 1/4 cup sliced red onions
- 1/4 cup shredded lettuce
- 2 tablespoons plain Greek yogurt
- 1 tbsp. fresh lemon juice
- 1 tsp. dried dill
- Salt and pepper to taste

Instructions:

1. In a small bowl, mix together the Greek yogurt, lemon juice, dried dill, salt, and pepper to make the dressing.
2. Cut open the pita breads to form pockets.
3. Spread the dressing inside each pita pocket.
4. Divide the turkey, cucumbers, tomatoes, red onions, and shredded lettuce evenly between the two pita pockets.
5. Serve immediately and enjoy!

Nutritional Information (per serving):
Cal: 250 | Fat: 3g | Chol: 30mg | Sod: 300mg | Carbs: 32g | Fiber: 6g | Sugars: 4g | Pro: 26g

18. Mediterranean Naan Pizza

Preparation time: 20 minutes
Servings: 2

Ingredients:

- 2 whole wheat naan bread
- 1/2 cup hummus
- 1/2 cup cherry tomatoes, halved
- 1/4 cup sliced Kalamata olives
- 1/4 cup crumbled feta cheese
- 2 tablespoons chopped fresh parsley
- 1 tbsp. extra virgin olive oil
- 1/2 tsp. dried oregano
- Salt and pepper to taste

Instructions:

1. Preheat the oven to 400°F (200°C).
2. Place the naan bread on a baking sheet.
3. Spread an even layer of hummus on each naan bread.
4. Top with cherry tomatoes, Kalamata olives, and crumbled feta cheese.
5. Drizzle with extra virgin olive oil and sprinkle with dried oregano, salt, and pepper.
6. Bake in the preheated oven for about 10 minutes, or until the edges are crispy and the toppings are heated through.
7. Remove from the oven and sprinkle with chopped fresh parsley.
8. Slice the naan pizzas and serve hot.

Nutritional Information (per serving):
Cal: 320 | Fat: 16g | Chol: 15mg | Sod: 500mg | Carbs: 35g | Fiber: 6g | Sugars: 3g | Pro: 11g

19. Avocado Toast with Tomato

Preparation time: 10 minutes
Servings: 2

Ingredients:

- 2 slices whole wheat bread
- 1 ripe avocado
- 1 small tomato, sliced
- 1 tbsp. fresh lemon juice
- 1/4 tsp. red pepper flakes (optional)
- Salt and pepper to taste
- Fresh cilantro or basil leaves for garnish (optional)

Instructions:

1. Toast the slices of whole wheat bread until golden and crispy.
2. In a small bowl, mash the ripe avocado with a fork until smooth.
3. Stir in the fresh lemon juice, red pepper flakes (if using), and season with salt and pepper to taste.
4. Spread the mashed avocado mixture evenly onto each slice of toasted bread.
5. Top the avocado spread with tomato slices.
6. Garnish with fresh cilantro or basil leaves if desired.
7. Serve immediately and enjoy!

Nutritional Information (per serving):
Cal: 200 | Fat: 11g | Chol: 0mg | Sod: 80mg | Carbs: 23g | Fiber: 7g | Sugars: 2g | Pro: 4g

20. Whole Wheat Pizza Dough

Preparation time: 1 hour 30 minutes (includes rising time)
Servings: 8

Ingredients:

- 2 cups whole wheat flour
- 1 cup all-purpose flour
- 1 tsp. active dry yeast
- 1 tsp. honey
- 1 cup warm water
- 1 tbsp. olive oil
- 1/2 tsp. salt

Instructions:

1. In a small bowl, dissolve the honey in warm water. Sprinkle the yeast over the water and let it sit for about 5 minutes until foamy.
2. In a large mixing bowl, combine the whole wheat flour, all-purpose flour, and salt.
3. Make a well in the center of the dry ingredients and pour in the yeast mixture and olive oil.
4. Stir the ingredients together until a dough starts to form.
5. Transfer the dough onto a lightly floured surface and knead for about 5-7 minutes until the dough becomes smooth and elastic.
6. Shape the dough into a ball and place it in a greased bowl, turning once to coat.
7. Cover the bowl with a clean kitchen towel or plastic wrap and let the dough rise in a warm place for about 1 hour until it doubles in size.
8. Preheat the oven to 450°F (230°C) and place a pizza stone or baking sheet in the oven to preheat.
9. Punch down the dough to release the air and divide it into 8 equal portions.
10. On a lightly floured surface, roll out each portion into a round or oval shape, about 1/4 inch thick.
11. Transfer the rolled dough onto a piece of parchment paper.
12. Top the dough with your favorite pizza toppings and slide the parchment paper with the pizza onto the preheated pizza stone or baking sheet.
13. Bake for about 12-15 minutes until the crust is golden brown and crispy.
14. Remove the pizza from the oven and let it cool for a few minutes before slicing and serving.

Nutritional Information (per serving):
Cal: 185 | Fat: 3g | Chol: 0mg | Sod: 147mg | Carbs: 35g | Fiber: 6g | Sugars: 1g | Pro: 7g

21. Caprese Stuffed Baguette

Preparation time: 15 minutes
Servings: 4

Ingredients:

- 1 baguette
- 2 ripe tomatoes, sliced
- 8 ounces fresh mozzarella cheese, sliced
- 1/2 cup fresh basil leaves
- 2 tablespoons balsamic glaze
- Salt and pepper to taste

Instructions:

1. Slice the baguette into 1-inch thick slices.
2. Preheat the oven to 375°F (190°C).
3. Arrange the baguette slices on a baking sheet and toast them in the oven for about 5 minutes until they are lightly crispy.
4. Remove the toasted baguette slices from the oven and let them cool slightly.
5. On each baguette slice, layer a slice of tomato, a slice of mozzarella cheese, and a fresh basil leaf.
6. Drizzle the stuffed baguette slices with balsamic glaze.
7. Season with salt and pepper to taste.
8. Serve the Caprese stuffed baguette slices immediately as an appetizer or light snack.

Nutritional Information (per serving):
Cal: 239 | Fat: 10g | Chol: 36mg | Sod: 220mg | Carbs: 23g | Fiber: 1g | Sugars: 3g | Pro: 14g

22. Veggie Packed Focaccia Bread

Preparation time: 2 hours 15 minutes
Servings: 12

Ingredients:

- 3 cups all-purpose flour
- 2 teaspoons active dry yeast
- 1 tsp. sugar
- 1 1/4 cups warm water
- 2 tablespoons olive oil
- 1 tsp. salt
- 1 cup cherry tomatoes, halved
- 1/2 cup sliced bell peppers
- 1/2 cup sliced red onions
- 1/4 cup sliced black olives
- 2 tablespoons chopped fresh rosemary
- Salt and pepper to taste

Instructions:

1. In a small bowl, combine the yeast, sugar, and

warm water. Let it sit for about 5 minutes until the yeast is activated and foamy.

2. In a large mixing bowl, combine the flour, olive oil, and salt. Pour in the yeast mixture and mix well until a dough forms.
3. Transfer the dough to a floured surface and knead for about 5-7 minutes until it becomes smooth and elastic.
4. Place the dough in a greased bowl, cover it with a clean kitchen towel, and let it rise in a warm place for about 1 hour or until doubled in size.
5. Preheat the oven to 425°F (220°C).
6. Punch down the risen dough and transfer it to a greased baking sheet. Press and stretch the dough to fill the baking sheet evenly.
7. Using your fingertips, make indentations all over the surface of the dough.
8. Arrange the cherry tomatoes, bell peppers, red onions, and black olives on top of the dough. Sprinkle with chopped rosemary.
9. Drizzle the top of the dough with olive oil and season with salt and pepper to taste.
10. Bake in the preheated oven for 20-25 minutes or until the bread is golden brown and cooked through.
11. Remove the focaccia from the oven and let it cool slightly before slicing and serving.

Nutritional Information (per serving):
Cal: 178 | Fat: 4g | Chol: 0mg | Sod: 195mg | Carbs: 31g | Fiber: 1g | Sugars: 1g | Pro: 4g

23. Spinach and Feta Pizza

Preparation time: 30 minutes
Servings: 4

Ingredients:

- 1 whole wheat pizza dough (store-bought or homemade)
- 1 cup fresh spinach leaves
- 1/2 cup crumbled feta cheese
- 1/4 cup sliced black olives
- 1/4 cup sliced red onions
- 1/4 cup diced tomatoes
- 1/4 tsp. dried oregano
- Freshly ground pepper to taste

Instructions:

1. Preheat the oven according to the instructions on the pizza dough package or to 425°F (220°C) if using homemade dough.
2. Roll out the pizza dough on a floured surface to your desired thickness and shape.
3. Transfer the rolled dough to a baking sheet or pizza stone.
4. Spread a thin layer of tomato sauce over the dough, leaving a small border around the edges.

5. Arrange the spinach leaves evenly over the sauce.
6. Sprinkle the crumbled feta cheese, black olives, red onions, and diced tomatoes over the spinach.
7. Sprinkle dried oregano and freshly ground pepper over the toppings.
8. Place the pizza in the preheated oven and bake for about 15-20 minutes or until the crust is golden brown and the cheese has melted.
9. Remove from the oven and let it cool for a few minutes before slicing and serving.

Nutritional Information (per serving):
Cal: 240 | Fat: 6g | Chol: 16mg | Sod: 350mg | Carbs: 37g | Fiber: 5g | Sugars: 3g | Pro: 11g

24. Whole Grain Garlic Knots

Preparation time: 1 hour 30 minutes
Servings: 12

Ingredients:

- 2 cups whole wheat flour
- 1 cup all-purpose flour
- 1 package (2 1/4 teaspoons) active dry yeast
- 1 tsp. sugar
- 1 tsp. salt
- 1 cup warm water
- 2 tablespoons olive oil
- 2 cloves garlic, minced
- 2 tablespoons chopped fresh parsley

Instructions:

1. In a large bowl, combine the whole wheat flour, all-purpose flour, yeast, sugar, and salt.
2. Add the warm water and olive oil to the dry ingredients. Mix until a dough forms.
3. Knead the dough on a floured surface for about 5-7 minutes or until smooth and elastic.
4. Place the dough in a greased bowl, cover with a clean kitchen towel, and let it rise in a warm place for 1 hour or until doubled in size.
5. Preheat the oven to 375°F (190°C) and line a baking sheet with parchment paper.
6. Punch down the dough and divide it into 12 equal-sized pieces.
7. Roll each piece into a rope about 8 inches long.
8. Tie each rope into a knot and place the knots on the prepared baking sheet.
9. Bake the knots in the preheated oven for 12-15 minutes or until golden brown.
10. While the knots are baking, in a small bowl, combine the minced garlic and chopped parsley.
11. When the knots are done, remove them from the oven and brush them with the garlic and parsley mixture.
12. Serve the garlic knots warm.

Nutritional Information (per serving):
Cal: 130 | Fat: 3g | Chol: 0mg | Sod: 195mg | Carbs: 23g | Fiber: 3g | Sugars: 0.5g | Pro: 4g

25. Greek Yogurt Cinnamon Bread

Preparation time: 1 hour 30 minutes
Servings: 12

Ingredients:

- 2 cups whole wheat flour
- 1 cup all-purpose flour
- 1 tsp. baking powder
- 1/2 tsp. baking soda
- 1/2 tsp. salt
- 1 tsp. ground cinnamon
- 1/2 cup unsweetened applesauce
- 1/2 cup honey
- 2 eggs
- 1 cup plain Greek yogurt
- 1 tsp. vanilla extract

For the Cinnamon Sugar Topping:

- 2 tablespoons granulated sugar
- 1 tsp. ground cinnamon

Instructions:

1. Preheat the oven to 350°F (175°C). Grease a 9x5-inch loaf pan and set aside.
2. In a large bowl, whisk together the whole wheat flour, all-purpose flour, baking powder, baking soda, salt, and ground cinnamon.
3. In a separate bowl, whisk together the applesauce, honey, eggs, Greek yogurt, and vanilla extract until well combined.
4. Pour the wet ingredients into the dry ingredients and stir until just combined. Be careful not to overmix.
5. Pour the batter into the prepared loaf pan and smooth the top with a spatula.
6. In a small bowl, combine the granulated sugar and ground cinnamon for the topping. Sprinkle the mixture evenly over the batter in the loaf pan.
7. Bake in the preheated oven for 50-60 minutes or until a toothpick inserted into the center of the bread comes out clean.
8. Remove the bread from the oven and let it cool in the pan for 10 minutes. Then transfer the bread to a wire rack to cool completely.

Nutritional Information (per serving):
Cal: 200 | Fat: 1.5g | Chol: 30mg | Sod: 180mg | Carbs: 43g | Fiber: 3g | Sugars: 21g | Pro: 7g

Desserts

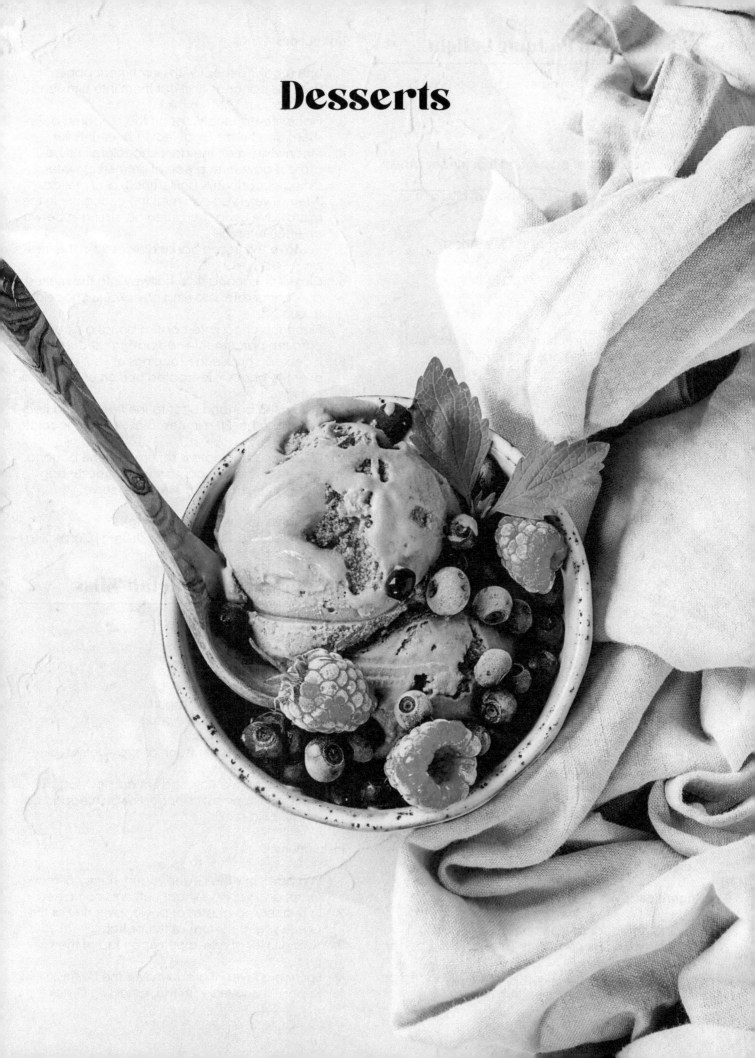

1. Berry Chia Pudding Delight

Preparation time: 10 minutes + chilling time
Servings: 4

Ingredients:

- 1 cup unsweetened almond milk (or any other non-dairy milk)
- 1 cup mixed berries (strawberries, blueberries, raspberries)
- 3 tablespoons chia seeds
- 1 tbsp. honey (optional, for sweetness)
- 1/2 tsp. vanilla extract

For the toppings:

- Fresh berries
- Chopped nuts (such as almonds or walnuts)
- Unsweetened shredded coconut

Instructions:

1. In a blender, combine the almond milk, mixed berries, honey (if using), and vanilla extract. Blend until smooth.
2. Pour the berry mixture into a bowl and add the chia seeds. Stir well to combine.
3. Let the mixture sit for about 5 minutes, then stir again to make sure the chia seeds are evenly distributed.
4. Cover the bowl with plastic wrap or a lid and refrigerate for at least 4 hours or overnight, until the mixture thickens and forms a pudding-like consistency.
5. Once chilled, give the chia pudding a good stir to break up any clumps.
6. Divide the pudding into serving bowls or glasses.
7. Top each serving with fresh berries, chopped nuts, and a sprinkle of unsweetened shredded coconut.
8. Serve chilled and enjoy!

Nutritional Information (per serving):
Cal: 110 | Fat: 5g | Chol: 0mg | Sod: 30mg | Carbs: 14g | Fiber: 7g | Sugars: 6g | Pro: 3g

2. Dark Chocolate Banana Bites

Preparation time: 10 minutes + freezing time
Servings: 4

Ingredients:

- 2 large bananas, ripe but firm
- 4 ounces dark chocolate (at least 70% cocoa), chopped
- Optional toppings: chopped nuts, shredded coconut, chia seeds, dried fruit

Instructions:

1. Line a baking sheet with parchment paper.
2. Peel the bananas and cut them into bite-sized slices, about 1/2 inch thick.
3. Place the banana slices on the prepared baking sheet and freeze for at least 1 hour until firm.
4. Meanwhile, melt the dark chocolate in a heatproof bowl over a pan of simmering water, stirring occasionally until smooth and melted. Alternatively, you can melt the chocolate in the microwave using short intervals, stirring in between each interval.
5. Remove the frozen banana slices from the freezer.
6. Dip each banana slice halfway into the melted dark chocolate, allowing any excess chocolate to drip off.
7. Place the chocolate-coated banana slices back onto the parchment-lined baking sheet.
8. If desired, sprinkle the toppings of your choice over the chocolate-coated portion of the banana slices.
9. Return the banana bites to the freezer and freeze for another 30 minutes to allow the chocolate to set.
10. Once the chocolate is set, transfer the banana bites to an airtight container or a freezer bag.
11. Store in the freezer until ready to serve.

Nutritional Information (per serving):
Cal: 160 | Fat: 8g | Chol: 0mg | Sod: 0mg | Carbs: 24g | Fiber: 3g | Sugars: 14g | Pro: 2g

3. Greek Yogurt Parfait Bliss

Preparation time: 10 minutes
Servings: 2

Ingredients:

- 1 cup non-fat Greek yogurt
- 1 tbsp. honey or maple syrup
- 1/2 tsp. vanilla extract
- 1 cup mixed berries (such as strawberries, blueberries, raspberries)
- 1/4 cup granola (low-sodium and low-sugar)
- Optional toppings: chopped nuts, shredded coconut, chia seeds

Instructions:

1. In a bowl, mix the Greek yogurt, honey or maple syrup, and vanilla extract until well combined.
2. In two serving glasses or bowls, layer half of the Greek yogurt mixture at the bottom.
3. Add a layer of mixed berries on top of the yogurt.
4. Sprinkle a layer of granola over the berries.
5. Repeat the layers with the remaining Greek

yogurt, berries, and granola.

6. If desired, sprinkle your choice of optional toppings on the top layer.
7. Serve immediately and enjoy!

Nutritional Information (per serving):
Cal: 180 | Fat: 1g | Chol: 0mg | Sod: 40mg | Carbs: 32g | Fiber: 4g | Sugars: 18g | Pro: 15g

4. Baked Apple Crisps

Preparation time: 10 minutes
Baking time: 2 hours
Servings: 4

Ingredients:

- 4 medium-sized apples (any variety)
- 1 tbsp. lemon juice
- 1 tsp. ground cinnamon
- Optional: 1-2 teaspoons honey or maple syrup (for added sweetness)

Instructions:

1. Preheat your oven to 200°C (400°F) and line a baking sheet with parchment paper.
2. Wash the apples thoroughly and remove the core. You can peel the apples if desired, but leaving the skin on adds more fiber.
3. Slice the apples into thin, even slices. You can use a mandoline or a sharp knife for this.
4. In a bowl, toss the apple slices with lemon juice to prevent browning.
5. Arrange the apple slices in a single layer on the prepared baking sheet.
6. Sprinkle the ground cinnamon evenly over the apple slices. If desired, drizzle the honey or maple syrup over the top.
7. Place the baking sheet in the preheated oven and bake for 1.5 to 2 hours, or until the apple slices are crispy and lightly golden. Make sure to check on them occasionally to prevent burning.
8. Once baked, remove from the oven and let the apple crisps cool completely before serving.
9. Enjoy the baked apple crisps as a healthy and delicious snack!

Nutritional Information (per serving):
Cal: 70 | Fat: 0g | Chol: 0mg | Sod: 0mg | Carbs: 18g | Fiber: 3g | Sugars: 13g | Pro: 0g

5. Chocolate Avocado Mousse

Preparation time: 10 minutes
Baking time: 2 hours
Servings: 4

Ingredients:

- 2 ripe avocados
- 1/4 cup unsweetened cocoa powder
- 1/4 cup honey or maple syrup
- 1 tsp. vanilla extract
- Optional toppings: fresh berries, chopped nuts, or grated dark chocolate

Instructions:

1. Cut the avocados in half, remove the pits, and scoop the flesh into a blender or food processor.
2. Add the cocoa powder, honey or maple syrup, and vanilla extract to the blender.
3. Blend the ingredients until smooth and creamy, scraping down the sides as needed.
4. Taste the mixture and adjust the sweetness if desired by adding more honey or maple syrup.
5. Transfer the mousse to serving dishes or small bowls.
6. Cover the dishes and refrigerate for at least 2 hours to allow the mousse to set and chill.
7. Before serving, you can top the mousse with fresh berries, chopped nuts, or grated dark chocolate for added flavor and texture.
8. Enjoy the chocolate avocado mousse as a satisfying and healthier dessert option!

Nutritional Information (per serving):
Cal: 220 | Fat: 14g | Chol: 0mg | Sod: 10mg | Carbs: 28g | Fiber: 7g | Sugars: 17g | Pro: 3g

6. Fruit Salad Medley

Preparation time: 15 minutes
Servings: 4

Ingredients:

- 2 cups mixed berries (strawberries, blueberries, raspberries)
- 2 medium oranges, peeled and segmented
- 1 large apple, diced
- 1 cup seedless grapes, halved
- 1 tbsp. fresh lemon juice
- 1 tbsp. honey (optional, for added sweetness)
- Fresh mint leaves for garnish (optional)

Instructions:

1. In a large bowl, combine the mixed berries, orange segments, diced apple, and halved grapes.
2. Drizzle the fresh lemon juice over the fruit to prevent browning and add a refreshing tang.
3. If desired, you can add a tbsp. of honey to enhance the sweetness of the fruit.
4. Gently toss the fruit salad to evenly distribute the flavors.

5. Let the fruit salad sit for a few minutes to allow the flavors to meld together.
6. Garnish the fruit salad with fresh mint leaves for a pop of color and added freshness.
7. Serve the fruit salad medley as a healthy and delicious side dish or snack.

Nutritional Information (per serving):
Cal: 80 | Fat: 0.4g | Chol: 0mg | Sod: 2mg | Carbs: 20g | Fiber: 3.4g | Sugars: 15g | Pro: 1g

7. Frozen Yogurt Berry Bark

Preparation time: 10 minutes
Freezing time: 4 hours
Servings: 6

Ingredients:

- 2 cups plain Greek yogurt
- 2 tablespoons honey or maple syrup (optional, for added sweetness)
- 1 tsp. vanilla extract
- 1 cup mixed berries (strawberries, blueberries, raspberries)
- 2 tablespoons unsweetened shredded coconut

Instructions:

1. Line a baking sheet with parchment paper or a silicone baking mat.
2. In a mixing bowl, combine the Greek yogurt, honey or maple syrup (if using), and vanilla extract. Stir until well combined.
3. Spread the Greek yogurt mixture evenly onto the prepared baking sheet, forming a rectangular shape about 1/4 inch thick.
4. Scatter the mixed berries and shredded coconut over the Greek yogurt, pressing them gently into the surface.
5. Place the baking sheet in the freezer and let it freeze for at least 4 hours or until completely firm.
6. Once frozen, remove the bark from the baking sheet and break it into pieces of desired size.
7. Serve the Frozen Yogurt Berry Bark immediately or transfer it to an airtight container and store in the freezer.

Nutritional Information (per serving):
Cal: 98 | Fat: 2g | Chol: 3mg | Sod: 27mg | Carbs: 11g | - Fiber: 1g | Sugars: 9g | Pro: 8g

8. Coconut Macaroon Drops

Preparation time: 15 minutes
Baking time: 15 minutes
Servings: 12

Ingredients:

- 2 cups shredded unsweetened coconut
- 1/4 cup honey or maple syrup
- 2 tablespoons coconut flour
- 2 large egg whites
- 1 tsp. vanilla extract
- Pinch of salt

Instructions:

1. Preheat your oven to 350°F (175°C). Line a baking sheet with parchment paper.
2. In a mixing bowl, combine the shredded coconut, honey or maple syrup, coconut flour, egg whites, vanilla extract, and a pinch of salt. Stir until well combined.
3. Using a tbsp. or a cookie scoop, drop rounded mounds of the coconut mixture onto the prepared baking sheet.
4. Bake in the preheated oven for about 15 minutes or until the edges of the macaroons turn golden brown.
5. Remove from the oven and let the macaroons cool completely on the baking sheet before serving.

Nutritional Information (per serving):
Cal: 86 | Fat: 6g | Chol: 0mg | Sod: 11mg | Carbs: 8g | - Fiber: 2g | Sugars: 5g | Pro: 1g

9. Lemon Poppy Seed Muffins

Preparation time: 15 minutes
Baking time: 20 minutes
Servings: 12

Ingredients:

- 1 1/2 cups whole wheat flour
- 1/2 cup almond flour
- 1/4 cup honey or maple syrup
- 2 tablespoons poppy seeds
- 1 tbsp. lemon zest
- 1 tsp. baking powder
- 1/2 tsp. baking soda
- 1/4 tsp. salt
- 3/4 cup unsweetened almond milk (or any non-dairy milk)
- 1/4 cup lemon juice
- 1/4 cup unsweetened applesauce
- 1 tsp. vanilla extract
- 2 tablespoons coconut oil, melted
- 1 tbsp. lemon juice (for the glaze)
- 1 tbsp. honey or maple syrup (for the glaze)

Instructions:

1. Preheat your oven to 350°F (175°C). Line a muffin

tin with paper liners.

2. In a large bowl, whisk together the whole wheat flour, almond flour, honey or maple syrup, poppy seeds, lemon zest, baking powder, baking soda, and salt.
3. In a separate bowl, whisk together the almond milk, lemon juice, applesauce, vanilla extract, and melted coconut oil.
4. Pour the wet ingredients into the dry ingredients and stir until just combined. Do not overmix.
5. Divide the batter evenly among the muffin cups, filling each about 3/4 full.
6. Bake in the preheated oven for about 18-20 minutes, or until a toothpick inserted into the center comes out clean.
7. While the muffins are baking, prepare the glaze by whisking together the lemon juice and honey or maple syrup in a small bowl.
8. Remove the muffins from the oven and let them cool in the pan for a few minutes. Then transfer them to a wire rack to cool completely.
9. Drizzle the glaze over the cooled muffins. Allow the glaze to set before serving.

Nutritional Information (per serving):
Cal: 162 | Fat: 6g | Chol: 0mg | Sod: 107mg | Carbs: 23g | Fiber: 3g | Sugars: 10g | Pro: 4g

10. Mango Sorbet Swirl

Preparation time: 10 minutes
Freezing time: 4 hours
Servings: 4

Ingredients:

- 3 large ripe mangoes, peeled and chopped
- 1 tbsp. lemon juice
- 1 tbsp. honey or maple syrup (optional, for added sweetness)
- Fresh mint leaves, for garnish

Instructions:

1. Place the chopped mangoes in a blender or food processor. Add the lemon juice and honey or maple syrup (if desired). Blend until smooth and creamy.
2. Pour the mango mixture into a shallow container or baking dish.
3. Place the container in the freezer and let it freeze for about 2 hours, or until partially set.
4. After 2 hours, remove the container from the freezer and use a fork to stir and break up any ice crystals that have formed.
5. Return the container to the freezer and let it freeze for another 2 hours, or until completely set.
6. Once the sorbet is completely frozen, remove it from the freezer and let it sit at room temperature for a few minutes to soften slightly.

7. Use a spoon or an ice cream scoop to swirl and scoop the mango sorbet into serving bowls or glasses.
8. Garnish with fresh mint leaves and serve immediately.

Nutritional Information (per serving):
Cal: 102 | Fat: 0.6g | Chol: 0mg | Sod: 3mg | Carbs: 26.1g | Fiber: 2.6g | Sugars: 23.4g | Pro: 1.2g

11. Peanut Butter Banana Bites

Preparation time: 10 minutes
Servings: 2

Ingredients:

- 1 ripe banana
- 2 tablespoons natural peanut butter (unsalted and no added sugar)
- 1 tbsp. unsweetened shredded coconut (optional, for garnish)
- 1 tbsp. chopped nuts (e.g., almonds, walnuts, or peanuts) (optional, for garnish)

Instructions:

1. Peel the banana and cut it into thick slices, about 1/2 inch thick.
2. Spread a small amount of peanut butter on top of each banana slice.
3. If desired, sprinkle the shredded coconut and chopped nuts over the peanut butter.
4. Repeat the process for the remaining banana slices.
5. Serve immediately and enjoy!

Nutritional Information (per serving):
Cal: 136 | Fat: 6.5g | Chol: 0mg | Sod: 3mg | Carbs: 18.6g | Fiber: 3.3g | Sugars: 8.6g | Pro: 4.5g

12. Strawberry Frozen Yogurt Cups

Preparation time: 10 minutes
Freezing time: 4 hours
Servings: 6

Ingredients:

- 2 cups frozen strawberries
- 1 cup plain Greek yogurt (unsweetened)
- 1 tbsp. honey (optional, for sweetness)
- Fresh strawberries, sliced (for garnish)

Instructions:

1. In a blender or food processor, combine the frozen strawberries, Greek yogurt, and honey (if using). Blend until smooth and creamy.

Line a muffin tin with paper or silicone liners.
2. Divide the strawberry yogurt mixture evenly among the muffin cups.
3. Top each cup with a sliced strawberry for garnish.
4. Place the muffin tin in the freezer and freeze for at least 4 hours or until the yogurt cups are firm.
5. Once frozen, remove the yogurt cups from the muffin tin and transfer them to a sealed container for storage in the freezer.
6. Serve the frozen yogurt cups directly from the freezer and enjoy!

Nutritional Information (per serving):
Cal: 59 | Fat: 0.4g | Chol: 2mg | Sod: 15mg | Carbs: 11.6g | Fiber: 1.9g | Sugars: 8.5g | Pro: 3.7g

13. Almond Date Energy Balls

Preparation time: 15 minutes
Servings: 12

Ingredients:

- 1 cup pitted dates
- 1 cup almonds
- 2 tablespoons unsweetened cocoa powder
- 1 tbsp. almond butter
- 1 tbsp. honey (optional, for added sweetness)
- 1/2 tsp. vanilla extract
- Unsweetened shredded coconut (for rolling, optional)

Instructions:

1. Place the pitted dates, almonds, cocoa powder, almond butter, honey (if using), and vanilla extract in a food processor.
2. Process the ingredients until they come together into a sticky dough-like consistency.
3. Scoop out small portions of the mixture and roll them into bite-sized balls using your hands.
4. If desired, roll the energy balls in shredded coconut for additional flavor and texture.
5. Place the energy balls in an airtight container and refrigerate for at least 30 minutes to firm up.
6. Serve and enjoy these delicious and energizing Almond Date Energy Balls!

Nutritional Information (per serving):
Cal: 112 | Fat: 5.5g | Chol: 0mg | Sod: 0mg | Carbs: 15.3g | Fiber: 2.6g | Sugars: 11.3g | Pro: 2.7g

14. Cinnamon Baked Apples

Preparation time: 40 minutes
Servings: 4

Ingredients:

- 4 medium-sized apples (such as Granny Smith or Honeycrisp)
- 2 tablespoons honey
- 1 tsp. ground cinnamon
- 1/4 tsp. ground nutmeg
- 1/4 cup chopped walnuts (optional)

Instructions:

1. Preheat the oven to 375°F (190°C).
2. Core the apples using an apple corer or a small knife, leaving the bottoms intact.
3. In a small bowl, combine the honey, cinnamon, and nutmeg.
4. Place the cored apples in a baking dish and spoon the honey mixture evenly over each apple.
5. If desired, sprinkle the chopped walnuts over the apples.
6. Bake the apples in the preheated oven for 25-30 minutes or until they are tender.
7. Remove the baked apples from the oven and let them cool for a few minutes before serving.
8. Serve the Cinnamon Baked Apples warm and enjoy the delicious and cozy flavors!

Nutritional Information (per serving):
Cal: 147 | Fat: 1.9g | Chol: 0mg | Sod: 2mg | Carbs: 36.4g | Fiber: 5.5g | Sugars: 27.2g | Pro: 0.9g

15. Raspberry Chia Seed Jam

Preparation time: 15 minutes
Servings: Makes about 1 cup of jam

Ingredients:

- 2 cups fresh or frozen raspberries
- 2 tablespoons chia seeds
- 2 tablespoons honey or maple syrup (optional, for sweetness)
- 1 tsp. lemon juice (optional, for flavor)

Instructions:

1. In a saucepan, heat the raspberries over medium heat until they start to break down and release their juices. Use a spoon to mash them slightly.
2. Stir in the chia seeds and continue cooking for about 5-7 minutes, stirring occasionally, until the mixture thickens.
3. If desired, add honey or maple syrup to sweeten the jam and lemon juice for a touch of brightness. Stir well to combine.
4. Remove the saucepan from heat and let the jam cool for a few minutes.
5. Transfer the jam to a clean jar or container and

let it cool completely. It will continue to thicken as it cools.

6. Once completely cooled, cover the jar and re-frigerate for at least 2 hours or overnight to allow the jam to set.

7. Serve the Raspberry Chia Seed Jam on toast, yogurt, oatmeal, or use it as a topping for pancakes or desserts. Enjoy!

Nutritional Information (per serving):
Cal: 19 | Fat: 0.7g | Chol: 0mg | Sod: 0.8mg | Carbs: 3.2g | Fiber: 1.5g | Sugars: 1.4g | Pro: 0.5g

16. Pineapple Coconut Popsicles

Preparation time: 10 minutes
Freezing time: 4-6 hours
Servings: Makes about 6 popsicles

Ingredients:

- 2 cups fresh pineapple chunks
- 1 cup unsweetened coconut milk
- 2 tablespoons honey or maple syrup (optional, for sweetness)
- 1 tsp. vanilla extract

Instructions:

1. In a blender, combine the pineapple chunks, coconut milk, honey or maple syrup (if using), and vanilla extract. Blend until smooth and well combined.

2. Taste the mixture and adjust the sweetness if needed by adding more honey or maple syrup.

3. Pour the mixture into popsicle molds, leaving a little space at the top for expansion.

4. Insert popsicle sticks into the molds.

5. Place the molds in the freezer and let them freeze for 4-6 hours, or until completely solid.

6. Once the popsicles are frozen, remove them from the molds by running them under warm water for a few seconds. Gently pull on the sticks to release the popsicles.

7. Serve immediately and enjoy these refreshing Pineapple Coconut Popsicles!

Nutritional Information (per serving):
Cal: 68 | Fat: 4.4g | Chol: 0mg | Sod: 3mg | Carbs: 7.5g | Fiber: 0.7g | Sugars: 5.5g | Pro: 0.5g

17. Vanilla Chia Pudding Cups

Preparation time: 5 minutes (plus chilling time)
Servings: Makes 2-3 servings

Ingredients:

- 1 cup unsweetened almond milk (or any non-dairy milk of your choice)
- 1/4 cup chia seeds
- 1 tbsp. pure maple syrup (or sweetener of your choice)
- 1 tsp. vanilla extract

Optional Toppings:

- Fresh berries
- Sliced almonds
- Unsweetened shredded coconut
- Cinnamon

Instructions:

1. In a bowl, combine the almond milk, chia seeds, maple syrup, and vanilla extract. Stir well to make sure the chia seeds are fully incorporated into the mixture.

2. Let the mixture sit for 5 minutes, then stir again to prevent clumping. Repeat this process one or two more times over the next 15 minutes.

3. Cover the bowl with plastic wrap or transfer the mixture to individual serving cups or jars.

4. Place the chia pudding cups in the refrigerator and let them chill for at least 2 hours or overnight to allow the chia seeds to absorb the liquid and thicken the pudding.

5. Before serving, give the pudding a good stir to make sure the texture is smooth and even.

6. Top the chia pudding cups with your favorite toppings such as fresh berries, sliced almonds, shredded coconut, or a sprinkle of cinnamon.

7. Enjoy your Vanilla Chia Pudding Cups as a healthy and satisfying breakfast, snack, or dessert!

Nutritional Information (per serving):
Cal: 100 | Fat: 5g | Chol: 0mg | Sod: 4mg | Carbs: 11g | Fiber: 7g | Sugars: 3g | Pro: 4g

18. Blueberry Oatmeal Cookies

Preparation time: 15 minutes
Baking time: 12-15 minutes
Servings: Makes about 12 cookies

Ingredients:

- 1 cup old-fashioned oats
- 1/2 cup whole wheat flour
- 1/4 cup almond flour
- 1/4 cup unsweetened applesauce
- 1/4 cup pure maple syrup
- 2 tablespoons coconut oil, melted
- 1 tsp. vanilla extract
- 1/2 tsp. baking powder
- 1/4 tsp. cinnamon
- Pinch of salt
- 1/2 cup fresh or frozen blueberries

Instructions:

1. Preheat the oven to 350°F (175°C). Line a baking sheet with parchment paper.
2. In a large mixing bowl, combine the oats, whole wheat flour, almond flour, baking powder, cinnamon, and salt. Mix well.
3. In a separate bowl, whisk together the applesauce, maple syrup, melted coconut oil, and vanilla extract.
4. Pour the wet ingredients into the dry ingredients and stir until well combined.
5. Gently fold in the blueberries, being careful not to crush them.
6. Drop rounded tablespoons of dough onto the prepared baking sheet, spacing them about 2 inches apart.
7. Flatten each cookie slightly with the back of a spoon.
8. Bake in the preheated oven for 12-15 minutes, or until the edges are golden brown.
9. Remove from the oven and let the cookies cool on the baking sheet for a few minutes before transferring them to a wire rack to cool completely.
10. Once cooled, store the cookies in an airtight container.

Nutritional Information (per serving):
Cal: 85 | Fat: 3.5g | Chol: 0mg | Sod: 23mg | Carbs: 12g | Fiber: 2g | Sugars: 4g | Pro: 2g

19. Watermelon Fruit Pizza

Preparation time: 20 minutes
Servings: 6

Ingredients:

- 1 small seedless watermelon
- 1 cup Greek yogurt
- 1 tbsp. honey (optional)
- Assorted fruits (such as berries, kiwi, pineapple, and grapes), sliced

Instructions:

1. Slice the watermelon into rounds, about 1 inch thick. You can adjust the size of the rounds based on your preference.
2. Place the watermelon rounds on a serving platter or individual plates.
3. In a small bowl, mix the Greek yogurt with honey (if desired) to sweeten it.
4. Spread a thin layer of Greek yogurt on each watermelon round, just like you would spread sauce on a pizza crust.
5. Arrange the sliced fruits on top of the Greek yogurt layer, creating a colorful and vibrant display.

6. Serve the watermelon fruit pizza immediately and enjoy!

Nutritional Information (per serving):
Cal: 94 | Fat: 0.4g | Chol: 2mg | Sod: 23mg | Carbs: 20g | Fiber: 1.2g | Sugars: 17g | Pro: 4g

20. Chocolate Dipped Strawberries

Preparation time: 15 minutes
Servings: 4

Ingredients:

- 1 pint fresh strawberries
- 3 ounces dark chocolate, chopped
- Optional toppings: chopped nuts, shredded coconut, sprinkles

Instructions:

1. Rinse the strawberries under cold water and pat them dry with a paper towel.
2. In a microwave-safe bowl, melt the dark chocolate in the microwave in 30-second intervals, stirring in between, until smooth and melted.
3. Dip each strawberry into the melted chocolate, holding it by the stem or using a toothpick inserted into the top. Allow any excess chocolate to drip off.
4. Place the dipped strawberries on a parchment-lined baking sheet or plate.
5. If desired, sprinkle or roll the chocolate-dipped strawberries in optional toppings such as chopped nuts, shredded coconut, or sprinkles.
6. Place the baking sheet or plate in the refrigerator for about 10 minutes to allow the chocolate to set.
7. Once the chocolate is firm, remove the strawberries from the refrigerator and transfer them to a serving plate.
8. Serve the chocolate-dipped strawberries immediately or store them in the refrigerator until ready to enjoy.

Nutritional Information (per serving):
Cal: 110 | Fat: 6g | Chol: 0mg | Sod: 1mg | Carbs: 14g | Fiber: 3g | Sugars: 9g | Pro: 2g

21. Banana Split Yogurt Parfait

Preparation time: 10 minutes
Servings: 2

Ingredients:

- 1 cup low-fat Greek yogurt
- 1 ripe banana, sliced

- 1/4 cup fresh strawberries, sliced
- 2 tablespoons chopped walnuts
- 1 tbsp. dark chocolate chips
- 2 tablespoons unsweetened shredded coconut
- Optional toppings: honey or maple syrup for drizzling

Instructions:

1. In two parfait glasses or bowls, layer half of the Greek yogurt in the bottom.
2. Top the yogurt with half of the sliced banana, sliced strawberries, chopped walnuts, dark chocolate chips, and shredded coconut.
3. Repeat the layers with the remaining ingredients, starting with the yogurt and finishing with the shredded coconut.
4. Drizzle the top of each parfait with a small amount of honey or maple syrup if desired.
5. Serve immediately and enjoy!

Nutritional Information (per serving):
Cal: 220 | Fat: 9g | Chol: 5mg | Sod: 40mg | Carbs: 25g | Fiber: 4g | Sugars: 13g | Pro: 14g

22. Mixed Berry Smoothie Bowl

Preparation time: 10 minutes
Servings: 2

Ingredients:

- 1 cup frozen mixed berries (such as strawberries, blueberries, and raspberries)
- 1 ripe banana
- 1/2 cup unsweetened almond milk (or any preferred milk)
- 1/4 cup plain Greek yogurt
- 1 tbsp. chia seeds
- Toppings: fresh berries, sliced banana, granola, shredded coconut, nuts, or seeds

Instructions:

1. In a blender, combine the frozen mixed berries, ripe banana, almond milk, Greek yogurt, and chia seeds.
2. Blend until smooth and creamy, adding more almond milk if needed to reach the desired consistency.
3. Pour the smoothie mixture into two bowls.
4. Top each bowl with your favorite toppings, such as fresh berries, sliced banana, granola, shredded coconut, nuts, or seeds.
5. Serve immediately and enjoy!

Nutritional Information (per serving):
Cal: 180 | Fat: 4g | Chol: 0mg | Sod: 30mg | Carbs: 33g | Fiber: 8g | Sugars: 16g | Pro: 6g

23. Orange Granita Delight

Preparation time: 5 minutes (plus freezing time)
Servings: 4

Ingredients:

- 4 large oranges
- 2 tablespoons honey or maple syrup (optional)
- Fresh mint leaves (for garnish)

Instructions:

1. Cut the oranges in half and squeeze out the juice into a bowl, removing any seeds.
2. Optional: If you prefer a sweeter granita, you can add honey or maple syrup to the orange juice and stir until well combined.
3. Pour the orange juice mixture into a shallow dish or pan.
4. Place the dish or pan in the freezer and let it freeze for about 1 hour.
5. After 1 hour, use a fork to scrape the partially frozen mixture, breaking up any ice crystals.
6. Return the dish or pan to the freezer and repeat the scraping process every 30 minutes for the next 2-3 hours, or until the mixture is completely frozen and has a granita-like texture.
7. Once the granita is fully frozen, remove it from the freezer and use a fork to fluff and break up the ice crystals.
8. Spoon the orange granita into serving glasses or bowls.
9. Garnish with fresh mint leaves.
10. Serve immediately and enjoy the refreshing Orange Granita Delight!

Nutritional Information (per serving):
Cal: 50 | Fat: 0g | Chol: 0mg | Sod: 0mg | Carbs: 13g | Fiber: 2g | Sugars: 9g | Pro: 1g

24. Peach Yogurt Popsicles

Preparation time: 10 minutes (plus freezing time)
Servings: 6

Ingredients:

- 2 cups fresh or frozen peaches, peeled and sliced
- 1 cup plain Greek yogurt
- 2 tablespoons honey or maple syrup
- 1 tsp. vanilla extract

Instructions:

1. In a blender or food processor, add the peaches, Greek yogurt, honey or maple syrup, and vanilla extract.

2. Blend until smooth and well combined.
3. Taste the mixture and adjust the sweetness by adding more honey or maple syrup if desired.
4. Pour the mixture into popsicle molds, leaving a little space at the top for expansion during freezing.
5. Insert popsicle sticks into the molds.
6. Place the molds in the freezer and let them freeze for at least 4-6 hours, or until completely firm.
7. Once the popsicles are frozen, remove them from the molds by running them under warm water for a few seconds.
8. Serve immediately or store the popsicles in a zip-top bag or container in the freezer for later enjoyment.

Nutritional Information (per serving):
Cal: 80 | Fat: 0.5g | Chol: 0mg | Sod: 20mg | Carbs: 17g | Fiber: 1g | Sugars: 15g | Pro: 5g

25. Pistachio Rice Pudding

Preparation time: 10 minutes
Cooking time: 25 minutes
Chilling time: 2 hours (optional)
Servings: 4

Ingredients:

- 1/2 cup Arborio rice (or any short-grain rice)
- 2 cups unsweetened almond milk
- 2 tablespoons honey or maple syrup
- 1/4 tsp. vanilla extract
- 1/4 cup shelled pistachios, chopped

Instructions:

1. In a medium-sized saucepan, combine the rice and almond milk.
2. Bring the mixture to a boil over medium heat, then reduce the heat to low and simmer for about 20-25 minutes, or until the rice is tender, stirring occasionally.
3. Stir in the honey or maple syrup and vanilla extract. Mix well.
4. Remove the saucepan from the heat and let the pudding cool to room temperature.
5. If desired, cover the pudding and refrigerate for at least 2 hours to chill.
6. Divide the pudding into serving bowls or glasses.
7. Sprinkle the chopped pistachios over the top of each serving.
8. Serve the pistachio rice pudding chilled or at room temperature.

Nutritional Information (per serving):
Cal: 200 | Fat: 5g | Chol: 0mg | Sod: 50mg | Carbs: 36g | Fiber: 2g | Sugars: 13g | Pro: 4g

Meal Plan

This food plan was created using the recipes given in the book. The combination of recipes was chosen according to the principles of the DASH diet so each day will never exceed 2,200 to 2,500 mg of sodium. Be careful to use salt sparingly.

DAY	BREAKFAST	LUNCH	DINNER
1	Spinach Veggie Omelet	Quinoa Stuffed Bell Peppers	Lemon Herb Baked Cod
2	Berry Overnight Oats	Roasted Vegetable Quinoa Bowl	Greek Beef Skewers
3	Whole Wheat Pancake Delight	Caprese Quinoa Stuffed Tomatoes	Garlic Parmesan Chicken Tenders
4	Mushroom Scrambled Eggs	Greek Orzo Salad	Grilled Lemon Pepper Chicken
5	Yogurt Berry Parfait	Spicy Cauliflower Rice Stir-Fry	Mediterranean Baked Sea Bass
6	Avocado Toast with Tomatoes	Ratatouille with Brown Rice	Herbed Baked Haddock Fillets
7	Veggie Breakfast Burrito	Zucchini Noodle Primavera	Balsamic Glazed Salmon
8	Quinoa Apple Bowl	Tomato and Mozzarella Farro Salad	Mediterranean Turkey Burgers
9	Smoked Salmon Bagel Delight	Veggie-Packed Brown Rice Pilaf	Beef and Lentil Soup
10	Blueberry Spinach Smoothie	Eggplant Parmesan Casserole	Ginger Soy Glazed Sea Bass
11	Zucchini Frittata Delight	Greek Salad Delight	Paprika Baked Chicken Wings
12	Almond Butter Toast Delight	Quinoa Avocado Salad Bowl	Lemon Rosemary Chicken Thighs
13	Turkey Mushroom Egg Scramble	Cucumber Tomato Salad	Tangy BBQ Pork Ribs
14	Berry Kale Yogurt Smoothie	Sweet Potato and Black Bean Tacos	Spicy Cajun Blackened Catfish
15	Cottage Cheese Peach Delight	Mediterranean Pasta Salad	Moroccan Spiced Beef Stew
16	Mango Coconut Quinoa Bowl	Cauliflower "Potato" Salad	Pesto Grilled Mahi-Mahi
17	Fruit-Topped Waffle Delight	Cilantro Lime Quinoa Salad	Teriyaki Glazed Tuna Steaks
18	Spinach Mushroom Breakfast Wrap	Whole Grain Garlic Knots	Spinach and White Bean Soup
19	Kiwi Chia Pudding Delight	Greek Yogurt Chicken Salad	Herbed Chicken Quinoa Bowl
20	Almond Cereal with Berries	Watermelon Feta Salad	Beef and Quinoa Stuffed Peppers
21	Sweet Potato Hash Browns	Tangy Coleslaw with Apple	Honey Mustard Pork Loin
22	Turkey Bacon Breakfast Sandwich	Cucumber Greek Yogurt Dip	Grilled Salmon Skewers
23	Cottage Cheese Fruit Salad	Roasted Vegetable Salad Bowl	Lemon Herb Baked Cod
24	Veggie Breakfast Quesadilla	Mango Spinach Salad	Garlic Parmesan Chicken Tenders
25	Banana Almond Butter Smoothie	Orzo Pasta Salad Delight	Greek Lemon Chicken Skewers
26	Lemon Garlic Roasted Asparagus	Berry Walnut Salad Medley	Cilantro Lime Turkey Breast
27	Caprese Salad Skewers	Mediterranean Chickpea Salad	Herb Roasted Pork Tenderloin
28	Baked Zucchini Fries	Spaghetti Squash with Marinara	Beef and Mushroom Stir-Fry
29	Chia Pudding	Minestrone Soup	Stir-fried Tofu

DAY	BREAKFAST	LUNCH	DINNER
30	Spicy Edamame Stir-Fry	Quinoa Black Bean Salad	Paprika Baked Chicken Wings
31	Stuffed Mushroom Caps	Tuna Salad Lettuce Wraps	Honey Glazed Pork Chops
32	Fresh Tomato Bruschetta	Roasted Vegetable Quinoa Bowl	Moroccan Chickpea Soup
33	Avocado Cucumber Salsa	Greek Orzo Salad	Ginger Soy Glazed Sea Bass
34	Steamed Broccoli with Lemon	Tomato and Mozzarella Farro Salad	Greek Lemon Chicken Skewers
35	Baked Sweet Potato Wedges	Veggie-Packed Brown Rice Pilaf	Beef and Bean Chili
36	Spinach and Feta Stuffed Peppers	Cucumber Tomato Salad	Lemon Herb Baked Cod
37	Cilantro Lime Quinoa Salad	Cauliflower "Potato" Salad	Teriyaki Chicken Skewers
38	Roasted Brussels Sprouts	Quinoa Avocado Salad Bowl	Garlic Parmesan Turkey Meatballs
39	Greek Yogurt Vegetable Dip	Mediterranean Pasta Salad	Lemon Rosemary Chicken Thighs
40	Grilled Eggplant Slices	Watermelon Feta Salad	Balsamic Glazed Salmon
41	Black Bean Hummus	Tangy Coleslaw with Apple	Herb Roasted Pork Tenderloin
42	Stuffed Cherry Tomatoes	Roasted Vegetable Salad Bowl	Greek Beef Skewers
43	Baked Parmesan Zucchini Rounds	Orzo Pasta Salad Delight	Pesto Grilled Mahi-Mahi
44	Cucumber Greek Yogurt Dip	Berry Walnut Salad Medley	Tangy BBQ Turkey Meatloaf
45	Roasted Cauliflower Bites	Mediterranean Chickpea Salad	Garlic Parmesan Chicken Tenders
46	Mediterranean Stuffed Olives	Spaghetti Squash with Marinara	Curry Lime Turkey Skewers
47	Steamed Green Beans with Almonds	Greek Salad Delight	Lemon Dill Chicken Kabobs
48	Quinoa Stuffed Bell Peppers	Quinoa Black Bean Salad	Paprika Baked Chicken Wings
49	Zesty Kale Chips	Tuna Salad Lettuce Wraps	Honey Glazed Pork Chops
50	Guacamole-Stuffed Cucumber Bites	Roasted Vegetable Quinoa Bowl	Moroccan Chickpea Soup
51	Tomato Basil Soup	Greek Orzo Salad	Ginger Soy Glazed Sea Bass
52	Lentil Vegetable Stew	Tomato and Mozzarella Farro Salad	Greek Lemon Chicken Skewers
53	Chicken Noodle Soup	Veggie-Packed Brown Rice Pilaf	Beef and Bean Chili
54	Minestrone Soup Delight	Cucumber Tomato Salad	Lemon Herb Baked Cod
55	Butternut Squash Bisque	Cauliflower "Potato" Salad	Teriyaki Chicken Skewers
56	Gazpacho with Fresh Veggies	Quinoa Avocado Salad Bowl	Garlic Parmesan Turkey Meatballs
57	Spinach Tortellini Soup	Watermelon Feta Salad	Lemon Rosemary Chicken Thighs
58	Chunky Vegetable Chowder	Tangy Coleslaw with Apple	Balsamic Glazed Salmon
59	Mushroom Barley Soup	Roasted Vegetable Salad Bowl	Herb Roasted Pork Tenderloin
60	Spicy Black Bean Soup	Orzo Pasta Salad Delight	Greek Beef Skewers

Bonus

Would you like to download my cookbook with 50 recipes for diabetes now?

It's easy!

Scan this QR Code and follow all the directions!

If there are problems and you can't download the recipes, email me at
bonus.violetharmond@gmail.com and I'll be happy to help!

Made in United States
Troutdale, OR
02/11/2024

17586049R00071